Decolonising Multilingualism in Africa

CRITICAL LANGUAGE AND LITERACY STUDIES

Series Editors: Professor **Alastair Pennycook** (*University of Technology, Sydney, Australia*) and Professor **Brian Morgan** (*Glendon College/York University, Toronto, Canada*) and Professor **Ryuko Kubota** (*University of British Columbia, Vancouver, Canada*)

Critical Language and Literacy Studies is an international series that encourages monographs directly addressing issues of power (its flows, inequities, distributions, trajectories) in a variety of language- and literacy-related realms. The aim with this series is twofold: (1) to cultivate scholarship that openly engages with social, political, and historical dimensions in language and literacy studies, and (2) to widen disciplinary horizons by encouraging new work on topics that have received little focus (see below for partial list of subject areas) and that use innovative theoretical frameworks.

All books in this series are externally peer-reviewed.

Full details of all the books in this series and of all our other publications can be found on http://www.multilingual-matters.com, or by writing to Multilingual Matters, St Nicholas House, 31-34 High Street, Bristol BS1 2AW, UK.

Other books in the series

Hybrid Identities and Adolescent Girls: Being 'Half' in Japan
Laurel D. Kamada

Decolonizing Literacy: Mexican Lives in the Era of Global Capitalism
Gregorio Hernandez-Zamora

Contending with Globalization in World Englishes
Mukul Saxena and Tope Omoniyi (eds)

ELT, Gender and International Development: Myths of Progress in a Neocolonial World
Roslyn Appleby

Examining Education, Media, and Dialogue under Occupation: The Case of Palestine and Israel
Ilham Nasser, Lawrence N. Berlin and Shelley Wong (eds)

The Struggle for Legitimacy: Indigenized Englishes in Settler Schools
Andrea Sterzuk

Style, Identity and Literacy: English in Singapore
Christopher Stroud and Lionel Wee

Language and Mobility: Unexpected Places
Alastair Pennycook

Talk, Text and Technology: Literacy and Social Practice in a Remote Indigenous Community
Inge Kral

Language Learning, Gender and Desire: Japanese Women on the Move
Kimie Takahashi

English and Development: Policy, Pedagogy and Globalization
Elizabeth J. Erling and Philip Seargeant (eds)

Ethnography, Superdiversity and Linguistic Landscapes: Chronicles of Complexity
Jan Blommaert

Power and Meaning Making in an EAP Classroom: Engaging with the Everyday
Christian W. Chun

Local Languaging, Literacy and Multilingualism in a West African Society
Kasper Juffermans

English Teaching and Evangelical Mission: The Case of Lighthouse School
Bill Johnston

Race and Ethnicity in English Language Teaching
Christopher Joseph Jenks

Language, Education and Neoliberalism: Critical Studies in Sociolinguistics
Mi-Cha Flubacher and Alfonso Del Percio (eds)

CRITICAL LANGUAGE AND LITERACY STUDIES: 26

Decolonising Multilingualism in Africa

Recentering Silenced Voices from the Global South

Finex Ndhlovu and Leketi Makalela

MULTILINGUAL MATTERS
Bristol • Blue Ridge Summit

DOI https://doi.org/10.21832/NDHLOV3354
Library of Congress Cataloging in Publication Data
A catalog record for this book is available from the Library of Congress.
Names: Ndhlovu, Finex, author. | Makalela, Leketi, author.
Title: Decolonising Multilingualism in Africa: Recentering Silenced Voices from the Global South/Finex Ndhlovu and Leketi Makalela.
Description: Bristol, UK; Blue Ridge Summit, PA: Multilingual Matters, 2021. | Series: Critical Language and Literacy Studies: 26 | Includes bibliographical references and index. | Summary: "This book interrogates and problematises African multilingualism as it is currently understood in language education and research. It challenges the enduring colonial matrices of power hidden within mainstream conceptions of multilingualism that have been propagated in the Global North and then exported to the Global South"— Provided by publisher.
Identifiers: LCCN 2021011127 (print) | LCCN 2021011128 (ebook) | ISBN 9781788923347 (paperback) | ISBN 9781788923354 (hardback) | ISBN 9781788923361 (pdf) | ISBN 9781788923378 (epub) | ISBN 9781788923385 (kindle edition)
Subjects: LCSH: Multilingualism—Africa. | Language policy—Africa. | Decolonization—Africa.
Classification: LCC P115.5.A35 N37 2021 (print) | LCC P115.5.A35 (ebook) | DDC 306.446096—dc23
LC record available at https://lccn.loc.gov/2021011127
LC ebook record available at https://lccn.loc.gov/2021011128

British Library Cataloguing in Publication Data
A catalogue entry for this book is available from the British Library.

ISBN-13: 978-1-78892-335-4 (hbk)
ISBN-13: 978-1-78892-334-7 (pbk)

Multilingual Matters
UK: St Nicholas House, 31-34 High Street, Bristol BS1 2AW, UK.
USA: NBN, Blue Ridge Summit, PA, USA.

Website: www.multilingual-matters.com
Twitter: Multi_Ling_Mat
Facebook: https://www.facebook.com/multilingualmatters
Blog: www.channelviewpublications.wordpress.com

Copyright © 2021 Finex Ndhlovu and Leketi Makalela.

All rights reserved. No part of this work may be reproduced in any form or by any means without permission in writing from the publisher.

The policy of Multilingual Matters/Channel View Publications is to use papers that are natural, renewable and recyclable products, made from wood grown in sustainable forests. In the manufacturing process of our books, and to further support our policy, preference is given to printers that have FSC and PEFC Chain of Custody certification. The FSC and/or PEFC logos will appear on those books where full certification has been granted to the printer concerned.

Typeset by Deanta Global Publishing Services, Chennai, India
Printed and bound in the UK by the CPI Books Group Ltd.
Printed and bound in the US by NBN.

Finex – *To the memory of my son, Sindiso, for closing all the gaps at home while I was away on project trips that culminated in this book.*

Leketi – *To my two beloved daughters, Leleti and Koketso, and to all students of multilingualism.*

Contents

Series Editors' Preface		viii
Preface		xvi
1	Myths We Live By: Multilingualism, Colonial Inventions	1
2	Unsettling Colonial Roots of Multilingualism	26
3	Unsettling Multilingualism in Language and Literacy Education	37
4	Decolonising Multilingualism in Higher Education	55
5	Decolonising Multilingualism in National Language Policies	75
6	African Vehicular Cross-Border Languages, Multilingualism Discourse	94
7	African Multilingualism, Immigrants, Diasporas	108
8	Multilingualism from Below: Languaging with a Seven Year Old	131
9	Recentring Silenced Lingualisms and Voices	155
	Index	177

Series Editors' Preface

Applied linguistics is often subject to various 'turns' as they sweep across the social sciences: we've seen social, somatic, sensory, ecological, performative, discursive, spatial, material, ontological, practice-based and other turns come and go. Some have a more lasting effect, while others engender a brief period of excitement and then dissipate. Two contemporary turns of particular importance to the field that intersect in this book are the multilingual and the decolonial. Both are of real significance for socio- and applied linguists, the one urging us to understand multilingualism not just as common, but as the norm, the starting point from which any studies of language use, language education, or language learning should flow; the other urging us to change the ways in which knowledge in the field is tied to coloniality, to ways of thinking embedded in inequitable historical and contemporary global relations. The important question raised by this book, however, is how these two emphases work together: what needs to be done from a decolonial perspective to change the ways that multilingualism is understood, particularly in contexts of the Global South?

Unlike some of the other turns from cultural studies, geography, or anthropology, the *multilingual turn* (May 2014) seems central to applied linguistics, and one we perhaps like to 'own' since it is so obviously close to our core concerns. Indeed, this book is published by Multilingual Matters, who have always considered multilingualism as the necessary starting point. This emphasis emerged in part as a reaction to perceived increases in multilingualism in cities in the Global North, as studies or migration, mobility and community language use revealed the scale of urban linguistic complexity. This newfound interest has been critiqued for a lack of historicity (diversity has been around a long time), a fascination with linguistic diversity at the expense of other significant factors in migrant lives (sociolinguists may find language diversity intriguing, but migrants have more pressing concerns in their lives to do with housing, employment, education, discrimination and so on), an obsession with urban contexts (while cities may intensify the contiguity of difference, non-urban contexts may be equally diverse), an emphasis on fluidity over fixity (flexible language use may indeed be common, but people are nonetheless confronted by the static and rigid norms of institutional language regulations) and a lack of geopolitical awareness (what has been seen as remarkable diversity in the Global North is the norm in the Global South).

Whatever misgivings there may be about some of this recent reframing of multilingualism, it nonetheless puts 'multilingualism from below' – the use of varied linguistic resources by people going about their daily lives, rather than the elite multilingualism of those from privileged linguistic-educational backgrounds – centre stage in a new era of linguistic-ethnographically-informed research. In conjunction with this move, studies of language learning and use more generally have started to turn a critical eye on the ways that monolingualism (and the strange idea that such a state is really possible) has been assumed to be the starting point for analysis. We need instead to start our sociolinguistic and psycholinguistic analyses with multilingualism rather than monolingualism as the norm. This shifting focus, which has been slow to gain ground in the narrowly normative domains of second language acquisition (SLA) studies, has also started to raise questions about other common and taken-for-granted ideas in the field, such as first and second languages, native speakers, code-switching, and so on. Attention has been drawn to the monolingual bias in SLA, which tends to assume that people speak one identifiable language, after which they learned another. Reacting to the ways SLA has 'erased bilingualism and multilingualism from the object of inquiry', Ortega (2019: 24) calls for an understanding of 'multilingualism as the central object of inquiry'. Despite some concerns about how multilingualism has been framed within this new focus, it has become, according to May (2014: 1), 'the topic du jour, at least in critical applied linguistics'.

Looking more broadly at the social sciences, meanwhile, Maldonado-Torres (2007) suggests that a *decolonial turn* is under way, a 'shift in knowledge production of similar nature and magnitude to the linguistic and pragmatic turns' (2007: 261). This decolonial turn 'involves interventions at the level of power, knowledge, and being through varied actions of decolonization' (2007: 262). Across a wide range of academic fields – economics, philosophy, anthropology, international relations, religious studies, psychology, among others – there has been a call to decolonise knowledge. In the field of ecology, Ferdinand (2019) shows how environmentalism hides behind a universalist narrative that overlooks the colonial, patriarchal and slavery foundations of modernity that have to be addressed if environmental equality is to become a reality. Connell (2018: 405) argues for the importance of decolonising sociology, a project that 'requires rethinking the composition of sociology's workforce and changing the conditions in which it produces and circulates knowledge'. This is, she reminds us, a process of redistribution of both knowledge and resources.

As these remarks make clear, this is not just an epistemological question, but also both an ontological one, and a project to address institutional structures, racism, curricula, social interactions, forms of funding and more. These are broad challenges that necessitate understanding Eurocentrism as a structural problem, perpetuated by people, institutions, texts, conferences, and many aspects of our academic disciplines (Richardson, 2018). The solution to these exclusionary frameworks of knowledge is not through 'rhetorics of inclusion' (Furo, 2018: 282) – moves to include ideas from the Global South, people of colour, Indigenous knowledges into the curriculum (though these are of course part of the picture) – but a much deeper questioning of the procedures of knowledge production. We should also be cautious, as Zeleza (2017) warns, not to limit a decolonial project to the undoing of colonial frameworks of knowledge, lest we overlook the many other forms of knowledge and ways of being that have always existed beyond the grasp of colonialism. And as Kubota (2019) cautions, a project to decolonise applied linguistics can only be successful to the extent that it makes questions of race and gender central. Mignolo and Walsh (2018: 17) emphasise the need for *decolonial insurgency* that would align with other forms of praxis and pedagogy '*against* the colonial matrix of power in all of its dimensions, and *for* the possibilities of an otherwise'.

So what happens when the multilingual and decolonial turns come together? While in some ways they may appear to sit comfortably alongside each other – the multilingual turn perhaps suggests a decolonising of the monolingual bias in applied linguistics – their relationship, as the authors of this book suggest, is a far more complex one. As Mufwene (2020: 290) comments, the idea of *decolonial linguistics* 'entails reducing the Western bias and hegemony in how languages of the global South and the (socio)linguistic behaviours of their speakers and writers are analysed'. It is not enough, therefore, just to emphasise multilingualism over monolingualism: what is at stake here is a far more extensive questioning of how we think about languages. Can we bring perspectives on multilingualism developed in the Global North to bear on language and education elsewhere, or does this become yet another form of knowledge colonisation? If the idea of multilingualism and associated views of language, language use and education are premised on understandings of language from the Global North – a view of languages as countable entities or an assumption that small-scale multilingualism is unsustainable – does the idea of multilingualism provide new terrain for discussion of language and diversity, or do its origins in the Global North render it inevitably compromised (Pennycook & Makoni, 2020)?

For the authors of *Decolonising Multilingualism in Africa*, many of the common ways of thinking about multilingualism, as exemplified in notions such as mother tongue education, bilingual education, or multilingual language policies need critical interrogation. They simply do not match the ways in which languages are used or understood in many African contexts. So the point is indeed not that a focus on multilingualism can constitute a decolonial enterprise, but rather that multilingualism itself is in need of decolonisation. The multilingual and decolonial turns rub up against each other. As Ndhlovu (2018: 118) puts it, while the invocation of 'high-sounding metaphors of human rights, anti-imperialism and biodiversity resonate with contemporary international conversations around social justice and equity issues', they struggle to achieve much because 'standard language ideology remains ensconced as the only valid and legitimate conceptual framework that informs mainstream understandings of what is meant by "language"'. This is not a question of language standardisation – the problem that language revival projects generally need to reduce language variety to a much narrower set of options – but that these projects all too often operate with a constricted understanding of what language is and how it operates.

The straitjacket of monolingual thought is not so easily thrown off. The monolingual/ multilingual dichotomy 'misdirects and misrepresents the notion of language diversity' (Ndhlovu, 2018: 118). Monolingual mindsets go far deeper than favouring monolingualism over multilingualism, or viewing multilingualism in monolingual terms: The issue at stake is a set of deep-seated language ideologies, or *language ideological assemblages* (Kroskrity, 2021) that are in need of a much more profound decolonising. The problem more broadly is that any approach to language education that assumes, for example, that there must be a dominant community language misses the point of Southern multilingualisms. There is a major gap in thinking about educational multilingualism, especially in Southern contexts, 'a singular failure to engage with the nature of multilingualism in these areas and how multilingualism can be harnessed as a resource, say, in a sector like education' (Mwaniki, 2018: 36). The problem with 'language-specific approaches', Nakata (2007: 175-6) points out, is that whether they focus on bilingual education, English as a second language, or local languages, they assume 'that all students have a common language'. The idea of a *multilingua franca* (Makoni & Pennycook, 2012), by contrast, views language as a multilayered chain that is constantly combined and recombined and in which 'secondary' language learning takes place more or less simultaneously with language use. In many Southern contexts, Global North concepts of languages, mother tongues or multilingualism do not reflect the ways languages are used and understood, which can be better described as forms of *multilanguaging* (Makalela, 2018).

The notion of translanguaging has been a point of contention in these debates. For García, (2019: 162) translanguaging has 'the potential to decolonize our conception of language and, especially, language education'. Translanguaging, as both ideology and pedagogy, can challenge the ways in which bilingualism and multilingualism are commonly construed as the use of separate, named languages – ideas that 'consolidated power among white majorities while stigmatising the practices of multilingual speakers' (García, 2019: 166) – opening up spaces for different ways of doing language pedagogy. Yet notions such as translanguaging have been critiqued on the grounds that to 'lay claim to an uncovering or (re-) discovering of multilingualism as more than the sum of languages understood as monolingual entities' by scholars from Europe and North America (and writing predominantly in English) 'appears ahistorical and dislocated from the experiences and scholarship of marginalised and minoritised people who live in both the geopolitical north and south' (Heugh & Stroud, 2018: 2).

This recent scholarship, Heugh and Stroud argue, not only appropriates, and claims as new, ideas that have been long circulating in the Global South, but also does so from a position that views multilingualism as a 'singular phenomenon' rather than embracing the full implications of a 'plurality of multilingualisms' (2018: 6-7). Here we confront one of the difficult issues of the uneven push and pull between North and South, as terms are taken up, reworked, reinvested with meaning, rejected, and so on. We know that the Global South is generally highly multilingual, and that this multilingualism is not best described via the language frameworks of the Global North. So what is the best way forward: to see how the idea of translanguaging can fit language use in the Global South, or to look for quite different ways of approaching the topic? Makalela (2018:

4; and this book) talks of *ubuntu translanguaging*, the view that in the context of complex multilingualism, 'no language is complete without another'.

We have to ensure that neo-colonial assumptions about language, culture and revitalisation, these ways of categorising and theorising 'Indigenous languages using norms for major global languages', or 'Western constructs of what "language" is when engaging in Indigenous language research, teaching, and advocacy', are put aside, in favour of local control of language reclamation projects (Leonard, 2017: 15). In short, we have to 'decolonise "language"' (Leonard, 2017: 32). We will not be able to change conditions of linguistic inequality on political grounds alone; it is only by also challenging linguistic paradigms that we can change the operations of language in terms of disparity and discrimination. Once language revitalisation is understood as 'an act of decolonisation', (Stebbins *et al.*, 2018: 237), the research process has to be seen in decolonial terms, involving different ways of understanding language and its relation to community and place, different relations between linguists and community members, different knowledge status between academic and community ways of knowing, different ways of writing and exploring voice. In this context, the subtitle of this book – *Recentering Silenced Voices from the Global South* – is an important reminder of what this is about.

This book is therefore a very welcome and very important addition to our series. Other books in this series – such as Higgins (2009) on English as a local language in east Africa, or Juffermans' (2015) on literacy practices in the Gambia – shed light on the ways in which language and literacy practices work at a local level in different parts of Africa. But the locus of enunciation of Ndhlovu and Makalela brings different perspectives, different voices, different kinds of knowledge to the table. As a similarly titled book from another Multilingual Matters series (Phipps, 2019) urges us, the challenge to decolonise multilingualism is a significant demand of our times, calling for the learning of non-colonial languages, the citing of scholars from the Global South, rethinking citation and copyright more generally, and a search for other ways of thinking and doing. Another book in this series reminds us that the task of critical applied linguistics is to *decolonise* language and literacy. The difference between official, standard and access-based approaches to education and grassroots, community, resistant education is that while the first 'aims to educate people to acquire skills and habits to fit and function in society *as it is* (unjust, organized in castes, individualistic, market-driven, etc.), the aim of alternative forms of education has always been the *decolonization* of minds' (Hernandez-Zamora, 2010: 200). It is towards such a decolonising goal that this book moves, suggesting that Motha's (2020) challenge as to whether a decolonial applied linguistics is possible may be answered (tentatively) in the affirmative: yes, it's possible, and this book is a very useful start in what is going to be a long and difficult struggle.

Alastair Pennycook
Ryuko Kubota
Brian Morgan

References

Connell, R. (2018) Decolonizing sociology. *Contemporary Sociology* 47 (4), 399–407.
Ferdinand, M. (2019) *Une écologie décolonniale*. Paris: Seuil.
Furo, A. (2018) *Decolonizing the Classroom Curriculum: Indigenous Knowledges, Colonialism, Logics and Ethical Spaces*. Ottawa: University of Ottawa.
García, O. (2019) Decolonizing foreign, second, heritage, and first languages: Implications for education. In D. Macedo (ed.) *Decolonizing Foreign Language Education: The Miseaching of English and Other Colonial Languages* (pp. 152–168). New York: Routledge.
Hernandez-Zamora, G. (2010) *Decolonizing Literacy: Mexican Lives in the Era of Global Capitalism*. Bristol: Multilingual Matters.
Heugh, K. and Stroud, C. (2018) Diversities, affinities and diasporas: A southern lens and methodology for understanding multilingualisms. *Current Issues in Language Planning* 20 (1), 1–15. https://doi.org/10.1080/14664208.2018.1507543.
Higgins, C. (2009) *English as a Local Language: Post-colonial Identities and Multilingual Practices*. Bristol: Multilingual Matters.
Juffermans, K. (2015) *Local Languaging, Literacy and Multilingualism in a West African Society*. Bristol: Multilingual Matters.
Kroskrity, P. (2021) Language ideological assemblages within linguistic anthropology. In A. Burkette and T. Warhol (eds) *Crossing Borders, Making Connections: Interdisciplinarity in Linguistics* (pp. 129–142). Berlin: Mouton de Gruyter.
Kubota, R. (2019) Confronting epistemological racism, decolonizing scholarly knowledge: Race and gender in applied linguistics. *Applied Linguistics* 41 (5), 712–732.
Leonard, W. (2017) Producing language reclamation by decolonising 'language'. In W. Leonard and H. De Korne (eds) *Language Documentation and Description* (pp. 15–36). London: EL Publishing.
Makalela, L. (2018) Introduction: Shifting lenses. In L. Makalela (ed.) *Shifting Lenses: Multilanguaging, Decolonisation and Education in the Global South* (pp. 1–8). Cape Town: CASAS.
Makoni, S. and Pennycook, A. (2012) Disinventing multilingualism: From monological multilingualism to multilingual francas. In M. Martin-Jones and A. Blackledge (eds) *The Routledge Handbook of Multilingualism* (pp. 439–453). Abingdon: Routledge.
Maldonado-Torres, N. (2007) On the coloniality of being: Contributions to the development of a concept. *Cultural Studies* 21 (2–3), 240–270.

May, S. (2014) Introducing the 'multilingual turn'. In S May (ed.) *The Multilingual Turn: Implications for SLA, TESOL and Bilingual Education* (pp. 1–6). Abingdon: Routledge.

Mignolo, W. and Walsh, C. (2018) *On Decoloniality: Concepts, Analytics, Praxis.* Durham: Duke University Press.

Motha, S. (2020) Is an antiracist and decolonizing applied linguistics possible? *Annual Review of Applied Linguistics* 40, 128–133.

Mufwene, S. (2020) Decolonial linguistics as paradigm shift: A commentary. In A. Deumert, A Storch and N. Shepherd (eds) *Colonial and Decolonial Linguistics: Knowledges and Epistemes* (pp. 289–300). Oxford: Oxford University Press.

Mwaniki, M. (2018) Language and literacy education in complexly multilingual contexts: Reflections for theory and practice. In L. Makalela (ed.) (2018) *Shifting Lenses: Multilanguaging, Decolonisation and Education in the Global South* (pp. 21–44). Cape Town: CASAS.

Nakata, M. (2007) *Disciplining the Savages: Savaging the Disciplines.* Canberra: Aboriginal Studies Press.

Ndhlovu, F. (2018) *Language, Vernacular Discourse and Nationalisms: Uncovering the Myths of Transnational Worlds.* Cham: Palgrave Macmillan.

Pennycook, A. and Makoni, S. (2020) *Innovations and Challenges in Applied Linguistics from the Global South.* Abingdon: Routledge.

Phipps, A. (2019) *Decolonising Multilingualism: Struggles to Decreate.* Bristol: Multilingual Matters.

Richardson, W. (2018) Understanding Eurocentrism as a structural problem of "undone science." In G. Bhambra, D. Gebriel and K. Nisancioglu (eds) *Decolonizing the University* (pp. 231–247). London: Pluto Press.

Stebbins, T., Eira, K. and Couzens, V. (2018) *Living Languages and New Approaches to Language Revitalisation Research.* Abingdon: Routledge.

Zeleza, P. (2017) The Decolonization of African Knowledges. Address at the 9th Africa Day Lecture, University of Free State, Bloemfontein, South Africa.

Preface

In 1930, the Government of Southern Rhodesia (present-day Zimbabwe) commissioned Clement Martyn Doke – a linguist from Witwatersrand University – to carry out what was to be a far-reaching project on the unification of language varieties spoken on the Zimbabwe plateau. This was the same year that Finex's mother, Laizah Ndhlovu (nee Mpofu, okaSipukanana) was born. Doke's brief was to reconcile and coordinate language development activities that had been initiated by close to a dozen missionary organisations. Efforts by missionary organisations were, at the time, fragmented and fraught with numerous disagreements centring on orthographic conventions for literacy and educational purposes. Then in 1931, Doke developed a uniform orthography for the whole area that came to be known as Mashonaland. He named the new standard language Shona, which from that time has come to be known as the 'language' and identity marker of more than 75% of Zimbabwe's population. This means that the Shona language as we know it today came into existence at about the same time that Finex's mother was born. She is now 91. The biggest language spoken in Zimbabwe is, therefore, less than 100 years old.

The story of Shona on the Zimbabwe plateau is a classic example of how colonially invented (and imposed) linguistic and identity categories have emerged throughout Africa, Latin America, Asia, the Indian subcontinent and other formerly colonised regions of the world. Seen through the lens of ideologies of enumeration, linguistic categories constructed under the aegis of colonial linguistics (Errington, 2001, 2008) have come to frame and underpin mainstream notions of African multilingualism. In *Decolonising Multilingualism in Africa*, we spotlight those discursive and metalinguistic elements of colonial ideologies of language as an entry point into the project of decolonising multilingualism in postcolonial contexts of the Global South. We question and challenge the phenomenology of multilingualism from Southern and decolonial perspectives.

We base our understanding of the Global South on definitions provided by several Southern and decolonial theorists, including Raewyn Connell (2014), John Comaroff and Jean Comaroff (2011), Baoventura de Sousa Santos (2011) and Alastair Pennycook and Sinfree Makoni (2020). According to de Sousa Santos (2011: 39), the Global South is 'a metaphor for human suffering caused by capitalism and colonialism on the global level, as well as for the resistance that seeks to overcome or minimize such suffering'. And as Isabelle Léglise (2019) advises, such definition of 'Southern' or the Global South captures a phenomenon that exists both in the North and in countries of the South. This means that instead of following a discourse that might seem to suggest the world is split into two geographical zones, the Global South is to be understood as a geopolitical, metaphorical and epistemological concept (Pennycook & Makoni, 2020) that refers to experiences or conditions of colonial exploitation, exclusion, epistemological extraversion (Hountonji, 1997) and marginalisation that are common to diverse societies at the global scale. In the pages that follow, we build on this conceptual framing of the Global South to unsettle the colonial legacy of the mainstream notion of multilingualism and then suggest alternative paradigms that accord with the histories and ontologies of the majority of people around the world.

Numerous previous research reports on colonial linguistics have shone a light on the problematic nature of standard language ideologies (see e.g. Errington, 2001, 2008; Fardon & Furniss, 1994; Makoni, 1998; Makoni & Pennycook, 2007; Severo, 2016). However, the body of similar work focusing on the problematic nature of the phenomenology of multilingualism in African and other comparable Southern contexts remains largely thin and disparate. A 2012 collection of essays by Jan Blommaert and others aptly titled *Dangerous Multilingualism: Northern Perspectives on Order, Purity and Normality* is one of the few emerging and quite contemporary interventions that advance lines of argument we are pushing in this project (Blommaert *et al.*, 2012). Nevertheless, though Blommaert and his colleagues raise some compelling arguments about how language in society has changed, they do not provide a genuine departure from mainstream notions of multilingualism that remain anchored on regimes of language shaped by colonialism. Their analysis is based on the idea that the mainstream view on multilingualism (which we challenge in this book) is real. Our position is that like the standard language ideology, the mainstream understanding of multilingualism is pre-eminently colonial and needs to be decolonised. We draw on insights from decolonial epistemology and qualitative ethnographic data from African communities to support our argument. We use these in generating new ideas and fruitful pathways to augment current efforts that advance alternative understandings of multilingualism – by specifically drawing attention to the 'significance of local knowledge about language' (Pennycook, 2008: 21). In doing so, we join and push forward the ongoing decolonial project that has gathered momentum since the turn of the 21st century. The book also contributes to an increasing body of scholarship, which can be construed as constituting a Southern critique into multilingualisms motivated by a desire to decolonise research into the social sciences and humanities.

References

Blommaert, J., Leppänen, S., Pahta, P., Virkkula, T. and Räisänen, T. (eds) (2012) *Dangerous Multilingualism: Northern Perspectives on Order, Purity and Normality*. London: Palgrave Macmillan.

Comaroff, J. and Comaroff, J.L. (2011) *Theory from the South: Or How Euro-America is Evolving toward Africa*. Boulder, CO: Paradigm.

Connell, R. (2014) Margin becoming centre: For a world-centred rethinking of masculinities. *NORMA: International Journal of Masculinities Studies* 9 (4), 217–231.

De Sousa Santos, B. (2011) Épistémologies Du Sud. *Études Rurales* 187, 21–49.

Errington, J. (2001) Colonial linguistics. *Annual Review of Anthropology* 30, 19–30.

Errington, J. (2008) *Linguistics in a Colonial World: A Story of Language, Meaning, and Power*. Oxford: Blackwell.

Fardon, R. and Furniss, G. (1994) *African Languages, Development and the State*. London/New York: Routledge.

Hountonji, P. (1997) Introduction: Recentering Africa. In P.J. Hountonji (ed.) *Endogenous Knowledge: Research Trails* (pp. 1–39). Dakar: CODESRIA.

Léglise, I. (2019) Multilingualism and heterogeneous language practices: New research areas and issues in the Global South. *Language et Société, Maison des Sciences de L'homme*, Hal-02065599.

Makoni, S. (1998) African languages as European scripts: The shaping of communal memory. In S. Nuttall and C. Coetzee (eds) *Negating the Past: The Making of Memory in South Africa* (pp. 242–248). Oxford: Oxford University Press.

Makoni, S. and Pennycook, A. (eds) (2007) *Disinventing and Reconstituting Languages*. Clevedon: Multilingual Matters.

Pennycook, A. (2008) Language-free linguistics and linguistics-free languages. In A. Mahboob and N. Knight (eds) *Questioning Linguistics* (pp. 18–31). Newcastle upon Tyne: Cambridge Scholars Publishing.

Pennycook, A. and Makoni, S. (2020) *Innovations and Challenges in Applied Linguistics from the Global South*. London/New York: Routledge.

Severo, C.G. (2016) The colonial invention of languages in America. *Alfa: Revista de Linguistica* 60 (1), 11–27. http://dx.doi.org/10.1590/1981-5794-1604-1.

1 Myths We Live By: Multilingualism, Colonial Inventions

The things we supposedly know so foundationally about the notion of multilingualism and associated metalanguages are not as straightforward as they seem. In her ground-breaking book aptly titled *The Myths We Live By*, Mary Midgely (2003: 1), says 'Myths are no lies. Nor are they detached stories. They are imaginative patterns, networks of powerful symbols that suggest particular ways of interpreting the world. They shape its meaning'. Multilingualism is no exception. Mainstream notions of multilingualism and their metadiscourses have to be understood in this light – they are related to the larger global cultural, ideological, and mythic context. Looking at mainstream multilingualism as a product of myths that have crystallised into normative social reality is important. It points us away from over-reliance on parsimonious explanations, and towards critical awareness of the 'regimes of truth' about multilingualism discourse. Additionally, such critical awareness opens opportunities for greater engagement with how mainstream 'regimes of truth'– about language, multilingualism, multilingual education, multilingual national language policies and so on – impinge upon the mundane everyday human condition, including myths we live by.

In recent years, multilingualism has become a buzzword in public, political and scholarly debates and discourses around the world. It has come to represent and to be equated with best practices in numerable social and educational policy areas such as bi-(multi-)lingual education; social inclusion; immigrant social service provision; social and political equality; regional and continental integration; active citizenship participation; and inclusive education. The definitions and practical applications of multilingualism are characterised by a litany of competing and contested interpretations (Liu, 2016). In a 2009 article titled 'Multilingual Education Policy and Practice: Ten Certainties (Grounded in Indigenous Experience)', Nancy Hornberger (2009) paints a rosy picture of perceived promises of multilingualism in general and multilingual education in particular. She posits that

> Our 21st century entrance into the new millennium has brought renewed interest and contestation around [the multilingual] education alternative. Ethnolinguistic diversity and inequality, intercultural communication and contact, and global political and economic interdependence are more than ever acknowledged realities of today's world. (Hornberger, 2009: 1)

Hornberger (2009: 1) goes on to say that multilingual education 'offers the best possibilities for preparing coming generations to participate in constructing more just and democratic societies in our globalized and intercultural world'. She characterises multilingual education as constituting a wide and welcoming doorway towards the peaceful coexistence of peoples as well as the restoration and empowerment of communities and societies that have historically been oppressed – by such forces as global coloniality, racial ideologies, class, gender and so on. To this end, Hornberger postulates 10 certainties of multilingualism, which she argues hold the promise for equality and access to educational and socioeconomic opportunities, especially for indigenous and other peripherised communities around the world.

However, though Hornberger's arguments are insightful and push the envelope of academic discourses and language education policy conversations into previously uncharted territory, two problems beset her project: one phenomenological and the other philosophical. The phenomenological problem has to do with her notion of the 'lingual' that undergirds the 'ten certainties' of multilingual education advanced in her thesis. Like many other previous scholars who have advanced similar arguments, Hornberger adopts mainstream understandings of multilingualism that view languages more as quantifiable objects and less as relational social practices that are not always amenable to processes and procedures of enumeration. This problem runs across the lines of arguments posited in all 'ten certainties' of multilingual education – and applies to her discussion of multilingual education policy and practice in both indigenous and non-indigenous contexts.

The philosophical problem we find in Hornberger's thesis is one about the concept of 'certainties', which arguably betrays the positivist habits and practices of Euro-modernist epistemologies. While there is no doubt that multilingual education policy – however conceived or conceptualised – is a good starting point in tackling the pervasive effects of hegemonic monolingual policy frameworks, pitching it in terms of certainties seems quite untenable. How are we able to postulate certainties in a world of diverse peoples, cultures, knowledge systems and ontologies, and ways of reading and interpreting social realities? This conundrum becomes even more complex when considered in the context of indigenous communities where Hornberger's project is grounded. The language practices and epistemologies of indigenous communities are quite dynamic and excessively complex to fit within reductionist schemas of 'certainty' that are informed by the Euro-modernist positivist tradition. In other words, the notion of 'certainty' in the domain of knowledge and knowledge production has to be seen in terms of what it is: a historical construct whose emergence is located in the context of 'the larger history of the expansion of modern, Western reason' (Peet, 1997: 75).

Writing about the logics of Western reason, Raewyn Connell (2007) draws our attention to four geopolitical assumptions that underpin such discourses. First is the claim to universality whereby the very idea of mainstream social theory (including theories on multilingualism) involves talking about universals and generalisations as if the whole world was a homogeneous continuum. The fallacy of this claim rests on the fatalistic assumption that 'all societies are knowable in the same way and from the same point of view' (Connell, 2007: 44). The second contour is that of reading from the centre; that is, the notion of 'certainty' constructs a social world read through the eyes of the metropole and not through an analysis of the metropole's action on the rest of the world. What is overlooked here is the fact that the experiences of the colonised cannot be fully represented in models that arose out of a colonial metropolitan reading of the world.

The third contour of mainstream discourses originating from the Global North is one that Connell (2007) calls 'gestures of exclusion'. This is about the total absence or marginalisation of theorists from the colonised world/Global South in metropolitan texts and discourses on multilingualism. In those exceptional instances where material culture and ideas from the colonised world are acknowledged, they are rarely considered part of the mainstream dialogue of theory. Riding on the back of colonial ethnography and social anthropological frameworks emphasising the modern/pre-modern distinction, Euro-modernist multilingualism discourses render the cultures and thought processes from the Global South irrelevant and treat them as belonging to a world that has been surpassed. This leads us to the fourth contour, which has been termed 'grand erasure'. The point here is that when empirical knowledge and theorisation about humanity in general are seen as coming solely from a positivist tradition (with its emphasis on certainty and universality), the immediate effect 'is erasure of the experience[s] of the majority of humankind from the foundations of social thought' (Connell, 2007: 46). Connell elaborates this line of argument in her more recent publications where she shows how the global metropole (Global North) has monopolised the domain of social scientific theorisation, while the global periphery (Global South) is relegated to the supply of raw data. Ultimately, concepts, methodologies and agendas from the South have remained largely unrecognised, marginalised and absent from mainstream social science theorisations (Connell, 2014, 2018, 2019).

In this book, we extend Connell's thesis and use it as an entry point in challenging Hornberger's framing of multilingualism in terms of certainties. Taking after Connell, we suggest that there is no singular universal notion or understanding of multilingualism. Rather, we posit that there are multiple conceptions of multilingualism that intersect with and reflect diverse global ontologies and experiences of living with languages – and these must necessarily include perspectives from the Global South. As Connell (2014: 217) advises, a world-centred, rather than a metropole-centred, approach to knowledge production, is what we need. This entails adopting an epistemological stance that requires rethinking (or unthinking) familiar concepts by posing a new set of questions we address from new perspectives that are yet to be tried and tested.

Linda Tuhiwai Smith (2012: i–xiv) (whom Hornberger cites a couple of times in her project) raises at least four objections to research agendas that proceed through the reification of conventional Euro-modernist paradigms. The first is that we need to develop counter-practices of research that are relevant to the agenda of 'disrupting the current hegemonic rules of research'. Secondly, she suggests that we need to 'articulate research practices that arise out of the specificities of epistemology and methodology rooted in people's cultural experiences'. The third is about how stories of research, examples of projects, critical examination and mindful reflection must be woven together to make meaningful and practical designs. In her fourth objection, Smith (2012: ii) says 'we need new ways of knowing and discovering, and new ways to think about research in order to demonstrate the possibilities of re-imagining research as an activity that can be pursued outside the narrow box of the scientific experimental design'. This is essentially about integrating praxis, theory, action and reflection in ways that provoke revolutionary thinking about the way we do research. These alternative trajectories suggested by Smith and shared by many other scholars (indigenous and non-indigenous alike[1]) would be inconceivable if we were to follow the logic of 'certainty' in our engagement of multilingualism discourses and multilingual education policies.

In a book aptly titled *Uncertainties of Knowledge*, Immanuel Wallerstein (2004) says

I believe that we live in a very exciting era in the world of knowledge, precisely because we are living in a systemic crisis that is forcing us to reopen the basic epistemological questions and look to structural reorganizations of the world of knowledge. It is *uncertain* whether we shall rise adequately to the intellectual challenge, but it is there for us to address. We engage our responsibility as scientists/scholars in the way in which we address the multiple issues before us at this turning point in our structures of knowledge. (Wallerstein, 2004: 58; author's emphasis)

This is a poignant reminder about the need to be open-minded in our research agendas. That is to say, we need to set aside grand narratives about universal 'certainties' in a world where the boundaries of epistemologies are in constant flux. The epistemologies of the South that underpin the overarching argument we advance in this book 'choose to build bridges between comfort zones and discomfort zones and between the familiar in the fields of struggle and oppression' (de Sousa Santos & Meneses, 2020: xviii). As Wallerstein reminds us in the above quotation, because the structures of knowledge are uncertain, we have no other choice but to continuously revisit epistemological questions, including ones that seem settled and have now crystallised into some kind of common-sense/traditional orthodox. Multilingualism presents us with some such questions that seem to have been settled and yet remain troubling due to myriad uncertainties around them.

(1) What language ideologies and ideologies of (or about) language underwrite the concept of multilingualism from a policy perspective and from an academic practitioner's perspective?
(2) What political-economic conditions are feeding into and sustaining the ongoing multilingualism discourse, including those discourses that inform ideas on immigrant and diaspora identities?
(3) What does the current framing of the multilingualism discourse reveal and hide about languages and their users?
(4) What are the assumptions and blind spots of the current understanding of multilingualism as a discourse and as a policy framework in immigrant and diaspora contexts?
(5) What promises do non-academic understandings of language in society hold for the development of nuanced and contextually relevant conceptions of multilingualism and its applications?
(6) Would Africa-centred conceptions of multilingualism be possible and what would their applications look like when seen from the perspective of decolonial epistemology?

In addressing these and related questions, we take the debate on linguistic ideologies and multilingualism in a new direction that is two-pronged. The first is that of interrogating and problematising the 'multilinguality' of African multilingualism as currently understood in language education; social policy settings; and in the community and society. The second is about mapping out what a socially realistic notion of multilingualism would look like if we take into account the voices of currently marginalised and ignored African communities of practice – both on the African continent and in the diasporas.

For the above reasons, the way we look at current mainstream understandings of multilingualism and multilingual education policy and practice is not as optimistic as the rosy picture painted in Hornberger's 10 certainties. We see the task at hand as that of how to build a different kind of knowledge about multilingualism and associated discourses on language in society. We argue that though mainstream understandings of multilingualism have prevailed for a long time, they have, at the same time, remained attached to a set of unpromising associations with language as an enumerable object (as opposed to language as process). The tendency to view multilingualism as the panacea for social, economic and educational inequalities ignores the dirty history of multilingualism discourse in the exploitation of colonised societies. On this point, we share Sinfree Makoni's (1998: 244) caution about the misleading and deceptive nature of such discourses as they 'derive their strength through a deliberate refusal to recollect that in the past multilingualism has always been used to facilitate the exploitation of Africans'. This specifically relates to the human rights-inspired multilingualism discourse in countries such as South Africa that overlooks the history of the Bantu language education policies of the apartheid era, which were designed not only to divide Africans but also to ensure Africans received a sub-standard form of education (Makoni, 1998, 2003). But this was actuated through the façade of promoting the use of indigenous African languages in educating African children.

There is, therefore, a compelling need to re-examine mainstream discourses, praxes and applications of multilingualism so we can fully understand how languages are regarded differently in various contexts and timespans. Writing with specific reference to the origins of sociolinguistics as an academic discipline, Conrad Koener says

> the appearance of a cover term for a particular field of research does not necessarily signal the beginning of a discipline, but it marks the point at which professional identification of a particular enterprise is regarded as desirable by at least some of its practitioners. (Koener, 1991: 65)

Koener's caution about sociolinguistics is equally relevant to how we should be looking at the discourse and praxis of multilingualism today. Both the phenomenology and conceptual architecture of what constitutes multilingualism in present-day African societies were co-constructed with the equally problematic and contested colonial notions of 'tribe' and 'tribalism' (Chimhundu, 2005; Ranger, 1985, 1989). This was part of the colonial project of inventing African identities that would ultimately enhance administrative convenience through the political control and manipulation of the 'native' 'colonial subject'. Bernard Cohn (1996) and later, Janina Brutt-Griffler (2006) could not have put it any better when they said that the colonisers sought to exercise *command over language* as a way to produce new *languages of command*.

It was within the context of these colonial imaginaries of African 'tribal' identities and 'African languages' that the current discourse of African multilingualism emerged. The problem with colonially inherited notions of African multilingualism is that they mystify the value of linguistic resources by treating them as separate autonomous entities (Canagarajah, 2011). And yet, as the most recent and quite contemporary sociolinguistics scholarship shows, languages are, in fact, products of the deeply social and cultural activities in which people engage for meaning making (Pennycook, 2010).

Several leading international scholars of sociolinguistics have questioned and challenged the very essence of African languages as we know them today. Some, such as Makoni and Alastair Pennycook (2007), have gone as far as characterising African languages as invented categories that need to be disinvented; and as semiotic artefacts of colonial archives of knowledge that betray the 'coloniality of language' (Ndhlovu, 2019) endemic in the postcolonial African body politic. These colonial imaginings of multilingualism sustain the very idea of African language diversity that abounds in mainstream academic social policy and practitioner conversations. This story of colonial inventions of languages and the colonial roots of mainstream notions of multilingualism is not unique to Africa. Rather, it is ubiquitous in other comparable regions of the Global South, such as Asia and Latin America.

The Burden of the 'Mono' in Multilingualism

There is a strong element of 'mono' thinking or mindset embedded in the current mainstream notion of multilingualism. This is traceable to the problematic concept of the 'monolingual mindset', which has been the subject of recent academic enquiry in the context of multilingualism and language education, particularly in immigrant and diasporic contexts.

Michael Clyne (2005, 2008) popularised the notion of the monolingual mindset in Australia against the backdrop of the declining use of migrant languages due to negative attitudes towards such languages by some sections of Australian society. Most Australians, mainly those from Anglo backgrounds, are said to have a latent belief that proficiency in many languages is, in fact, an exception rather than a norm for most people. Locating it within political and public policy statements symptomatic of conservative politics in Australia, Clyne (2008) says that a monolingual mindset is about seeing everything in terms of a single language.

> This includes (a) regarding monolingualism as the norm and plurilingualism (whether bi- or multilingualism) as exceptional, deviant, unnecessary, dangerous or undesirable, (b) not understanding the links between skills in one language and others, and (c) reflecting such thinking in social and educational planning. (Clyne, 2008: 348)

While many societies have had long histories of compartmentalising language in this way and treating certain varieties or dialects as superior to others, these attitudes have intensified since the rise of Western European Enlightenment. The twin processes of colonial imperialism and Christian modernity have had the most significant influence on the spread of monolingual thinking. As Clyne (2008: 349) elaborates further, 'important decisions in education and other public domains are [typically] made according to criteria assuming that monolingualism is the norm and that plurilingualism (using two or more languages) is exceptional, problematic or transitory'. The term 'monolingual' in particular has been examined by many other scholars including Ellis (2006: 176) who, like Clyne, says that an individual is monolingual if he/she 'does not have access to more than one linguistic code as a means of social communication'. In her review of some pioneering studies in sociolinguistics and educational linguistics, Ellis provides a taxonomy of the monolingual mindset. She breaks down this concept into three strands based on societal and institutional manifestations. First is the representation of monolingualism as 'the unmarked case' – that is, monolingualism as the normal or default situation while multilingualism is set as the exception. Monolingualism as a limitation or absence of skills is the second strand, which according to Ellis, is reflected mainly in academic discourses and in the framing of language education policies in schools and institutions of higher education. The third strand is that of monolingualism as a pathological state whereby the monolingual individual is said to be so 'because he or she has suffered from lack of opportunity to learn (or maintain) a second language through discriminatory policies and practices' (Ellis, 2006: 186).

Although we do share the concerns raised by both Clyne and Ellis around the notion of the monolingual mindset and its pervasive effects, we hold some reservations with the way they frame or conceptualise the 'mono' in monolingualism and – by extension – the 'multi' in multilingualism. Their critiques are largely anchored on approaches that posit the existence of 'languages' as given countable things that we all see/use and relate to in similar ways. Makoni and Pennycook (2007) have highlighted a glaring blind spot about how such scholarly approaches to diversity start with the enumerative strategy of counting languages and romanticising a plurality based on these putative language counts. The point of greater significance here is that the question of diversity is not necessarily or always a quantitative one. There are several other ways of how to talk about diversity without having to invoke the logics of quantity or enumerability. We provide the following two stories that we hope will help concretise the point we are arguing about, engaging with diversity in ways that sidestep the language of numbers and mono-epistemologies.

The first story is about Finex's father, James Mabuku Ndhlovu-Mhaso (1896–1994). He was born in October 1896, exactly one month after the Union Jack had been raised at Fort Salisbury to signal the formal occupation of Zimbabwe by the British Pioneer Column on 12 September of the same year. Finex's father died at the age of 98. He had never had the privilege of receiving formal colonial education, which could have introduced him to Western Euro-modernist systems of literacy and numeracy.[2] For this reason, James Mabuku Ndhlovu-Mhaso could neither read nor write, not even his own name. However, he had the good fortune of owning a very big herd of cattle – probably close to 200 – purchased through savings from the meagre salary he earned as a driver of ox-drawn wagons at the newly established mining towns of Que Que and Hartley. Each animal had a name and an identity based on the colour of its skin, the shape of its horns (or lack of them) and so on.

Decades later, Finex and his elder brothers became herd boys for these cattle, some of which would wander and get lost in the bush. Each time they brought the animals back home at the end of the day with some missing, Finex's father would easily tell which ones were missing and ask how they got lost. He would just look at the herd and ask in isiNdebele language:

Inkonyane kaNzimakazi ikuphi?
Kutheni uLentusi ngingamboni lapha?
Kanti ithokazi likaNsundukazi lilitshiyephi?

[Where is Nzimakazi's calf?
Why is Lentusi not here?
Where did you leave Nsundukazi's heifer?]

Remember, Finex's father had no knowledge of Euro-modernist enumerative logics of measuring diversity. However, he could always figure out the specific animals that were missing among the close to 200 of them. This tells us that he definitely had a clear sense of gauging diversity by following a route that does not start with the enumerative strategy. What we learn from this story is that people from different social and cultural traditions have differing ways of engaging with matters of diversity without necessarily having to invoke Euro-modernist habits and practices of literacy and numeracy. This type of knowledge about using one's senses to read and interpret social reality is missing from current mainstream conceptions of multilingualism and language diversity. It lays to rest several myths that we live by, including the common-sense assumption that the question of diversity is always a quantity question.

The second story is about Leketi's mother. Leketi grew up with a mother who never had the opportunity to attain formal schooling under apartheid South Africa. Going to the local shops to buy anything was always a mission impossible as both Leketi and his mother could not read price tags or understand Afrikaans, which was used in the stores near the farm areas. Their village, Leboeng, had a number of speakers who fluidly used Sepedi, Xitsonga and Siswati without boundaries.

Another observation of Leketi's mother was that under the adverse poverty conditions they experienced, she always had to ask for help from the neighbours. Leketi noticed particular ways in which communication and meaning making were made. His mother would go to a neighbour with the intention of asking for a sugar refill for her children to have tea before they went to school (they needed this energy boost to walk approximately 12 kilometres to school daily). She would go into the neighbour's house unannounced as such casual visits were always expected from anyone living in the village. Upon arrival, they would offer her something to eat and then general conversations would begin. These included all kinds of village stories (what is referred to as the 'goat of the road', which meant stories whose author is unknown, but they floated around and were believed to be true) and updates about experiences in wood gathering, seasonal changes, etc. These conversations would go on for half a day and on other occasions they would last for nearly the whole day – full of talking, eating and bonding. To end the talks, Leketi's mother would say 'goodbye' once and twice but without actually leaving. These goodbyes were a signal that she wanted something unspoken. In other words, saying goodbye more than once was known to be an indirect request for something as found in the Sepedi wording: 'Go laela gantshi ke maano a tlala' [many goodbyes are a connive for hunger relief]. The third goodbye was always a cue for the host to walk the visitor out. Leketi's mother would come to the third goodbye and at this point the host would walk her out as expected. Once she had moved out of the yard and the gate, she would make her request for a sugar refill known. If the host had an extra sugar portion to supply, they would walk back into the house for it and then Leketi's mother would go home. If the host had no sugar to offer, it would be at this point that it was safe to receive the negative news and walk away.

What we observe from the story is that the local people in this village have established literacy practices and ways of meaning making that are particular to this community. These ways of meaning making through indirection are funds of knowledge that often sit at odds with modern school literacy expectations where the maxim of straight to the point is valorised. In brief, there are African ways of meaning making that have always been marginalised through colonial and mono notions of literacy.

The significant point here is one about the need to write into our conversations those multiple and competing, yet equally legitimate ways of talking about diversity. Pennycook (2008) cautions about the unintended consequences of approaching diversity from a purely quantitative approach:

> By rendering diversity a quantity question of language enumeration, such approaches continue to employ the census strategies of colonialism while missing the qualitative question of where diversity lies. (Pennycook, 2008: 24)

Therefore, the persistent problem we find in mainstream approaches to multilingualism and language diversity is that they follow a mono-epistemic paradigm that exclusively focuses on standard countable language-things while turning a blind eye to several other ways of speaking about people's diverse language and communicative practices (Ndhlovu, 2015b). At the heart of the matter are questions of language conceptualisations and epistemologies. Our concern should not only be about the number of 'language' things or objects that are being recognised and validated in multilingual education and other social policy frameworks. Rather, the focus should be on how we conceive or conceptualise the 'lingual'. What is our concept of the 'lingual' in 'monolingualism' and 'multilingualism'? In advancing this view on language diversity, we echo Adamek's (2004: 4) concept of lingualism, which he uses 'to indicate linguistic practices in their broadest terms, including all attitudes, gestures, signs, and cultural activities related to language use'.

Our thesis also builds on and extends Ingrid Piller's (2016) critique of 'monolingual ways of seeing' that underpin multilingual education policies and academic research agendas. Piller opens her analysis by positing that what we see is constrained by what we expect to see based on our beliefs and knowledge. In the context of mainstream multilingualism research paradigms, she argues that English monolingualism undergirds contemporary ways of seeing what counts as valid academic research and forms of knowledge produced. With specific focus on research into multilingualism, she goes on to identify and unpack three aspects of monolingual ways of seeing. The first is about perceptions of multilingualism as generic and context-free. That is, 'monolingual ways of seeing multilingualism entail a very peculiar perspective that disguises its peculiarity as general and universalistic' (Piller, 2016: 28). The two consequences of this universalising tendency are that (a) monolingual ways of seeing are obscured from being recognised as particularistic; and (b) the need to examine the specificity and locality of monolingual ways of seeing is overlooked as it remains hidden behind the façade of universal relevance. This critique resonates with lines of argument advanced by decolonial and Southern theorists that we draw upon in this book.

The second monolingual way of seeing is one about the presentist view of multilingualism and the preoccupation with immediacy that does not pay much attention to the history of sociolinguistics research. According to Piller, contemporary monolingual ways of seeing direct researchers' attention to more recent societal (read colonial) conditions of the 19th and 20th centuries while overlooking linguistic diversity that has flourished for more than 3000 years (Piller, 2016: 28). Piller further argues that such obsession with an ahistorical and presentist view of research into multilingualism reflects 'a lack of knowledge about the historically longstanding awareness of vocal multiplicities, their sources, their intertwinings and, consequently the problems of interpretation that they present' (Piller, 2016: 29). In short, the presentist monolingual way of seeing ignores both the long-standing philosophical traditions exploring linguistic, social and epistemological diversity, and contexts (especially Southern and indigenous) where multilingualism is the normal state of being.

Piller describes the third monolingual way of seeing as being about a focus on the product of the monolingual academic text whereby material in languages other than English is rarely presented in the original. Instead, readers are denied the multilingual experience through the habit of translating from other languages into English as a way of admitting such material into the world of 'valid' and 'legitimate' epistemology. But, as Benjamin (2002: 254) advises, 'no translation however good it may be can have any significance as regards the original'. This is to say that the ontologies of given cultures and the experience of ontic categories, such as time and space, are rendered intelligible through the distinctiveness of a language (that is, language as process, a means of reading and interpreting social reality). Things in the world directly experienced and perceived in a system of thought, are made visible and sayable through the immediacy of enunciating in the languages of that particular experience or tradition.

However, this does not suggest that the problem of signifying meaning, or its deferral, is peculiar to translation between languages (Derrida, 1977, 2008). We acknowledge that hegemonic/subaltern relations between people can vex the production and interpretation of knowledge within a particular culture – including knowledge about such things as language diversity. Individuals and population groups, despite dialectical differences, can have shared monolingual habits, but be divided in their struggle for meaning and onto-epistemic visibility. The challenge of translating different systems of thought offers both problems and possibilities that transfer within and across the matrix of global cultures. For these reasons,

> Contemporary multilingualism research written in English offers, by and large, a monolingual reading experience. It is not uncommon to find that data from other languages are simply presented in translation; if non-English data are presented in the original, they are always accompanied by an English translation. In the typical contemporary English-language research article, the reader can comfortably go into monolingual mode; even if other language material appears in the article, the reader, if so inclined, does not need to pay attention and can skip it to simply concentrate on the English. (Piller, 2016: 30)

Piller's sentiments echo those of South African critical psychologist Desmond Painter (2011) who introduced the notion of the 'monolingual drone'. Painter uses the metaphor of the 'monolingual drone' as a summary term for the situation whereby researchers and educators lazily rely on the idea that English is a global lingua franca, an innocent 'link language'. In doing so, they inadvertently contribute 'to exactly that which we seek to disrupt when we critique the contemporary university's neoliberal rhetoric of "internationalisation" and "marketable knowledge"' (Painter, 2011: 1). Painter locates his characterisation of English as a 'monolingual drone' within broader discourses on neo-colonial relationships of knowledge production and consumption. Drawing on the example of South Africa where the majority of the population uses multiple language types, Painter says the preference for English monolingualism is problematic because it reflects elite hegemonic interests and not those of the majority of the population. In the domain of academic research and publication, the English 'monolingual drone' is evidenced by common assumptions of those who work in predominantly English language environments. Since literature is abundantly available in English in these environments, it can be easy to describe English medium literature as '*the* literature (as in: an overview of the literature; a search of the literature, etc), often not pausing to reflect on the parallel existence of other, linguistically different bodies of writing and publication' (Painter, 2011: 1).

This discourse of English as a self-evident academic language hides more than it reveals. The one thing it hides is that it presents itself as the ideological opposite of processes of exclusion: that in the midst of linguistic and cultural diversity, English is the mechanism of inclusion, of intercultural dialogue and understanding, of the obliteration of boundaries and of joint and borderless activity. But as the previous body of work in critical applied linguistics has shown (see e.g. Canagarajah, 1999; Pennycook, 1994, 2007; Phillipson, 2003), English is ideologically and culturally laden. The ubiquitous discourse that presents English as a 'neutral' and self-evident lingua franca for global academic exchanges is deceptive and misleading. It obscures the fact that for the majority of communities around the world, boundaries between languages are soft, blurry and in constant flux. One only has to watch South African television soap operas and listen to the everyday conversations of ordinary South Africans to get a sense of the dynamic nature of linguistic usages that defy the façade of language boundaries. This means for the majority of scholars from the Southern orbit of the globe, writing in monolingual mode is a futile exercise disconnected from the language practices of the communities for whom they are writing. It effectively amounts to the production and reproduction of the very same colonial matrices of power and epistemological hegemonies that are disconnected from the 'qualitative' multilingual practices of real people in real life.

It follows, therefore, from the above that monolingual mindsets, monolingual ways of seeing and monolingual drones are very powerful tools for entrenching epistemological inequities 'precisely because they are put forward as intellectual arguments and not as moral ones, and even less as political ones' (Wallerstein, 2004: 162). Consequently, the imposition of hegemonic language ideologies (albeit by stealth) in the conduct and communication of research about multilingualism 'permits groups controlling structures of knowledge to limit what can conceivably be observed in research, what kind of findings are seen to be plausible and therefore acceptable, and what kind of policy implications can be drawn from this knowledge' (Wallerstein, 2004: 162).

Inspired by Pierre Bourdieu's (1991) notion of linguistic habitus, Ingrid Gogolin (2002) introduced the multilingual habitus approach that we can draw upon as a counter-hegemonic strategy for addressing problems associated with 'monolingual drones', 'monolingual mindsets' and 'monolingual ways of seeing'. A multilingual habitus perspective seeks to accommodate and recognise those language practices that are generally ignored, marginalised and consigned to the peripheries of educational epistemologies and pedagogies (Ndhlovu, 2015b). In the context of education, a multilingual habitus approach is also about tapping into students' funds of knowledge (McIntyre *et al.*, 2001) whereby the totality of linguistic resources, communication codes and cultures of learning are harnessed and deployed towards epistemological renewal in our teaching and research agendas. Ndhlovu's (2015b) notion of ignored lingualism[3] extends the applications of multilingual habitus approaches in language education policy. Ignored lingualism is a summary term for those views about language that depart from traditional/orthodox understandings of what language diversity entails (Ndhlovu, 2015b: 406). Ignored lingualism also aligns with the translingual approaches widely advocated by Canagarajah (2011), García and Li Wei (2014) and Li Wei and Zhu (2013) among others – that draw attention to the promises of a multilingual habitus framing of educational policies.

Carol Benson (2014) identified at least five key contours and educational benefits of a multilingual habitus. First, it allows for the negotiation of language(s) of literacy and interaction among classroom participants. Second, a multilingual habitus approach allows for the design of learning goals in terms of the quality and usefulness of the competences of learners. Third, it provides opportunities for building on students' knowledge and experiences, thus promoting a systematic and holistic approach to engaging various types or forms of knowledge. The fourth benefit is about promoting the development of metalinguistic awareness among both educators and students as an integral part of conducting research and disseminating research outcomes. Fifth, a multilingual habitus approach encourages scaffolding meaning and using methods and other language types appropriate to students' needs and experiences.

Overall, multilingual habitus looks for opportunities to complement and support existing strengths and capacities as opposed to focusing on, and staying with, the problem or concern (Department of Education and Early Childhood Development, 2012). It represents 'a paradigm shift—a movement away from monolingual deficit-based approaches that fail to provide sufficient information about strengths and strategies to support students' learning and development' (Department of Education and Early Childhood Development, 2012: 6). A multilingual habitus perspective draws the attention of educators and policymakers to students' pre-existing strengths such as intellectual abilities, communication skills, language abilities, interpersonal skills, capacities, dispositions, interests and motivations. In short, a multilingual habitus is the direct opposite of a monolingual habitus in the sense that it makes 'the language(s) of teaching and learning explicit' (Benson, 2014: 293) through the development of appropriate methods, materials and assessments that reflect the language experiences of learners and the communities to which they belong.

Nevertheless, the lingering ghosts of monolingual mindsets, monolingual ways of seeing and monolingual drones remain. In the context of postcolonial Africa, multilingual policies in their current framing are not working. Could it be that the notions of 'multilingualism' being promoted are disconnected from societal language practices and expectations? If this were to be the case – as we posit in this book – what must we do?

This Book

In the following pages, we present eight distinct, yet interrelated themes that build on and extend into new directions the burgeoning social science scholarship on decolonial epistemology. The book searches for fruitful ways of exploring next steps in decolonising the discourse and praxis of multilingualism. Previous decolonial theorisations have posited five strands of coloniality: coloniality of power, coloniality of knowledge, coloniality of culture, coloniality of nature and coloniality of being (Quijano, 2000). This book seeks to contribute new points of method, theory and interpretation that will advance scholarly conversations on decolonial epistemology by adding a sixth strand: coloniality of language. We use the concept of coloniality of language to describe the ways in which notions of language and multilingualism in postcolonial societies still remain colonial. The book places the concept of coloniality of language at the centre of scholarship on decolonial epistemology. In doing so, it adds a new angle that pushes forward a more applied agenda to establish clear and empirically grounded frameworks designed to challenge the enduring colonial matrices of power hidden within mainstream conceptions of multilingualism and language diversity that were propagated in the Global North and then exported to the Global South under the aegis of colonial modernity and pushed through in the guise of universal epistemic relevance.

The premise of *Decolonising Multilingualism in Africa* is that mainstream understandings of multilingualism such as those that underpin multilingual education, mother tongue education, additive bilingual education and multilingual national language policies are problematic. These must be critically interrogated because they exemplify the subtle manifestation of 'coloniality of language'. Coloniality of language is a summary term for how notions of language, multilingualism and their applications in social and educational policy arenas in most postcolonial societies, remain colonial (Ndhlovu, 2020). All languages that are counted under dominant models of multilingualism (mostly under the banner of official and national languages) are semiotic social inventions that serve the colonial purpose of invisibilising other language practices. As was the case during the colonial/apartheid era, those languages that are recognised in mainstream notions of multilingualism programmes in a range of social policy, educational and political domains today inadvertently serve the purpose of hiding the homogenising and exclusionary intentions of such programmes. This is precisely because the same colonially invented versions of languages are being celebrated as bastions of sociolinguistic justice and equity in these domains. And yet, as we know, standard 'national languages' – also known as vernacular languages – were invented and then deployed towards sociocultural and political engineering processes that produced skewed versions of local native/indigenous identities (Brutt-Griffler, 2006; Makoni, 1998; Ndhlovu, 2009; Ranger, 1989). It is here that the notion of 'coloniality of language' advanced in this book is a useful analytical lens. It sheds new light on why there is really nothing new, novel or progressive about current bi-/multilingual or additive bilingual education policies that rest on colonially invented conceptions of African multilingualism, as we know it today. In this vein, this book is a first step towards a counter-hegemonic project that seeks to challenge the legacy of colonial language ideologies that currently undergird mainstream multilingualism research and theorisation.

We note and acknowledge the commendable progress made by previous scholars in unmasking colonial matrices of power that underwrite the notion of language as a standard enumerable construct. However, some blind spots remain. Questions around the phenomenology of multilingualism itself and the conceptual frameworks that shape common-sense assumptions about language diversity have so far not been adequately addressed in the form of a systematic body of work such as a scholarly book or research monograph. What we currently have is a plethora of theorisations that are not tied together by a coherent and cogent cross-cutting theme. As we have indicated above, there remain several theoretical and empirical questions around what constitutes meaningful and holistic understandings of multilingualism in formerly colonised regions of the world – beyond the mere enumeration of multiple 'language-things'.

In a recent book titled *Metaphors of Multilingualism*, Rainer Guldin (2020) spotlights this very issue and argues that notwithstanding the emergence of new approaches, the traditional monolingual point of view is still significantly influencing present-day attitudes towards multilingualism. Guldin focuses on shifts both in the choice and in the use of metaphors across a selection of humanities and social disciplines to trace the radical redefinition of multilingualism that has taken place over the last decades. *Decolonising Multilingualism in Africa* joins this body of emerging and quite contemporary work. It is a first attempt to weigh into these contested issues by specifically interrogating the phenomenology of African multilingualism and implications for relevant communities of scholars and policymakers.

However, the pathway we follow in searching for answers to questions at the centre of the book, does not intend to be doctrinaire. Neither do we seek to answer these questions in the abstract. Rather, we deploy a combination of innovative theorisation, commitment to empirical evidence and methodological rigour. Consequently, some chapters are based on data from in-depth narrative ethnographic studies with African communities – both on the continent and in the diaspora. We leverage the potential of decolonial epistemology to act as a unifying force in our attempt to draw scholarly attention to those marginalised and ignored African notions of multilingualism. A significant part of our agenda is to untangle complex meanings and understandings of multilingualism through culturally relevant modes of engagement with non-academic communities. The overall intention is to find connections, points of confluence and opportunities for the transfer of methods and concepts, not only among members of academic communities, but also between them and non-academic communities. This way, we hope to develop alternative ways for charting next steps in solving practical language-related problems in educational and other social policy areas – in ways that mitigate the limitations of conventional or Euro-modernist versions of multilingualism. This is about forging collaborative research with non-academic communities as equal partners, whereby social scientists are willing to learn at the feet of community leaders, women, the youth, refugees, migrants – the subaltern so to speak. It is about listening to the stories of ordinary men and women, and using such stories to generate concept notes that inform discourses and policy frameworks on language and literacy education and on many other social, economic and political domains where language is implicated.

Organisation

This book consists of nine chapters as follows. Chapter 1 introduces the book and lays out its theoretical and empirical contributions to the topic of multilingualism and language ideologies. It starts by reviewing mainstream beliefs and fallacies about the meanings and social applications of multilingualism. A key argument advanced is that by examining alternative conceptualisations of multilingualism – specifically those from the Global South – and transposing them onto a range of socioeconomic, political and cultural domains, we can begin to develop a fruitful and revised consideration of the role of language in society.

Chapter 2 provides a historiographical account of the colonial origins of standard languages and, by extension, the common-sense view that regards multilingualism as simply an accumulation of numerable 'language-things' (Ndhlovu, 2014). The argument is that current mainstream understandings of multilingualism and its entailments have to be seen in the context of the larger colonial archive of knowledge where an ideology of languages as separate, autonomous objects in the world, things that could be classified, arranged and deployed as media of exchange was developed. Both the phenomenology and conceptual architecture of what constitutes multilingualism in many African countries – and indeed in nearly all countries around the world – were co-constructed with the equally problematic and contested colonial notions of 'tribes' and 'tribalism'. The significant point advanced in this chapter is this: current understandings of African multilingualism that are tied to colonial language ideologies are part of the broader political project of global coloniality – the obsession with creating hierarchies of humanity, albeit by stealth. A critique of the rather simplistic embrace of colonial language ideologies as underpinning pillars of African multilingual policy frameworks concludes the chapter.

In Chapter 3, we turn to the applied interests of multilingualism in the domains of language and literacy education. Language and literacy education is one area that has received quite a lot of policy intervention at the international, national and sub-national levels. Such policy interventions are couched in terms such as mother tongue education, bilingual education, additive bilingual education, second/third additional languages education, multilingual education and many more. This chapter broadens and further extends these established paradigms by problematising the phenomenology of multilingualism as currently used and understood in the field of language and literacy education. It uses qualitative data that was collected through community-based participatory research in the Limpopo and Mpumalanga provinces of South Africa. The goal is to shed new light on how local community understandings of multilingualism can inform, shape and influence expert academic and practitioner practices and discourses on language and literacy education. This is about adopting a bottom-up approach whereby conventional wisdom is inverted. The chapter concludes by arguing that instead of teaching communities about multilingualism and literacy, academic experts and educators need to speak less and listen more to the stories, views, opinions and wisdom of real people, speaking in their real everyday languages, about their real multilingual and literacy practices.

Following on the arguments made in Chapter 3, the fourth chapter focuses on the place of multilingualism in higher education. The chapter argues that one of the crises of postcolonial African higher education is that it continues to perpetuate conservative models and discourses on training and skills development. Most African institutions of higher learning are increasingly embracing multilingualism policy frameworks as part of national agendas on transforming the higher education sector through curriculum reform and epistemological renewal. However, although the intentions and ideals are good, the so-called multilingual approaches are dogged by endemic principles of neoliberal practices and beliefs that have created myths and fallacies about multilingualism. In this chapter, we challenge those conventional and predominant higher education teaching and learning approaches that are masqueraded as a multilingual medium of instruction. Drawing specifically on contemporary theories that look at languages as transient and borderless, the chapter proposes alternative ways of seeing the multilingual medium of instruction by harnessing the diversity of language practices and communicative resources of university students. The overall goal is to bring the social fabric of wider society into our epistemological and pedagogical imaginings of a decolonised African higher education sector. Case studies include institutional language policies of universities in southern Africa.

In Chapter 5, we turn the focus on multilingual national language policies. We argue that regardless of domain – whether education/educational linguistics, media, business, law and so on – language policy always necessarily implicates several issues that are economic, political, cultural and developmental. For this reason, we approach the discourse and praxis of language policy in a manner that recognises and integrates all these separate, but intricately connected, disciplinary perspectives. The argument is that we need to draw on a much wider battery of critical, reflective and more progressive views on language policies that not only question but also proffer alternatives to canonical models of language policy and planning regimes. This chapter, therefore, adds a new angle to conversations on postcolonial African multilingual national language policies. It brings to light those intricate linkages between language policymaking, the interests of politics and the exigencies of fashioning linguistic and cultural uniformity. We introduce the concept of 'coloniality of language' as an explanatory paradigm for how notions of multilingual national language policy regimes in postcolonial Africa have largely remained colonial. The conclusion is that mainstream models of multilingual national language policies that are widely celebrated in most postcolonial African countries exemplify the subtle manifestation of 'coloniality of language'.

Chapter 6 turns to those omissions and blind spots of projective conclusions about the potential of African vehicular cross-border languages and how such assumptions are shaped by dominant, neoliberal and Euro-modernist ideologies of language and multilingualism. We argue that the proposition that African vehicular cross-border languages are best positioned to facilitate African integration is underpinned by a hegemonic and colonial philosophy that misdirects the African multilingualism debate. This becomes apparent when the perceived utility of vehicular cross-border languages is considered against the backdrop of contestations around language definition traditions. The chapter concludes with a critical analysis of perceptions about the ability of vehicular cross-border languages to resolve the anticipated intercultural communication problems of an integrated Africa.

In Chapter 7, we turn to prospects for 'dis-inventing' and 're-constituting' (Makoni & Pennycook, 2007) African multilingualism in immigrant and diasporic contexts. The chapter uses data from narrative ethnographic studies on the language practices of African migrants in rural and regional Australia to support the proposition that we need to look closely at the communicative practices of mobile people in order to sharpen our understanding of multilingualism. At the heart of the chapter is the question: What can we learn about multilingualism from the language practices, mobilities, and social and cultural experiences of migrants and diasporas? In addition to the decolonial turn, the chapter is built around the mobility paradigm (Salazar et al., 2017), an approach that seeks to include the historic movement of people with the contemporary importance of individuals' contributions to society. Following this framework of analysis, the chapter provides a laser-like focus on African migrants' comments and take on things (no matter how insignificant they might seem on the surface), in order to apprehend underlying and collective discourses. In paying particular attention to people's mobilities, movements, encounters, exchanges and mixtures, the chapter brings the voices and perspectives of immigrants and diasporas into the multilingualism debate. The overall conclusion is that the stories of research participants and researchers' mindful reflection on them need to be meticulously woven together in developing new, meaningful and broad-based theories of multilingualism.

Chapter 8 reviews the autoethnographic method in multilingualism research. The chapter tells and analyses a story about Finex's casual and unplanned encounter with Omphile, a seven-year-old boy in Johannesburg, South Africa. Omphile and Finex interacted using communicative practices that confirmed the anti-conventional theories of multilingualism posited in this book. The story also challenges the methods that support empirical observations of mainstream multilingualism research and common-sense assumptions about how language works in everyday real life. A major line of argument advanced in the chapter is one about the promises that autoethnographic approaches hold for researching multilingualism in ways that sidestep the language and methods of the positivist tradition. It is argued that in the same way that contemporary sociolinguistics theorisations remind us about how communication is not limited to determinate languages or codes, research does not have to be limited to controlled, systematic scientific methods. The framework of autoethnography reviewed in this chapter is one example of a praxis that is anti-methodological and, thus in line with many of the anti-foundational premises of the entire book.

We conclude with Chapter 9 that presents what we hope constitute fruitful ideas for Africa-centred conceptions of multilingualism. Tying together narrative stories about the language practices of African communities discussed in the entire book, the chapter argues that a more fruitful and broader conception of multilingualism is, after all, possible. The alternative conceptions of multilingualism posited in this chapter also try to capture and articulate transnational frames needed to comprehend the cultural identities and language practices of a world characterised by diverse and very many epistemological traditions.

Notes

(1) See e.g. Chilisa (2011), Novoa (2015) and Salazar *et al.* (2017).
(2) In light of what we now know about how Euro-modernist colonial education systems were designed to erode the ontological density of 'colonial subjects', we now believe that Finex's father was among the few lucky ones to escape or survive the pervasive effects of hegemonic epistemological impositions that brainwash.
(3) See Chapter 9 for a more detailed discussion of 'ignored lingualism' and the promises it holds for pushing the multilingualism discourse towards more fruitful pathways.

References

Adamek, P.M. (2004) Habits of household lingualism. *TESEL E-Journal* 8 (1), 1–24. See http://tesel-ej.org/ej29/a1.html.
Benjamin, W. (2002) The task of the translator. In M. Bullock and M. Jennings (eds) *Selected Writings Volume 1* (pp. 253–263). Cambridge, MA: Harvard University Press.
Benson, C. (2014) Towards adopting a multilingual habitus in educational development. In C. Benson and K. Kosonen (eds) *Language Issues in Comparative Education: Inclusive Teaching and Learning in Non-Dominant Languages and Cultures* (pp. 283–299). Rotterdam/Boston/Taipei: Sense Publishers.
Bourdieu, P. (1977) *Outline of a Theory of Practice*. Cambridge: Cambridge University Press.
Brutt-Griffler, J. (2006) Language endangerment, the construction of indigenous languages and World English. In M. Pütz, J.A. Fishman and J.N. Aertselaer (eds) *Along the Routes to Power: Explorations of Empowerment through Language* (pp. 35–54). Berlin/New York: Mouton de Gruyter.
Canagarajah, S. (1999) *Resisting Linguistic Imperialism in English Teaching*. Oxford: Oxford University Press.
Canagarajah, S. (2011) Codemeshing in academic writing: Identifying teachable strategies of translanguaging. *The Modern Language Journal* 95 (3), 401–417.
Chilisa, B. (2012) *Indigenous Research Methodologies*. Los Angeles, CA/London: Routledge.
Chimhundu, H. (1992) Early missionaries and the ethnolinguistic factor during the invention of tribalism in Zimbabwe. *Journal of African History* 44, 87–109.
Clyne, M.G. (2005) *Australia's Language Potential*. Sydney: University of New South Wales Press.
Clyne, M.G. (2008) The monolingual mindset as an impediment to the development of plurilingual potential in Australia. *Sociolinguistic Studies* 2 (3), 347–365.
Cohn, B.S. (1996) *Colonialism and Its Forms of Knowledge*. Princeton, NJ: Princeton University Press.

Connell, R. (2007) *Southern Theory: The Global Dynamics of Knowledge in Social Science.* Crows Nest: Allen & Unwin.
Connell, R. (2014) Margin becoming centre: For a world-centred rethinking of masculinities. *NORMA: International Journal of Masculinities Studies* 9 (4), 217–231.
Connell, R. (2018) Decolonizing sociology. *Contemporary Sociology* 47 (4), 339–407.
Connell, R. (2019) *The Good University: What Universities Actually Do and Why It's Time for Radical Change.* London: Zed Books.
Department of Education and Early Childhood Development (2012) *Strength-based Approach. A Guide to Writing Transition Learning and Development Statements.* Australia: State of Victoria.
de Sousa Santos, B. and Meneses, M.P. (2020) Preface. In B. de Sousa Santos and M.P. Meneses (eds) *Knowledges Born in the Struggle: Constructing Epistemologies of the Global South* (pp. xiv–xviii). London/New York: Routledge.
Derrida, J. (1977) *Limited Inc: abc.* Baltimore, MD: Johns Hopkins University Press.
Derrida, J. (2008) *Writing and Difference.* Abington: Routledge and Keenan.
Ellis, E. (2006) Monolingualism: The unmarked case. *Estudios de Sociolingüística* 7 (2), 173–196.
García, O. and Li Wei (2014) *Translanguaging: Language, Bilingualism and Education* Basingstoke: Palgrave Macmillan.
Guldin, R. (2020) *Metaphors of Multilingualism: Changing Attitudes towards Language Diversity in Literature, Linguistics and Philosophy.* London/New York: Routledge.
Hornberger, N.H. (2009) Multilingual education policy and practice: Ten certainties (grounded in indigenous experience). *Language Teaching* 42 (2), 197–211.
Koener, K. (1991) Toward a history of modern sociolinguistics. *American Speech* 66 (1), 57–70. See http://www.jstor.org/stable/455434.
Li, W. and Zhu, H. (2013) Translanguaging identities: Creating transnational space through flexible multilingual practices amongst Chinese university students in the UK. *Applied Linguistics* 34 (5), 516–535.
Liu, W. (2016) Conceptualising multilingual capabilities in anglophone higher degree research education: Challenges and possibilities for reconfiguring language practices and policies. *Education Sciences* 6 (39), 1–12.
Makoni, S. (1998) African languages as European scripts: The shaping of communal memory. In S. Nuttall and C. Coetzee (eds) *Negating the Past: The Making of Memory in South Africa* (pp. 242–248). Oxford: Oxford University Press.
Makoni, S. (2003) From misinvention to disinvention of language: Multilingualism and the South African constitution. In S. Makoni, G. Smitherman, A.F. Ball and A.K. Spears (eds) *Black Linguistics: Language, Society, and Politics in Africa and the Americas* (pp. 132–151). London & New York: London.
Makoni, S. and Pennycook, A. (eds) (2007) *Disinventing and Reconstituting Languages.* Clevedon: Multilingual Matters.
McIntyre, E., Rosebery, A. and González, N. (eds) (2001) *Classroom Diversity: Connecting Curriculum to Students' Lives.* Portsmouth, NH: Heinemann.
Midgely, M. (2003) *The Myths We Live By.* London/New York: Routledge.
Ndhlovu, F. (2009) *The Politics of Language and Nation Building in Zimbabwe.* Bern: Peter Lang.
Ndhlovu, F. (2014) *Becoming an African Diaspora in Australia: Language, Culture, Identity.* Houndmills: Palgrave Macmillan.
Ndhlovu, F. (2015a) *Hegemony and Language Policies in Southern Africa: Identity, Integration, Development.* Newcastle upon Tyne: Cambridge Scholars Publishing.

Ndhlovu, F. (2015b) Ignored lingualism: Another resource for overcoming the monolingual mindset in language education policy. *Australian Journal of Linguistics* 35 (4), 398–414.
Ndhlovu, F. (2020) Post-colonial language education or coloniality of language by stealth? In A. Abdelhay, S.B. Makoni and C.G. Severo (eds) *Language Planning and Policy: Ideologies, Ethnicities and Semiotic Spaces of Power* (pp. 133–151). Newcastle upon Tyne: Cambridge Scholars Publishing.
Novoa, A. (2015) Mobile ethnography: Emergence, techniques and its importance to geography. *Human Geographies* 9 (1), 97–107.
Painter, D. (2011) The Monolingual Drone: Language and Critical Psychology, Part 1. See https://southernpsychologies.wordpress.com/2011/12/03/the-monolingual-drone-language-and-critical-psychology-part-1/ (accessed 15 October 2019).
Peet, R. (1997) Social theory, postmodernism, and the critique of development. In G. Benko and U. Strohmayer (eds) *Space and Social Theory: Interpreting Modernity and Postmodernity* (pp. 72–87). Oxford: Blackwell.
Pennycook, A. (1994) *The Cultural Politics of English as an International Language*. London: Longman.
Pennycook, A. (2007) *Global Englishes and Transcultural Flows*. New York: Routledge.
Pennycook, A. (2008) Language-free linguistics and linguistics-free languages. In A. Mahboob and N. Knight (eds) *Questioning Linguistics* (pp. 18–31). Newcastle upon Tyne: Cambridge Scholars Publishing.
Pennycook, A. (2010) *Language as a Local Practice*. London/New York: Routledge.
Phillipson, R. (2003) *English Only Europe? Challenging Language Policy*. London: Routledge.
Piller, I. (2016) Monolingual ways of seeing multilingualism. *Journal of Multicultural Discourses* 11 (1), 25–33.
Quijano, A. (2000) Coloniality of power, ethnocentrism, and Latin America. *Nepantla* 1, 533–580.
Ranger, T.O. (1985) *The Invention of Tribalism in Zimbabwe*. Gweru: Mambo Press.
Ranger, T.O. (1989) Missionaries, migrants and the Manyika: The invention of ethnicity in Zimbabwe. In L. Vail (ed.) *The Creation of Tribalism in Southern Africa* (pp. 118–150). London: James Currey.
Salazar, N.B., Elliot, A. and Roger, N. (eds) (2017) *Methodologies of Mobility: Ethnography of Experiment*. New York/Oxford: Berghahn.
Smith, L.T. (2012) *Decolonizing Methodologies: Research and Indigenous Peoples* (2nd edn). London/New York: Zed Books.
Wallerstein, I. (2004) *Uncertainties of Knowledge*. Philadelphia, PA: Temple University Press.

2 Unsettling Colonial Roots of Multilingualism

Introduction

This chapter provides a historiographical account of the colonial origins of standard languages and, by extension, the common-sense view about multilingualism as simply an accumulation of numerable 'language-things' (Ndhlovu, 2014). The argument is that current mainstream understandings of multilingualism and its entailments have to be seen in the context of the larger colonial archive of knowledge where an ideology of languages as separate, autonomous objects in the world, things that could be classified, arranged and deployed as media of exchange, was developed (Makoni & Pennycook, 2007). Both the phenomenology and conceptual architecture of what constitutes multilingualism in many African countries – and indeed in nearly all countries around the world – were co-constructed with the equally problematic and contested colonial notions of 'tribes' and 'tribalism'. This was part of the colonial project of inventing African identities that would ultimately enhance administrative convenience through the political control and manipulation of the 'native' 'colonial subject'. The other key point advanced in this chapter is this: the current understanding of African multilingualism that is tied to colonial language ideologies is part of the broader political project of global coloniality – the obsession with creating hierarchies of humanity, albeit by stealth. A section that provides a robust critique of the rather uncritical embrace of colonial language ideologies as underpinning pillars of African multilingual policy frameworks concludes the chapter.

Colonial Linguistics and African Multilingualism

The vast and expansive body of scholarship critical of what has come to be known as colonial linguistics (see e.g. Brutt-Griffler, 2006; Errington, 2001, 2008; Fardon & Furniss, 1994; Makoni, 1998; Severo,

2016; Zeleza, 2006) has ably demonstrated that named 'African languages' as we know them today are as recent as colonialism itself. They do not predate the emergence of this dark side of the history of humankind. Named African languages that form the basis for the discourse and praxis of African multilingualism and multilingual education policies are remnants of the Euro-modernist colonial matrix of power. In this vein, Joseph Errington (2001, 2008) advises that as other texts by historians, cultural anthropologists and literary theorists have been, the writings of early colonial linguists (including those who worked under the auspices of Christian missionary societies) must be scrutinised. Such a critical look is necessary because it is imperative for us to understand why and how

> Actions of colonial agents outran their own intent, and colonial linguistic work likewise had uses and effects beyond those foreseen or intended by its authors. It was grounded in institutions and animated by interests that legitimized simple views of enormously complex situations and that licensed what were often fantasmatic representations of authoritative linguistic certainty in the face of spectacular ignorance. At issue here are the sources of such 'certainty', because they are bound up with enabling ideologies about hierarchies of languages and peoples on colonial territory and in precolonial pasts. (Errington, 2001: 20)

Cristine Severo (2016) builds on Errington's arguments to reflect on metalinguistic aspects of colonial linguistics projects in South America. Severo introduces the notion of 'discursivization' that she uses as an explanatory concept for how colonial discourses on language are not neutral, but constitute a paradigm of modernity, which is strongly rooted in both Christianity and Enlightenment. In the words of Severo (2016: 1), colonial discourses on language constitute 'a political colonial framework of exploitation and control of land, people and languages. [Such] discursivization of language in the colonial context produced differences, hierarchies and the naturalization of cultural and human inequalities'. Together with other scholars of similar persuasion, Severo and Errington remind us that colonial political interests of power and domination were at the heart of the 19th-century missionary projects of describing and documenting languages. They draw our attention to the colonial historiography of 'African languages' and 'indigenous American languages', and to how representations of linguistic structure by early colonial missionary-linguists and colonial interests shaped each other.

When the late scholar of African nationalist historiography, Terrence Osborne Ranger (1929–2015), pioneered the thesis of the 'invention of tribalism' in southern Africa, little did he know that this summary term of what was essentially a colonial project of manipulation and control would endure to this day. In his 1985 monograph titled *The Invention of Tribalism in Zimbabwe*, Ranger provides an informative account of the various ways by which early missionary organisations in Zimbabwe (then the British colony of Southern Rhodesia) colluded with the colonial government in the process of inventing linguistic and tribal identities for the indigenous people. The project of Christianisation provided a legitimising ideology for colonial rule and was part and parcel of westernisation imposed – from above and without – on Africa. Among the self-proclaimed colonial linguists were native affairs commissioners, missionaries, anthropologists, diarists, hunters and travellers. Hailing from diverse religious, social and political persuasions in the West, these self-proclaimed linguists participated in the collection of sociolinguistic information on what they termed 'the native tribes of Southern Rhodesia'. The majority of these researchers-cum-colonial agents 'did not have the necessary linguistic or phonetic training and they saw tribes everywhere and equated these tribes with dialects or languages' (Chimhundu, 1992: 81), let alone these ethnic groups' agreement to meddle with their own linguistic practices (Ndhlovu & Kamusella, 2018).

Ranger describes how, for instance, the American Methodist, the Anglican and the Catholic churches contributed to the creation of a Church Manyika Language, which was promoted through the mission school system to the exclusion of the Manayika ethnic group's traditional (read: non-Christian) leadership who employed a different dialect/sociolect (Ranger, 1989). This culminated in a situation in which, by 1930, people 'in Makoni, Umtali, and Inyanga districts and in the migrant diaspora' (Ranger, 1989: 141) began to accept (Church) Manyika as their identity to the exclusion of the pre-Christian non-colonial traditional identity and its linguistic practices. According to Ndhlovu and Kamusella (2018), the main objective of colonial administrations in developing a keen interest in local language issues was to contain identities that appeared 'fluid' and 'unreasonable' to them from the Western vantage within colonial contexts so as to facilitate European rule as colonialists saw fit. In other words, *divide et impera*. Language is an instrument of power. In the Manyika case, the dethroning of 'traditional Manyika' by 'Church Manyika' meant the shift in power over the Manyika ethnic group from its traditional leadership to the colonial administration, or the Manyika's loss of agency over their own culture and society.

The work of Clement Martyn Doke (1893–1980), then professor of linguistics at the University of Witwatersrand (South Africa), played a major role in providing the much needed (by colonialists) intellectual expertise for the invention of tribalised linguistic identities in Zimbabwe. Doke's 1931 report on the 'necessary' unification of the Shona dialects left an indelible mark on the terrain of Zimbabwean linguistic and identity conceptualisation that has endured in Zimbabwe to this day (Chimhundu, 2005; Ndhlovu, 2006). Such colonially constructed languages epitomised a systematic and deliberate effort towards developing colonial 'command over language', which would ultimately lead to the development of a 'language of command' for the better subjugation of the colonised (Brutt-Griffler, 2006). In the words of Ingrid Piller (2017):

> A language with a name is an invention and once it has been invented, an eo ipso [on its own account] claim about how that language is a direct expression of the culture associated with that language is never far away. Once a language has become accepted as a fact – once it has been named, described and codified in grammars and dictionaries – the relationship between that language and that culture seems self-evident. (Piller, 2017: 52)

This is precisely what happened during the process of inventing linguistic and tribal (ethnic) categories not only on the Zimbabwean plateau but also throughout the African continent south of the Sahara (Brutt-Griffler, 2006; Errington, 2008; Makoni, 1998; Ndhlovu, 2010), the Oceanic region, the Indian subcontinent and the Americas (Makoni & Pennycook, 2007). Southern Africa, in particular, is replete with several examples of ambiguities and contradictions that characterised the entire colonial project of inventing African languages, which were co-constructed with the modern African nation-state, and the ideology of the necessity to eradicate tribalism/ethnicity. This is well illustrated by the history of the Thonga language that is known by slightly different names within and across the borders of South Africa, Swaziland, Mozambique and Zimbabwe. Some of the names by which this language is known in these countries include Xichangana (Zimbabwe), Gwamba (Swaziland), Xitsonga (South Africa) and Ronga/XiRonga (Mozambique). Although Thonga has always been spoken in one form or another since precolonial times, it only emerged as a language-with-a-name (*Einzelsprache*) in the 19th century in the course of colonisation. The history of Thonga as we know it today is traced back to the work of two Swiss missionaries, Paul Berthoud (1847–1930) and Ernest Creux (1845–1929) who were sponsored by the Paris Missionary Society (Errington, 2008).

Both Berthoud and Creux had learned some version of Sesotho, which they had used for proselytising in some parts of southern Africa. However, after arriving in then Natal in 1872, they discovered that no one there spoke any variety of Sesotho. So, 'they took it upon themselves to learn the local language in order to spread their faith in that language' (Piller, 2017: 51). One thing they had not anticipated was the diversity of mutually intelligible language varieties in the Transvaal area, which they conveniently chose to ignore for two practical reasons. First, they did not have sufficient funds to print religious-instructional materials in more than one language. And second, like their fellow missionaries on the Zimbabwean plateau, they needed the Transvaal to be seen as one linguistically and culturally homogeneous unit. This would strengthen their 'Christianising claim' to the region in order to bar it from rival missionaries who were operating in the surrounding areas. In order to achieve their goal, Berthoud and Creux embarked on the twin process of describing and inventing a language they named Thonga. In this way, they could teach and control this language, and monopolise its written forms and uses to the exclusion of other missionaries who by default would be deemed 'incompetent' in this field. In the end, the two missionaries successfully established their version of Thonga (ethnic) identity by conflating the invented language and the cultural identity of the local populace. As Errington (2008: 116) observes, these missionaries' success in inventing Thonga was confirmed by later descriptions of the language as 'one of the most trustworthy and complete manifestations of the [Thonga people's] mind and the oldest element in the life of the tribe [...] the great bond which bound the Thonga clans together in the past centuries'.

The above account of the invention of Shona and Thonga as languages-with-names (*Einzelsprachen*) is slightly contradictory to the colonial processes of inventing southern African languages that are classified as belonging to the Sotho/Tswana and Nguni groups of languages. The former group includes Sepedi, Sesotho and Setswana, while the latter category includes Zulu, Xhosa, Siwati and Ndebele. Although the languages in each category are mutually intelligible (just like the varieties of Shona and Thonga), those missionaries and colonial academics who invented them did not treat the related languages as one unit – that is either as Nguni or Sotho/Tswana. Rather, the route they followed was the exact opposite of the one followed in the case of varieties of Thonga and Shona. In the words of Ndhlovu and Kamusella (2018), each of the varieties of Nguni and Sotho/Tswana was treated as a separate language in its own right, and as such was supplied with a distinct grammar, orthography and other reference works for literacy and religious/education instructional purposes.

To this day, the mutually intelligible varieties of both Nguni and Sotho/Tswana clusters are treated as separate languages in academic circles, in social policy frameworks and in the community and society at large. On the other hand, the mutually intelligible varieties of both present-day Shona and Thonga are treated as a single language. This clearly betrays the ironies, ambiguities and contradictions of colonial methodological tribalism (grafted on the equally ambivalent and culture-specific Western concept of a language) that continues to undergird mainstream academic research projects and reports on the social and political histories of the languages of southern Africa. However, the point of greater significance here is this: while the route followed in the invention of Thonga and Shona was different to that followed in the invention of Zulu, Xhosa, Siswati, Ndebele, Setswana, Sepedi and Sesotho, the dynamics and the outcome of the process were the same. Both processes were initiated, conducted and controlled by colonial agents in the service of colonial administrations, and both resulted in the implementation of the Western idea of a language as an institution, alongside the creation of countable, discrete objects (*Einzelsprachen*) – that were subsequently conflated with equally invented ethnocultural ('tribal' or 'ethnic') identities. Such created (or, more correctly, imposed) entities underpin current mainstream understandings of African multilingualism.

The colonial project of resolving administrative challenges through language standardisation was carried over and taken to new heights by postcolonial African regimes, presumably run by the colonised, for themselves and in their own interest. The colonial objective of inventing named (discrete) languages (*Einzelsprachen*) was to enhance administrative convenience for improved control over the colonised. Paradoxically, the same languages are popularised today as part of nation-state building via the route of multilingual policies in the postcolonial context (Ndhlovu, 2009). This shows that the postcolonial indigenous elites have unreflectively espoused the colonial ideological and cultural impositions as their own. However, in both colonial and postcolonial situations, control and manipulation are the main motivations. The push for linguistic homogenisation and cultural uniformity in postcolonial Africa was and continues to be motivated by quests for building national (that is, statewide) consensus premised on selected indigenous languages that are perceived as more 'authentic' (or indigenous) and better grounded in both pre- and post-imperial frameworks (Ndhlovu, 2008, 2014).

Consciously or not, Western and indigenous academics from across the humanities and social sciences have accumulated and shaped an overbearing intellectual capital that has helped obscure the fact that these hegemonic, Euro-modernist and fundamentalist versions of African languages were invented at the point of colonial encounters by colonisers and in their own interest. Named African languages (shaped in line with the Western idea of *Einzepsprache*) as we know them today are as recent as colonialism itself and do not predate this dark episode in the history of humanity, euphemistically known as the 'scramble for Africa'. This invites the following important questions. When academics, policymakers and other language practitioners talk about multilingualism in Africa, what is the object of their conversation? What is it that they are describing? Is it the diversity of languages-with-names (*Einzelsprachen*) or the diversity of languages as processes? And how far back do they go in time when they trace the social and political history of African multilingualism?

Overall, what the foregoing analysis shows is that at the heart of colonial linguistics (which shapes current notions of African multilingualism) were four interrelated forces that colluded and collided in complex ways: colonial imperialism; Christian modernity; modern nation-state ideologies; and technologies of orthography and orthodoxy. We explicate these below.

- *Christian modernity*: Doctrinal and prescriptive views on language may as well be traced to Christian missionary interests that proceed from biblical precepts about Jesus (and Christianity) as the only way: 'I am the way, the truth, and the life. No one comes to the Father except through me' (John 14:6). Christian proselytising currents such as these run through standard language ideological discourses that validate monolingual and mono-epistemological views as the norm, thereby foreclosing possibilities for multiple yet equally valid and legitimate ways of knowing. Missionary denominations working in different parts of colonised territories called into existence particular language types, which became the way. The recruitment of speakers followed through liturgical teachings and the mission school, thus producing social class hierarchies: elite versus subaltern, educated versus uneducated and so on. As covert vehicles for evangelical proselytisation, such invented languages have come to 'reflect conservative, nation-state ideologies inimical to the needs and conditions of communities in the global periphery' (Johnston, 2017).

- *Ideologies of the modern nation-state*: This is about the Euro-modernist catechism of one nation, one language, one people as the underpinning pillar of what Benedict Anderson (1991) characterises as an 'imagined community'. For Anderson, the nation is imagined in three respects. First, as limited because it has finite boundaries beyond which lie other nations. Second, as sovereign because the concept of a modern 'nation' was born in an age in which the Enlightenment and revolution were destroying the legitimacy of the divinely ordained, hierarchical dynastic realm. Third, as a community, because, regardless of the actual inequality and exploitation that may prevail in each, the nation is conceived as a deep, horizontal comradeship (Anderson, 1991: 7). Binaries and hierarchies of humanity (racial, ethnic, tribal, nativist) were the outcome of all three imaginings of the nation in colonial contexts. Colonial versions of African 'indigenous' languages perceived as more 'authentic' and better grounded in both pre- and post-imperial frameworks form the basis for the current mainstream multilingualism discourse (Ndhlovu, 2008, 2014).
- *Technologies of orthography and orthodoxy*: Subsequent to inventing particular types of languages, missionaries and other colonial linguists set about to develop writing systems. These then crystallised into some kind of orthodoxy to a point of being misconstrued as true representations of the speech forms and identities of colonial subjects. What ultimately ensued were binary categories supporting value judgements about hierarchies of humanity produced: fallacies of absences such as literacy versus oracy, civilised versus primitive, among others. At the heart of it all was the will to know about languages and the will to power (Foucault, 1986); or as Severo (2016) would say, it was about the science of the gaze, of observation. Christian missionary involvement in language matters has partly driven the interests of *colonial dispositif*: a 'set of practices and discourses [including] laws, documents, treaties, letters, cartography, travelers' notes, chronicles, artistic illustrations, grammars, word lists, translation of texts, invention & adaptation of alphabets' (Severo, 2016: 2). Print capitalism gave a new fixity to language, manifested via official dictionaries, grammars and etymologies, which served as a homogenising force that brought together the people through a colonially invented common language (Anderson, 1991; Ndhlovu, 2009).

The upshot of all three processes combined was the invention of a set of narratives emphasising the role of power to save, rescue and develop other people (Mignolo, 2011). These practices and discourses on languages, cultures and identities were at the service of the interests of 'the colonial archive of western knowledges about Africa and African identities and of indigenous knowledges that were to be suppressed, erased or lost under colonial rule' (Ndhlovu & Kamusella, 2018: 348). This, as Makoni (1998) would suggest, reduces African languages into colonial scripts in the shaping of European communal memory. Such were the sociopolitical and ideological conditions out of which emerged current mainstream discourses on multilingualism. The task at hand for us, therefore, is not to merely change the narratives of our histories, but transform our sense of what it means to live (Bhabha, 1994) with languages as individuals and communities of the Global South.

Conclusion

The sad admission is that the majority of mainstream academic researchers in Africa have unreflectively embraced the colonially invented 'tribal' turn by mimicking holus-bolus those notions of multilingualism sponsored and underwritten by colonial administrations, and then imposed by early colonial academics who were tasked by the former with the invention of African languages as we currently know them. The consequence of this imposition from without Africa has been the continued pursuit of scholarly legitimised tribalism (ethnicity), whereby the methodologies of conceptualising African languages reproduce and sustain colonially invented multilingual ideologies. What we see here is the persistence of a methodological tribalism (ethnicism) that is traceable to the heyday of colonial incursions in Africa. The challenge we are facing today is, therefore, both methodological and conceptual and revolves around two contending perspectives on language – that is, the Western imposition of languages and multilingualism as institutions, and language and multilingualism as indigenous discursive and communicative practices of speakers. How far back we go in time and history determines what we eventually choose to include in our conceptualisation of multilingualism. Ideally, it would be prudent to go back to a point that transcends the era of colonial encounters. Going back in time beyond the point of the colonial imposition, however necessary and laudable, is extremely difficult, due to the aforementioned unreflective internalisation of this colonial imposition by both indigenous scholars and populations concerned as the 'really existing' norm, which is erroneously perceived to have prevailed 'since times immemorial'.

References

Anderson, B. (1991) *Imagined Communities: Reflections on the Origin and Spread of Nationalism*. London: Verso.
Bhabha, H.K. (1994) *The Location of Culture*. London: Routledge.
Brutt-Griffler, J. (2006) Language endangerment, the construction of indigenous languages and world English. In M. Pütz, J.A. Fishman and J.N. Aertselaer (eds) *Along the Routes to Power: Explorations of Empowerment through Language* (pp. 35–54). Berlin/New York: Mouton de Gruyter.
Chimhundu, H. (1992) Early missionaries and the ethno-linguistic factor during the invention of tribalism in Zimbabwe. *Journal of African History* 44, 87–109.
Chimhundu, H. (2005) Introduction to Photographic Reprint of C.M. Doke. *The Unification of Shona Dialects*. Norway: ALLEX Project.
Errington, J. (2001) Colonial linguistics. *Annual Review of Anthropology* 30, 19–30.
Errington, J. (2008) *Linguistics in a Colonial World: A Story of Language, Meaning, and Power*. Oxford: Blackwell.
Fardon, R. and Furniss, G. (1994) *African Languages, Development and the State*. London/New York: Routledge.
Foucault, M. (1986 [1975]) *Discipline and Punish: The Birth of the Prison*. Harmondsworth: Peregrine.
Johnston, B. (2017) *English Teaching and Evangelical Mission: The Case of Lighthouse School*. Bristol: Multilingual Matters.
Makoni, S. (1998) African languages as European scripts: The shaping of communal memory. In S. Nuttal and C. Coetzee (eds) *Negotiating the Past: The Making of Memory in South Africa* (pp. 242–248). Oxford: Oxford University Press.
Makoni, S. and Pennycook, A. (eds) (2007) *Disinventing and Reconstituting Languages*. Clevedon: Multilingual Matters.
Mignolo, W.D. (2011) Epistemic disobedience and the decolonial option: A manifesto. *Transmodernity* 1 (2), 44–66.
Ndhlovu, F. (2006) Gramsci, Doke and the marginalization of the Ndebele language of Zimbabwe. *Journal of Multilingual and Multicultural Development* 27 (4), 302–318.
Ndhlovu, F. (2008) The politics of language and nationality in Zimbabwe: Nation building or empire building? *South African Journal of African Languages* 28 (1), 1–10.
Ndhlovu, F. (2009) *The Politics of Language and Nation Building in Zimbabwe*. Bern: Peter Lang.
Ndhlovu, F. (2010) Language policy, citizenship and discourses of exclusion in Zimbabwe. In S. Ndlovu and J. Muzondidya (eds) *Grotesque Nationalism in Africa: Essays on Zimbabwe* (pp. 195–215). Bern: Peter Lang.
Ndhlovu, F. (2014) *Becoming an African Diaspora in Australia: Language, Culture, Identity*. Houndmills: Palgrave Macmillan.
Ndhlovu, F. and Kamusella, T. (2018) Challenging intellectual colonialism: The rarely noticed question of methodological tribalism in language research. In T. Kamusella and F. Ndhlovu (eds) *The Social and Political History of the Languages of Southern Africa* (pp. 347–364). London: Palgrave Macmillan.
Piller, I. (2017) *Intercultural Communication: A Critical Introduction*. Edinburgh: Edinburgh University Press.
Ranger, T.O. (1989) Missionaries, migrants and the Manyika: The invention of ethnicity in Zimbabwe. In L. Vail (ed.) *The Creation of Tribalism in Southern Africa* (pp. 118–150). London: James Currey.

Severo, C.G. (2016) The colonial invention of languages in America. *Alfa: Revista de Linguistica* 60 (1), 11–28.

Zeleza, P.T. (2006) The inventions of African Identities and Languages: The discursive and developmental implications. In O.F. Arasanyin and M.A. Pemberton (eds) *Selected Proceedings of the 36th Conference on African Linguistics* (pp. 14–26). Somerville, MA: Cascadilla Proceedings Project.

3 Unsettling Multilingualism in Language and Literacy Education

Introduction

Language and literacy education is one area that has received a lot of policy interventions at the international, national and sub-national levels (García & Li Wei, 2014; Makoni & Pennycook, 2007). Some of the policy interventions are couched in such terms as mother tongue education, bilingual education, additive bilingual education, second or third additional languages, multilingual education and many more. The abundance of conceptual frameworks and models such as these is not surprising, thanks to the realities of the post(modern) world where print and electronic literacies are mundane. It is, however, apparent that these policy interventions are often misguided and do not yield positive outcomes to emancipate African children from the abyss of illiteracy and educational failure. The outcomes are largely predictable in that the cultural constructs that define ways of meaning making from African indigenous knowledge systems (IKS), epistemologies and culturally relevant pedagogies are residually ignored in both teacher education (higher education) and curriculum inscriptions which govern classroom practices.

This chapter proposes a rethink of the ways multilingualism is currently viewed in language and literacy education. It broadens and further extends the more established multi-literacies paradigm by problematising the phenomenology of multilingualism as currently used and understood in the field of language and literacy education. The chapter uses qualitative data that was collected through community-based participatory research (CBPR) in the Limpopo and Mpumalanga provinces of South Africa. The goal is to develop a model for how local community understandings of multilingualism can inform, shape and influence expert academic and practitioner practices and discourses on language and literacy education. This is about adopting a bottom-up approach whereby conventional wisdom is inverted. The chapter concludes by arguing that instead of teaching communities about multilingualism and literacy, academic experts and educators need to speak less and listen more to the stories, views, opinions and wisdom of real people, speaking in their real everyday languages, about their real multilingual and literacy practices.

Multilingualism Misconceived as a Disabler

To understand the African languages and literacy practices and how they have been influenced by colonial processes, one needs to look at the European Enlightenment period as the focal point. Current reading and writing literacy practices have always been lopsided towards a monoglossic orientation to the exclusion of the students' existing linguistic and cultural repertoires (Day & Park, 2005). This means that literacy in named standard languages such as English, French or any ex-colonial language takes precedence over local non-standardised languages. In those exceptional situations where local language literacy is supported, it is often in total isolation from the other languages spoken in the immediate community. Invariably, language and literacy education programmes have resulted in the segmentation of languages and literacy practices into hermetically sealed units (Makalela, 2015).

As already indicated in Chapter 2, the relevant body of post-colonial literature is replete with evidence that suggests the European monolingual ideology gave rise to territorialised languages that coincided with nation-state borders (Khosa, 2013). Drawing on the perceived strength of this frame of thinking (which had taken root in the process of building unitary modern states), research and education systems adopted the one-ness ideology to the extent that a popular view emerged about multilingualism as a sign of chaos, disorder not only for the nation, but also for one's individual mind. Baker (2011) and Makalela (2014b) report that it was in this connection that a false belief was formed that the use of more than one language is cognitively hazardous in creating mental confusion – what has come to be known as the fallacy of monolingual thinking. As observed elsewhere (Makalela, 2014a; May, 2014; Ricento, 2000), this orientation towards literacy and language abilities is imbued by the one-ness ideology of the European Enlightenment period of nation-states (i.e. one nation, one language) and the belief that using more than one language causes mental confusion (Baker, 2011; Makalela 2014b). These colonial Euro-modernist views on language need to be decolonised as a way to push back the frontiers of cognitive, sociolinguistic and social injustices that are endemic in mainstream literacy education practices.

Decolonising Literacy

Despite intentional policy interventions and government programmes (e.g. Read to Lead or Reading for Meaning campaigns in South Africa), there is very little conversation about how the indigenous literacies of the local people can be harnessed for literacy transformation (Makalela, 2018a). This goes against a plethora of research findings which recommend that the locally grounded literacy practices of indigenous communities throughout the world should be included as part of the mainstream schooling system to build inclusive communities (e.g. Hornberger, 2012; Lane, 2010; Williams, 2006). To do this with conviction, however, requires a realisation that orthodox literacy theories, pedagogies and beliefs are an outcome of a colonial system of domination and the nexus of cultural control over the local communities. Without this conviction, it follows that deficit models of literacy frameworks that favour mono-epistemic ideologies premised on colonial language ideologies continue to define school literacy practices. Such approaches ignore the foundations of literacy knowledge embedded in these communities (see e.g. Makalela, 2018a; Makoni, 2003; Mignolo, 2000).

Academic researchers from the Global South have not adopted a one-sided perspective. Rather, they have also concentrated on how students from these contexts are unable to fit into pristine models of literacy that were conceived and theorised from an outsider perspective (Mignolo, 2000). As Makalela (2018a) argues, most of these studies focus on learners' inability to grasp large chunks of text; the negative influences of their African languages on their acquisition of English literacy; wholesale borrowing of established teaching approaches from foreign contexts; and lack of parental involvement in the literacy activities of their children (see also Brock-Utne, 2015, 2016).

At the core of language and literacy education in Africa are monolingual and epistemic biases, which as pointed above, put ex-colonial languages at the centre to the exclusion of African languages and the way in which meanings are constructed from the logic of these languages. An African languages-centred perspective aligns neatly with the sociocultural approach pioneered by scholars such as Brian Street (2011) and James Paul Gee (2013) who view literacy as a sociocultural construction that involves intersections between school, home and community. In order to benefit from funds of knowledge brought into the schooling system, it is important to go beyond the technical skill to read or function within social contexts to include one's ontology (reasoning, thinking, way of living, means of looking at the world and behaviour in the world)

(Perry, 2012). From this point of view, literacy is a cultural construction implicated in the nexus of power relations between hegemonic colonial literacies and marginalised literacies.

The gap between colonial (by implication school) and marginalised literacies, on the one hand, and English and African languages, on the other hand, does not recognise literacy as an interactive and complex sociocultural process that manifests in multiple voices coming into contact with each other. It is in this connection that Mikhail Bakhtin (1981: 272) viewed an open space where each member of the community represents a voice of learning and knowing, and each voice contributes to dialogised *heteroglossia*[1] in which multiple layers of values are embodied. This shows that learners not only acquire the conventions and skills of reading, but they also learn sociocultural values that are attached to particular literacies. To date, schooling in Africa has meant the acquisition and application of literacies that are based on the linguistic typologies of ex-colonial languages with very little known about the sociocultural values attached to African languages. In the next section, we turn to African languages and literacy parameters.

African Languages and Literacy

Language is among the most significant factors in the survival of IK and it represents a window through which culture is practiced (Antone, 2000; Letseka, 2013). It is a way of coming to grips with the external world and developing a symbolism to represent it so that it can be talked about and thought about (Ouane & Glanz, 2010). From this viewpoint, languages become repositories of world views where values and teachings can be discerned from within their grammatical structure (Armstrong, 1995; Makalela, 2018a). This means that we expect indigenous African languages to have unique schema and categorisation systems that reflect their speakers' value in the world. Whereas reading and writing are used to drive what is discussed (content) in the academic environment, the holistic world view inferred from African languages implicates that speakers use all their senses to pay attention to both animate and inanimate objects (Makalela, 2018a, 2018b; Mawere, 2015).

On the contrary, the majority of classroom conversations in educational settings such as those we find in most African countries involve specialised English language where learners are expected to individually construct their own understanding of the concepts and language. These include questioning, describing, explaining, hypothesising, elaborating, verifying and sharing results. It is instructive to note that these academically accepted language conventions may contravene the social rules of discourse particular to African language speakers. Below is a discussion on rhetorical organisation schema to demonstrate a different way of knowing that is nested in African languages.

Paragraphing and Textual Coherence

One of the obvious and fundamental cultural differences between English and indigenous African languages with a Bantu grammatical and rhetorical structure is the level of directness and indirectness in information exchange. The English paragraph structure requires that one applies the Western maxim of straight to the point or first things first. Organisation of information shows the hierarchy of ideas with the dominant idea taking priority (topic sentence), followed by supporting sentences and a concluding sentence at the end of the paragraph. Bantu languages, on the other hand, follow an organising principle of circumlocution – a cultural construct underpinning high levels of indirection that is highly valued (Makalela, 2016, 2018a). Whereas rhetorical cohesion is internal in Germanic languages – that is, readers and writers negotiate their meaning from within the paragraph, Bantu languages denote a rhetorical organisation form where cohesion is external to the text or paragraph. In other words, readers/hearers are challenged to complete the thought expressed by using information external to the paragraph (contextual clues). Following the sense-making logic of the Germanic languages, English can be classified as a writer/speaker-responsible language (output driven) in the sense that responsibility is highly placed on the text producer to make themselves clear through a linear organisation of structure.

African languages, on the other hand, are reader/hearer-oriented languages in that the message receiver has a responsibility to figure out meaning from their rhetoric organisation system that is non-linear, flat and non-hierarchical. Circumlocution values an ecosystem of ideas that are holistic and integrated (inside and outside) where the environment ('beating about the bush') external to the idea presented is highly valued. Motlhaka and Makalela (2016) showed that this way of making sense is dialogic in nature – derived from a cultural locus of call-response communicative patterns that engage the reader/hearer fully as a critical and active participant in the process of meaning making. Figure 3.1 provides a visual representation of the different ways of knowing and making sense in English and African languages.

Figure 3.1 illustrates paragraph systems that either internalise or externalise textual cohesion. In Paragraph A (which typifies English), the

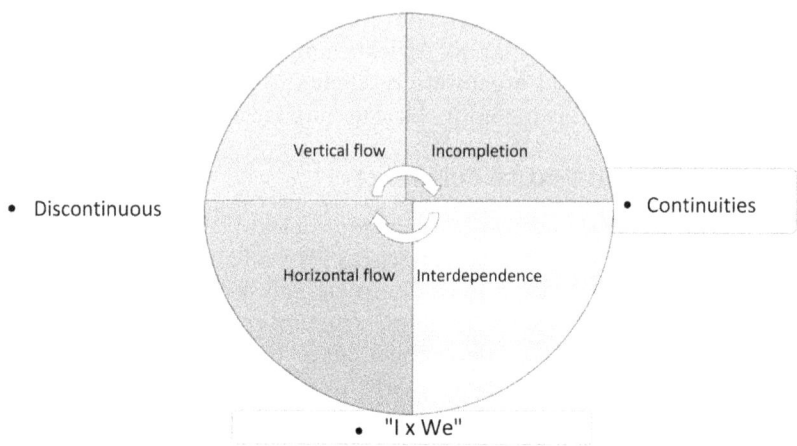

Figure 3.1 Ways of reading and writing the world

reader has relatively less responsibility in that ideas are neatly packed in a hierarchy that shows the order of importance. Because textual coherence is internal to the text, the type of language following this meaning-making process is writer responsible. That is, the writer has more responsibility to make herself or himself clear. Paragraph B (which typifies most African languages), on the other hand, requires readers to draw inferences (going external to the text) and connect the text with contextual information as a basis for meaning making. Here, the languages following this logic of meaning making are reader responsible. That is, it is the responsibility of the reader to figure out the meaning that is implicit, indirect and external to the text. It is in this connection that one is able to infer epistemological pathways and pedagogical choices relevant to speakers of English versus speakers of African languages as different. The logic represented in each language type is evidence of the accepted view that literacy should be understood as a sociocultural construction through interactions among participants (hearer and speaker). This sociocultural approach to languages means that languages are viewed as more than print-based language arts for gaining access to employment. Instead, literacy should reflect a broad approach that recognises the unique ways that indigenous people represent their experiences. Therefore, literacy includes a means of looking at the world and behaviour in the world (Makalela, 2016), which is deeply rooted in culture. The introduction of an IKS as an overarching organising principle for curriculum transformation allows for a deeper understanding of a culture where co-construction of meaning is highly valued. This implies that educators cannot stand outside of the indigenous languages to understand speakers of these languages, their ways of being and knowing.

Researching and Understanding Language and Literacy: Ubuntu Research Methodology

To decolonise language and literacy education in Africa, there is a need to value meaning-making processes that align with the African languages and literacy parameters. IK and languages take a holistic approach and pieces of information as inseparable like the people who hold them. In this connection, the core feature of IK methodologies is participatory and community centred in nature where knowledge is viewed as sociocultural and historical in orientation, especially if the goal is to reassert cultural identities. Keane and Malcolm (2004) argue that IK research has a negotiated purpose that focuses on indigenous thought and experience. Taking a cue from ways of making sense that are transversal and dialogic, African research methods should focus on the relationship between the researcher and the participants who, as we will show, assume different but complementary roles. In this relationship, the researcher and the participants are involved in co-constructing knowledge as equal agents and subjects of knowledge at the same time where the boundaries between the researcher, the researched and the participants are fluid. Blurring the fixity of the researcher–participant roles is consonant with the interdependence logic of the ubuntu value system that finds expression through the injunction: *motho ke motho ka batho* [I am because you are. You are because I am]. Although ubuntu is often a subject of controversy among philosophers who cast doubt on its relevance as a moral compass in contemporary African societies (e.g. Matolino & Kwindigwi, 2013), its currency in carving out an epistemology (what and how we come to know) and a research methodology (step-by-step approach to finding the truth) holds strong in its intimation of infinite relations between the provider and the taker of information: one is because the other is. In particular, the researcher and the researched can exchange roles and hold both roles at the same time to allow for multiple layers of truth that are corroborated and refined by both the individual (I) and the collective (We). One cannot be without the other. Mbiti described the key contours of ubuntu as follows:

> Only in terms of other people does the individual become conscious of his own being, his own duties, his privileges and responsibilities towards

himself and other people. Whatever happens to the individual happens to the whole group, and whatever happens to the whole group happens to the individual. The individual can only say: 'I am, because we are; and since we are, therefore I am'. This is a cardinal point in the understanding of the African view of man. (Mbiti, 1969: 106)

The cardinal point that simultaneously merges and demerges the individual and the group frames what we henceforth define as the ubuntu research methodology (URM) as a highly participatory and inclusive knowledge construction engagement. The participatory nature of the URM provides agency to the researched communities that are traditionally reified in abstraction as 'cold subjects' of research who value anonymity and confidentiality. The reiterative nature of the method, which is underlined by reversing and complementing roles, implicates a research process that uses mainly qualitative methods such as grounded theory and ethnography, and instruments that include interviews, focus groups, joint observation, home visitations, hearing stories and indigenous games. While quantitative measures are possible within this approach, data collection will typically be eclectic in that both the intended and unintended data is collected by both the researcher and the community participants who play both the researcher and participant roles at the same time. In order to facilitate multiple truths via the ubuntu lens, data analysis is a communal, repetitive and negotiated process. This information gathering process includes a rich environmental scan, commitment to the establishment of a rapport, carrying out sampling with the community, reiterative data collection and critical reflection. The ethics extend beyond traditional forms where anonymity and confidentiality are preserved, to a social contract where the results are disseminated with the participants as equal holders of the intellectual property. When taken together, the ubuntu methodological proposition requires a deeper engagement with challenges through inquiry, action and reflection that are participatory and community centred in nature along the fluid systems preferred within the ubuntu logic.

At the Hub for Multilingual Education and Literacies, we adopted a CBPR approach in order to engage elderly community members to become co-constructors of knowledge from inception to arriving at results (Makalela, 2018b). In the study reported in this chapter, we sought to fully engage research participants and derive an approach that would give full expression of the literacy practices and events understood from the point of view of the local communities. This was considered a radical departure from the traditional descriptors of *action research*, which entail taking planned action to improve a situation and simultaneously researching the change process in order to develop a theory about the situation. However, as shown in Makalela (2018a) and reiterated here, we recruited community stakeholders in a distinctly remote rural community in Mpumalanga province, South Africa, through planned meetings with key people of influence in the selected community to achieve a holistic and broad-based understanding of literacy based on IK.

The initial part of the project relied on establishing contact and a rapport between our university team and the community through key influential people. We addressed issues of trust and cooperation at this stage and ensured that everyone was clear about the goals and parameters of the project. We went for a walk around the community to understand the community environment through the eyes of a local partner researcher who knew the details of the community operations. This initial scan was useful in establishing the availability of infrastructural features such as a library, and the location of schools and other organisations in the community.

An initial recruitment meeting was held in a schoolyard, where a number of elders gathered specifically for this research process. People had been made aware of this meeting through a school, using a combination of word of mouth, posters and letters to parents who had school-going children. Following the information session, we interviewed key people including teachers, community leaders, principals, church leaders and six elders to get preliminary ideas on what they believed literacy meant in the community. The elders' age ranged from 65 to 85 years, and conversations were conducted in local African languages widely spoken in the community: Sepedi, SiSwati and Xitsonga. In this connection, we believed that the voice of the external researcher was incomplete without the voice of the internal researchers (the local community) in a complementary way that resonates with the principles of ubuntu.

Multilingual Data Collection and Researcher-Researched Analysis

Data collection involved reminiscing about literacy events, artefacts and activities. The selected elders presented a series of stories including fables, poetry and folktales, which were audio-recorded and transcribed. As part of the analysis, subsequent stages involved engagement through reflections, use of cultural cues, and ways of knowing that were revealed in the context or process of storytelling.

Key Lessons Learned from Researching African Languages and Literacies with Community Elders

The ways of researching African languages literacies discussed above provide for a theorisation and framework for decolonising language and literacy education. In tandem with the sociocultural lens applied in this study to understand literacy as a cultural product (Bakhtin, 1981; Gee, 2013; Street, 2011), the theme that cut across the narratives of the elderly is ubuntu as a type of African cultural competence that was evident throughout the contents of the stories shared and the processes involved in telling the stories. As explained above, ubuntu is a way of life premised on complex intersections between the individual *I*, and the collective *We*. As we have already indicated, African languages overlap in infinite relations of dependency where no one language is complete without the other. This practice was observed throughout the narratives that were shared in at least three named languages: Sepedi, Siswati and Xitsonga. This interwoven network of languages is best represented in a graph, as shown in Figure 3.2.

Figure 3.2 denotes a fluid and porous relationship where, in the first instance, languages operate within the humanity logic of 'I × We' (with × marking the intersection), which is translated from the African value system of ubuntu with its basic tenet *I am because you are; you are because I am*. In this context, languages are a representation of the human nature of belonging together as opposed to being completely separate entities. Because of their ubuntu, languages are in a constant and simultaneous process of deforming and reforming. As they do this, they overlap into one another to the extent that the boundaries between them are inconsequential to the meaning-making process and information flow.

The second aspect illustrated in the ubuntu translanguaging model is the notion of incompleteness (Nyamnjoh, 2015, 2017), which denotes the fact that no single entity is complete on its own. In the making of a multilingual speaker who uses an interwoven network of language systems to make sense of the world and a sense of who they are, no one language is complete without the other. This is evident from the narratives discussed above.

The third aspect of ubuntu translanguaging is interdependence. This means that the state of being incomplete leads to entities depending on each other for the total sum of meaning. Multilingual speakers use repertoires from different varieties to make sense of the world and have a deeper understanding of the social, economic and environmental realities around them.

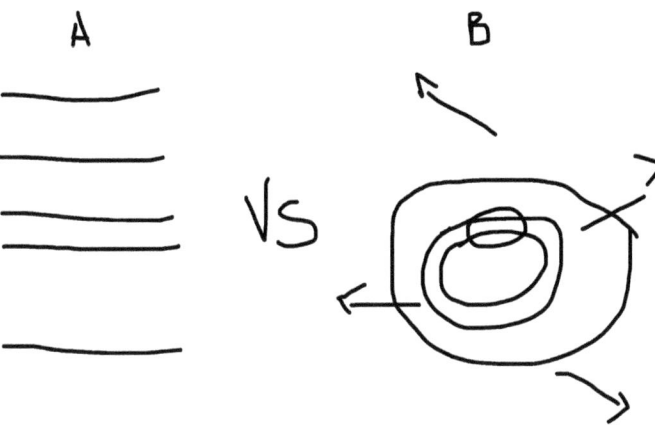

Figure 3.2 The ubuntu translanguaging/multilanguaging model (*Source*: Makalela, 2016)

The fourth tenet of ubuntu translanguaging shows the complexity of information flow where both horizontal and vertical mobility of information in communicative events take place. Whereas it is common for interlocutors to hear input in one language and give a response (output) in a different language, many African sociolinguistic realities allow for input in more than one language and output in more than one language in speech events. It is in this context that *multilanguaging* best describes this complex web of languages in use, with multiple flows of languages in an infinite relation of dependency. The key to the underlying multilanguaging formula is that the information flow and the interaction between languages are not linear, but circular and fluid without a terminal endpoint. This is reflected in the dialectic process of *discontinuation* on the one hand, and *continuation* on the other hand, where there is a constant disruption of language boundaries and simultaneous domestication of what is strange or new (that is, new fluid boundaries are being formed).

From the elderly community, we learned that a multidimensional pedagogy is prevalent in a non-formal and traditional African education system. In particular, we learned that learner-centred approaches from a plural perspective shared in a series of conversations and demonstrations with the community researchers involve both the learners and the teachers. It is both the teacher and the learner learning and at the same time the learner and the teacher teaching in such a fluid multidirectional way. This means that the teachers and learners are not separated into neat categories of learners' and teachers' roles. At the centre of the education enterprise is co-learning, where both the teachers and the learners acquire knowledge through shared learning. On the one hand, community-based learning means that individualised learning is not the first preference – children learn in a community of others within a community structure, usually outside of their home. Community-based learning ensures quality of instruction and learning through co-teaching and co-learning.

Another finding from the community-based research related to rhetorical expressions in the process of learning and teaching. I have shown that academic programmes use the paragraph system where topic sentences carry the main ideas usually in the first sentence of a paragraph. Contrary to this school-based practice, analysis of the elderly's stories and processes of telling revealed more complex ways of knowing, where ideas are not placed in a hierarchy of priority, but rather they are organised in a flat and circular pattern for readers/the audience to make sense of by picking out the main aspects for themselves. In other words, it is not up to the writer/speaker to determine what is the main idea. It is in this connection that we characterise African languages as *reader-* or *hearer-responsible languages* due to the strong demand they place on readers or an audience (Makalela, 2016). The use of songs, dance and creative entertainment by a group of community members as a way of communicating sensitive subjects shows that high levels of indirection are more effective in getting the message across than a direct and individualised focus. We argue that circumlocution, which does not recognise a hierarchy of ideas, is a pathway to receiving and to knowing information; it forms an epistemic roadmap and ontological orientation for speakers of indigenous African languages. In other words, their ways of knowing and being are found in flat and indirect communication patterns and this should be the basis for literacy development and induction in teacher education programmes in Africa.

Implications for Ubuntu Language and Literacy Pillars

The ubuntu language and literacy model, which leverages on interdependence, discontinuous continuation and rhetorical organisation mapping of circumlocution, suggests a few pillars that ground it in IK.

Community-based knowledge

The foregoing discussions suggest that within the ubuntu logic, everything is connected in a web of relationships. The matrix of the 'I' and 'we' denotes an ecosystem of learning where every subject matter introduced to learners should be examined and interpreted within its contexts. For example, texts that are used in schools and the methodology for teaching reading and writing need to be contextualised within the place (community). In this way, school literacy events and contents are located within the funds of knowledge that are external to the classroom. This view is also supported by the external orientation of meaning making (paragraphs), which challenges learners to go beyond the text as the first level of comprehension. This is in direct contrast with the abstraction of subject matter that is isolated from the local environmental factors and treated within the structural limitations of the texts in very surface and rudimentary ways. The key tenet of this pillar is that literacy instruction should be reflective of the learners' place – their environment which includes both animate and inanimate objects. As seen with the paragraph structure, the meaning-making process is incomplete without full engagement with the environment. This allows for mind and environment interactions as central to induction for meaningful literacy instruction. Thus, it is evident that literacy is not limited to printed text and surface engagement with writing or reading conventions.

Multiple perspectives and multilingualism

The notion of multiple perspectives writes off the one-ness ideology that persists in the current curricula configurations where only Western forms of knowledge and ways of knowing are represented. For example, there is an epistemic belief that using more than one language will create mental confusion and, as a result, the curriculum is designed for an ideal monolingual speaker while multilingual speakers with an African languages background are disproportionately disadvantaged. A multiple perspective seeks to integrate our best collective knowledge to construct the fullest and clearest picture of the situation or phenomenon studied. Multilingualism is leveraged as a resource for deeper learning and engagement with content. In other words, using more than one language for processing meaning while reading and writing in the same lesson is a cultural competence of multilingual speakers. UNESCO (2003) makes this point explicit:

> local languages are the means for preserving, transmitting, and applying traditional knowledge in schools. A bilingual or multilingual education allows the full participation of all learners; it gives learners the opportunity to confront, in the positive sense, the knowledge of their community with knowledge from elsewhere. (UNESCO, 2003: 17)

Here, we argue that African multilingualism would entail using more than one language in the same lesson for meaning making in what we refer to as ubuntu translanguaging. As supported by a body of research in the field, translanguaging as a pedagogical strategy allows for the realisation of metalinguistic awareness and a full range of perspectives. This view aligns with 21st-century competencies where learners should be able to reconcile tensions and engage in trade-offs. The nature of multilingual engagement supports metalinguistic awareness which heightens the learning process and evokes metacognition and meta-learning.

Everything in the universe lives

A holistic approach to language and literacy education requires a heightened awareness of the relationship between one's self and everything else in one's immediate environment. This pillar reiterates the ecological systems of knowledge and the infinite relations of dependency between humans and nature. In this ecological relationship of interdependence, there is no hierarchical order of superiority – humans are not superior to nature and therefore do not seek to control it. The paragraph structure in African languages demonstrates a cyclical and non-hierarchical world view.

Practical Implications for Teacher Education and Schools

There are far-reaching implications for the translanguaging techniques on teacher education. First, the discussions showed that student teachers who were trained through the translanguaging programme were able to utilise its techniques to improve school readers' word recognition skills and other literacy skills and events expected in the curriculum. We infer from these results that teacher education can induct pre-service teachers in the use of African languages as resources through translanguaging to teach reading, writing, listening and speaking.

Ecologically speaking, reading literacy can best be understood in a continuum of other local literacies that converge for early readers to emerge as multi-competent readers who use resources in a variety of languages around them. Translanguaging techniques provide the student teachers with tools to harness this literacy continuum.

The overall contribution of this study is to a broader social understanding of literacy reading options in Africa. This approach to literacy departs from early works that have always viewed reading literacy as an abstraction, an isolated cognitive activity and an independent variable that is removed from social contexts (Street, 1984). Beginning from a social approach to literacy, the present study involved the socialisation context of the learners as a literacy event and the affirmation of their own languages and then incrementally built towards the development of cross-linguistic awareness. In this way, meaning making was balanced in terms of the three systems that help children to make sense of the world around them: community, multilingualism and holistic approaches (everything lives). This three-dimensional view of meaning making was useful in the study as it affirmed an alternative way of looking at reading pedagogy. The following specific strategies for teaching learners in African language and literacy education contexts are relevant for our teacher education programme:

(a) Purposeful alternation of the language of input and output in reading instruction: translanguaging.
(b) Raising phonological awareness through contrasts with other languages.
(c) Student teachers' ability to use literature that taps into children's existing cultural repertoires.
(d) Resourcing and improving the print environment with local texts.
(e) Including contrastive analysis between languages, building on home language practices. (Makalela, 2014b)

While these principles are broad, their specific application can be tailor-made to fit comparable African language and literacy education contexts elsewhere. I have shown that the main translanguaging technique – purposeful alternation of the languages of input and output – helps to develop literacy in more than one language. Training teachers of language and literacy would imply undertaking a holistic approach as opposed to monolingual practices that have not proven successful in Africa.

Conclusion

This chapter sought to examine African language and literacy education practices and provide new ways to decolonise the current practices in schools. The chapter relied on an IK system framework to understand ways of knowing and being that are particular to African multilingual contexts. The village elders were involved as co-constructors of knowledge in gauging lessons from literate reminiscing and ways of telling indigenous stories. The central finding of the study presented here is that ubuntu translanguaging reflects a precolonial cultural competence, a heuristic method for identity affirmation and epistemic access for speakers with indigenous African language backgrounds. Drawing on the potential of antecedent knowledge systems and funds of knowledge based in the communities, we are able to build a framework by theorising language use relevant for local rural communities than the orthodox approaches that were introduced by colonial powers and extended by the schooling sector. At the core of the alternative literacy models is the value of multilingualism as a norm and a resource for educational purposes. The chapter revealed that ubuntu literacy takes effect in learner-centred environments where co-learning between learners and teachers is valorised. It also revealed a preference for a community-based learning approach where everything lives and where everything is not organised in a hierarchical structure.

Taken together, it seems plausible that academics and researchers should slow down and allow the communities to talk back, have a voice as co-constructors of knowledge. In this way, language and literacy education can transform, be decolonised and reflect African value systems as the base. More research is needed to augment the positions presented in this study.

Note

(1) Heteroglossia is a term used by Bakhtin to refer to the diversity of voices and styles of discourses from texts. It was originally understood as limited to literary texts, but it is widely used to include all forms of texts.

References

Antone, E. (2000) Empowering Aboriginal voice in Aboriginal education. *Canadian Journal of Native Education* 24 (2), 92–102.
Armstrong, J. (1995) Keepers of the earth. In T. Roszak, M.E. Gomes and A.D. Kanner (eds) *Ecopsychology: Restoring the Earth, Healing the Mind* (pp. 316–325). San Francisco, CA: Sierra Club Books.
Baker, C. (2011) *Foundations of Bilingual Education and Bilingualism* (5th edn). Bristol: Multilingual Matters.
Bakhtin, M. (1981) *The Dialogic Imagination: Four Essays*. Austin: University of Texas Press.
Brock-Utne, B. (2015) Language, literacy and democracy in Africa. In L. Makalela (ed.) *New Directions on Language and Literacy Education for Multilingual Classrooms in Africa* (pp. 15–33). Cape Town: Centre for Advanced Studies of African Society (CASAS).
Brock-Utne, B. (2016) The ubuntu paradigm in curriculum work, language of instruction and assessment. *International Review of Education* 62 (1), 29–44.
Day, R.R. and Park, J. (2005) Developing reading comprehension questions. *Reading in Foreign Language* 17 (1), 60–73.

García, O and Li Wei (2014) *Translanguaging: Language, Bilingualism and Education*. New York: Palgrave Macmillan.
Gee, J.P. (2013) *The Era of Anti-Education: Creating Smarter Students through Digital Learning*. New York: Palgrave Macmillan.
Hornberger, N.H. (ed.) (2012) *Indigenous Literacies in the Americas: Language Planning from the Bottom Up* (Contributions to the Sociology of Language, vol. 75). New York: Walter de Gruyter.
Keane, M. and Malcolm, C. (2004) Participatory research. In C. Malcolm (ed.) *Human Rights, Democracy, and Social Justice: Science and Mathematics Literacy in Disadvantaged Communities* (pp. 57–64). Durban: University of KwaZulu-Natal Press.
Khosa, R. (2013) *Let Africa Lead: African Transformational Leadership for 21st Century Business*. Johannesburg: Vezubuntu.
Lane, S. (2010) Valuing all pathways to literacy: An action research project with indigenous early childhood students. *Practically Primary* 15 (2), 7–10.
Letseka, M. (2013) Educating for ubuntu/botho: Lessons from indigenous education. *Open Journal of Philosophy* 3 (2), 337–344.
Makalela, L. (2014) Teaching indigenous African languages to speakers of other African languages: The effects of translanguaging for multilingual development. In L. Hibbert and C. van der Walt (eds) *Multilingual Universities in South Africa: Reflecting Society in Higher Education* (pp. 88–104). Bristol: Multilingual Matters.
Makalela, L. (2015) *New Directions in Language and Literacy Education*. Cape Town: CASAS.
Makalela, L. (2016) Ubuntu translanguaging: An alternative framework for complex multilingual encounters. *Southern African Linguistics and Applied Language Studies* 34 (3), 187–196.
Makalela, L. (2018a) Community elders' narrative accounts of ubuntu translanguaging: Learning and teaching in African education. *International Review of Education* 64 (6), 823–843.
Makalela, L. (ed.) (2018b) *Shifting Lenses: Multilanguaging, Decolonisation and Education in the Global South*. Cape Town: Centre for Advanced Studies of African Society (CASAS).
Makoni, S. (2003) From misinvention to disinvention of language: Multilingualism and the South African Constitution. In S. Makoni, G. Smithermann, A. Ball and A. Spears (eds) *Black Linguistics: Language, Society and Politics in Africa and the Americas* (pp. 132–149). London/New York: Routledge.
Makoni, S. and Pennycook, A. (eds) (2007) *Disinventing and Reconstituting Languages*. Clevedon: Multilingual Matters.
Matolino, B. and Kwindingwi, W. (2013) The end of ubuntu. *South African Journal of Philosophy* 32 (2), 197–205.
Mawere, M. (2015) Indigenous knowledge and public education in sub-Saharan Africa. *Africa Spectrum* 50 (2), 57–71.
May, S. (ed.) (2014) *The Multilingual Turn: Implications for SLA, TESOL and Bilingual Education*. New York: Routledge.
Mbiti, J.S. (1969) *African Religions and Philosophy*. London: Heinemann.
Mignolo, W. (2000) *Local Histories/Global Designs: Coloniality, Subaltern Knowledges, and Border Thinking*. Princeton, NJ: Princeton University Press.
Motlhaka, H. and Makalela, L. (2016) Translanguaging in an academic writing class: Implications for a dialogic pedagogy. *Southern African Linguistics and Applied Languages Studies* 34 (3), 251–260.

Nyamnjoh, F.B. (2015) Incompleteness: Frontier Africa and the currency of conviviality. *Journal of Contemporary African Studies* 33 (1), 48–63.

Nyamnjoh, F.B. (2017) *Drinking from the Cosmic Gourd: How Amos Tutuola can Change Our Minds*. Mankon, Bamenda: Langaa Research & Publishing.

Ouane, A. and Glanz, C. (2010) *Why and How Africa should Invest in African Languages and Multilingual Education: An Evidence- and Practise-Based Policy Advocacy Brief*. Hamburg: UNESCO Institute for Lifelong Learning (UIL). See http://unesdoc.unesco.org/images/0018/001886/188642e.pdf (accessed 25 September 2018).

Perry, K. (2012) What is literacy?: A critical overview of sociocultural perspectives. *Journal of Language and Literacy Education* 8 (1), 50–71.

Ricento, T. (2000) Historical and theoretical perspectives in language policy and planning. *Journal of Sociolinguistics* 4 (2), 196–213.

Street, B.V. (1984) *Literacy in Theory and Practice*. Cambridge: Cambridge University Press.

Street, B.V. (2011) Literacy inequalities in theory and practice: The power to name and define. *International Journal of Educational Development* 31 (6), 580–586. doi: 10.1016/j.ijedudev.2010.09.005

UNESCO (2003) *Convention for the Safeguarding of the Intangible Cultural Heritage*. Paris: UNESCO Publishing.

Williams, E. (2006) *Bridges and Barriers: Language in African Education and Development*. Manchester: St Jerome Publishing.

4 Decolonising Multilingualism in Higher Education

Introduction

Many universities in African countries have remained outposts of colonial knowledge systems despite the pretensions of postcolonial rhetoric in defence of their independence. The past few years have seen student unrest organised around the decolonisation of universities. In South Africa, two notable student movements emerged, namely, Rhodes Must Fall at the University of Cape Town and the Fees Must Fall movement, which saw all South African universities shut down for several weeks (Mwaniki et al., 2018; Ndlovu-Gatsheni, 2017). At the heart of these student protests was the call for greater access to higher education through the decolonisation of curricula and medium of instruction at South African universities. Despite these student-organised movements, the status quo has largely remained, with ex-colonial languages still exclusively used for learning, teaching and research. As observed throughout the world, this monolingual orientation prohibits multilingual students from a full expression of who they are and how they come to know (e.g. García & Li Wei, 2014; Gentil, 2011; Heller, 2007). Associatively, many universities prohibit students from drawing on their antecedent multilingual resources in favour of a unilingual approach, which marginalises their complex ways of meaning making and identity expression (e.g. García & Li Wei, 2014; Li Wei, 2018; Makalela, 2018b; Otheguy et al., 2017). In this connection, unilingual practices have mediated curricular programmes that favour the English-only approach in multilingually complex, versatile and ambiguous classroom environments (e.g. Robinson et al., 2018).

Yet, research has convincingly shown that monolingual bias at universities can be disrupted if classroom practices, curricula and policies build on the multiple repertoires of the students and acknowledge the linguistic fluidities that are embedded in one another (e.g. García, 2011; Li Wei, 2011). This undertaking requires a high degree of alertness, the adoption of a cultural approach to learning and teaching and a high level of acceptance of student's linguistic repertoires and African cultural competence where there is a constant disruption of language boundaries, artificial orderliness and simultaneous recreation of new discursive discourses (Makalela, 2015). In this chapter, we report on the effectiveness of using translingual practices among speakers of African languages in an institution of higher learning in South Africa. We propose the use of translanguaging for decolonising mainstream classrooms to encompass African language-speaking students' multilingual affordances to give them voice and access to knowledge in higher education institutions. We conclude by canvassing practical translingual activities and future research directions for adaptation in comparable contexts.

Monolingualism: A Colonially Inherited Problem for Africa

All evidence available on precolonial Africa suggests that fluid multilingualism has always been a cultural competence of speakers of African languages. In South Africa, for example, there is a record of linguistic interaction that dates to about 120,000 years ago when the Khoe and the San people settled in the country (Makalela, 2018b; Webb & Kembo-Sure, 2000). The Khoe and the San people interacted with each other in a variety of languages and with speakers of Bantu languages in the later part of history when speakers of Bantu languages settled in around 600 BC. Bantu language speakers are believed to carry a value system of interconnectedness referred to as ubuntu or botho as expressed in the slogan: 'I am because you are, you are because we are'. Research holds that the literacy records of these speakers were ignored (at best) or erased (at worst) by foreign anthropologists and linguists who wanted to propagate a view that 'peoples of Africa have not yet risen to the stage of education which can produce written records of important events or institutions' (Raum, 1993: 3). However, folklore, art, rock paintings and engravings reveal that there were diverse literacy forms and practices encoded in different languages through the trade of minerals, architecture and civilisation found in the Kingdom of Emperor Monomotapa, which stretched all over the southern African states (Cox, 1996; Makalela, 2005). Raum (1993), for example, is instructive in noting that

> the natives were able to record subjects apparently even of abstract nature, by means of incisions and to decipher them later, developing in conversation the subject thus recorded by reference to the tally. (Raum, 1993: 11)

These complex communication systems among people of different ethnic groupings suggest that more than one language was used for intercultural and interethnic cross-pollination that led to one of the early civilisation centres in the region – that of Mapungubwe in the Limpopo Valley. Makalela (2015) observed that the Khoe and the San who were hunters and guardsmen, respectively, shared resources and collaborated on complex social systems such as interethnic marriages. The Bantu language groups also had a history of cohabitation and cross-interethnic mobility before they came into contact with European settlers in 1652. During this time, they developed mining, trade and agriculture where crops and seeds were shared across a wider spectrum of cultural and linguistic affiliations. Visiting or finding another human being was highly valued – hence the expansion of family systems as seen in expressions such as 'younger mother' or 'elder father', 'stranger come to my home so that we grow' and 'it takes a village to bring up a child' (see Amadiume, 1987). This reveals that there was a continuum of language systems as well as inward and outward mobility between various ethnic or tribal communities. Because fluidity and coexistence characterised African multilingualism prior to colonisation, it is important to point out that communication and the transmission of knowledge occurred through language varieties spoken and understood across a wider spectrum of the current ethno-linguistic divides (Davidson, 1992).

These well-known African literacy traditions are currently missing from the teaching and learning practices and policies of higher education institutions. It has been well documented that academic literacy practices in Africa are still monolingual in orientation despite multilingual policies in official documents (see Hibbert & Van der Walt, 2014). In the case of South Africa, the Department of Education (DoE) expressed the conundrum of this policy–practice discord in the following terms:

> Language has been and continues to be a barrier to access and success in higher education; both in the sense that African and other languages have not been developed as academic/scientific languages and in so far as the majority of students entering higher education are not fully proficient in English and Afrikaans. (DoE, 2002: Clause 5)

> The challenge facing higher education is to ensure the simultaneous development of a multilingual environment in which all our languages are developed as academic/scientific languages, while at the same time ensuring that the existing languages of instruction do not serve as a barrier to access and success. (DoE, 2002: Clause 6)

The perspective represented in these policy documents is that speakers of African languages are proportionately disadvantaged compared to speakers of English and Afrikaans. In Clause 6, these languages are implicated in barring access and success of speakers of African languages. It is important to note here too that the Fees Must Fall movement sought social and academic justice as cogently represented by Ndlovu-Gatsheni (2017):

> What the RMF and FMF movements have successfully brought to the fore are the long-standing but unresolved issues of opening the doors of learning and education to everyone, as promised by the ANC in the Freedom Charter of 1955; rescuing the university from capture by neo-liberal market forces and repositioning it as a public good; rethinking and redefining the university as a truly African public institution serving African communities; rethinking and rearticulating the broader philosophical foundations of higher education in Africa to enhance relevance; financing and funding higher education to enable access; decolonising the epistemology, curricula and alienating institutional cultures of the universities; democratising student-staff relations to enhance teaching and learning; using indigenous languages for learning and teaching; ending the dehumanising outsourcing of black workers; as well as the depatriarchalisation, deracialisation and de-Westernisation of universities. (Ndlovu-Gatsheni, 2017: 25)

It is important to record here that both the legislative framework and the intentions of the decolonising movement by students have not moved South Africa and by extension other African countries from a history of language boxing (Makalela, 2014a; Makoni, 2003), where African languages were isolated into linguistic tribes. This aligns with the colonial policies of divide and rule and the apartheid separation policies of separate development, which led to 10 Bantustan homelands[1] and restrictions on crossing the homeland borders (Makalela, 2014b). In other words, higher education to date is not linguistically different from the periods of colonisation in Africa and apartheid specifically in South Africa.

Transforming through Ubuntu Translanguaging

Research on the nature of language in the postmodern school era has shifted focus from language structures to what speakers do with the language. The former is a technocratic approach that characterised mainstream thinking in the 19th and 20th centuries when the focus was on languages as autonomous entities that are capable of being placed in separate boxes. The latter is imbued by the degree to which 21st-century populations move within and between nation-states and it recognised the rapid ways in which people of different languages communicate across languages with no clear boundaries (García, 2009, 2011; Hornberger & Link, 2012; Makoni, 2003; Makoni & Pennycook, 2007). This gravitation from languages as static entities to fluid communicative repertoires positions multilingualism as the norm, not the exception or a challenge that needs to be resolved (García & Li Wei, 2014; Makalela, 2015).

As already stated above, Makalela (2015) has characterised language within a state of fuzziness that results from complex multilingual zones as a *discontinuation continuation*. That is, in hybrid language and people contact zones there is a constant disruption of the orderliness of language boundaries and a simultaneous recreation of new discursive ones. For most African multilingual speakers who grow up speaking up to six languages, input and output alternation is *the only way* to become, gain epistemic access and develop self-efficacy in education. In this connection, a preferred literacy methodology for such students should be porous, complex and value interdependence in tandem with the ancient African value systems of communication and indigenous ways of knowing (see Makalela, 2018b). Here, the contention is that the notion of languaging had always been an African interlingual experience that can be traced as far back as the 12th century in the Limpopo Valley (Makalela, 2018a). To account for this historical factor and to bring ubuntu values of interdependence and fluidity, the concept *ubuntu translanguaging* was coined to describe these complex African multilingual practices.

Ubuntu refers to an African humanism cultural pattern that values overlaps, continuity and crossovers between communities. It finds expression in the slogans: 'I am because you are; you are because we are; visitor please come to my home so we are complete' to value complex and multidirectional interdependence between people. While there is a general acceptance of ubuntu as a way of life for speakers of the Bantu language family in sub-Saharan Africa, reservations have been flagged by a number of scholars. van Binsbergen (2001), for example, argue that ubuntu denies individuality, fosters conformity and it is decontextualised. They also see it as a revivalist movement for an idea that has lost relevance in contemporary societies. Matolino and Kwindigwi (2013) argue that ubuntu has ended and that it is obsolete for contemporary African societies that are large and differentiated. They use examples of violence that can be seen in contemporary societies to argue that ubuntu is, *de facto*, dead. One of these is a Mozambican-born taxi driver who was dragged on a police van in South Africa as a form of police brutality meted against civilians. It is worth noting, however, that all these criticisms of ubuntu accorded it a utopian world view of perfectionism, which cannot be claimed of any value systems. Secondly, the complex and infinite relations of dependency between the individual and the collective are overlooked in these criticisms. For the record, the I and We relations suggest a coexistence of both inclusivity and exclusivity at the same time. In other words, individuality and collectivity do not become mutually exclusive. Third, speakers of Bantu languages practice ubuntu as their cultural competence that is rooted in their languages. It is in this connection difficult to argue that ubuntu is imposed on people whose languages are organised around the tenets of its logic (Makalela, 2019). These criticisms, therefore, are not sustainable as they are influenced by a utopian view, a one-ness ideology associated with Western epistemologies and the extraction of ubuntu outside of the logic of the Bantu languages to write off ubuntu as a philosophy, a way of life and a methodology.

The use of ubuntu in language teaching and language policies has been useful to undergird interdependence and the understanding that no one language is complete without the other. When the notions of incompleteness and interdependence as a normal way of life are recognised, it becomes useful to provide an accurate description of African multilingualism where speaking more than three languages and overlaps between these languages is a norm. This complex cycle of incompletion and multidirectional interdependence reflects discontinuation continuation (incompletion × interdependence = discontinuation continuation → *ubuntu translanguaging*) where the disruption of language boundaries and the creation of discursive speech repertoires occur simultaneously. It is in this connection that the ubuntu logic provides a fruitful and productive pathway to support the proposition that one language is incomplete without the other.

It should be stated that translanguaging as a pedagogic strategy in bilingual classrooms has its roots in the work of Cen Williams who studied Welsh–English bilingual secondary school learners' language practices in Wales (Baker, 2011; Li Wei, 2011). It has been expanded over time to refer to the alternation of all discursive discourses of input and output outside of the formal schooling environment (García, 2009) or a porous language practice of complex interdependence that defines African multilingualism prior to colonialism (Makalela, 2018a). The basic tenet of translanguaging is that it refers to a language communicative function of receiving an input in one language variant and giving an output in another language variant. When translanguaging is deployed in classroom contexts, bilingual learners are able to use more than one language for knowledge access and develop positive experiences at school (Creese & Blackledge, 2018).

As expanded by García (2009: 45), translanguaging includes multiple discursive practices that are perceived as 'more like an all-terrain vehicle whose wheels extend and contract, flex and stretch, making possible, over highly uneven ground, movement forward that is bumpy and irregular but also sustained and effective'. The all-terrain vehicle metaphor is instructive in showing that while it may seem bumpy and non-linear in its movement, there is logic and sense that enable it to accomplish its task. Like the logic of a moving all-terrain vehicle, multilingual speakers who use more than one language in the same utterance or in their input/output are able to make sense of the world and of who they are.

The languaging phenomenon can also be understood from a psycholinguistic perspective (Li Wei, 2011, 2018). In studying learners from a Chinese language background in England, Li Wei (2011: 1223) clarified languaging as the process of using language to gain knowledge, to make sense, to articulate one's thought and to communicate about using language. He observed that his multilingual learners 'were creative and critical as their communicative system moved seamlessly between different linguistic structures and systems, including different modalities, and went going beyond them' (Li Wei, 2011: 1223). He refers to the social space for multilingual language users as a 'translanguaging space', which is an ongoing space created for language practices where multilingual speakers are constantly involved in making strategic choices that are situation sensitive about the language systems they use to achieve their communicative goal (Li Wei, 2011: 1). These findings suggest that translanguaging practice is natural to multilingual speakers and that it is the best candidate for enhancing both the social sensitivities and the cognitive strength needed for learners to be successful at school.

Research on translanguaging is also bolstered by the general observation that monolingual programmes, under the auspices of maintenance bilingual education, have over decades achieved no more than to create two monolinguals in one body (e.g. Blommaert, 2010; Li Wei, 2011). García (2011) observes the outcomes of language separatism as follows:

> It was the strict separation of languages that enabled language minorities to preserve what was seen as their 'mother tongue', their 'ethnic language', while developing a 'second language' that would never be a 'first' or a 'native' one, for those designations were reserved for the language majority which inhabited a separate space. (García, 2011: 7)

As shown elsewhere, the main idea here is that a separatist view of language and the classifications of 'first', 'second' and 'mother tongue' do not fit the sociolinguistic realities of the majority of speakers in the 21st century. In order to take a more complex account of language use and match multilingual spaces in this century, the classroom language practices of multilingual learners should be characterised as consisting of a discursive practice of 'languaging'. According to García (2011: 7), languaging refers to 'social features that are called upon by speakers in a seamless and complex network of multiple semiotic signs'. This means that a language maintenance programme may not be desirable for multilingual learners because it encourages strict definitions of language as autonomous, bounded and pure as used by a specific group of people whose identity depends on it.

It is worth noting that most research on translanguaging has been undertaken at primary and secondary school levels. Well-known studies by Creese and Blackledge (2010) and Li Wei (2011) have come to the conclusion that bilinguals have the tenacity to transform restrictive monolingual landscapes and are able to create critical and creative spaces for themselves. These schools recorded success in their programmes, which are unmatched by monolingual counterparts.

As we have indicated above, the South African higher education system is infested with an inherited monolingual bias despite the policy proscribing multilingualism as the norm and a resource for academic studies. Some initiatives over the years have shown the positive effects of using multilingual approaches at several universities (Hibbert & Van der Walt, 2014; Madiba, 2014; Makalela, 2014a, 2014b, 2015). For example, Madiba (2014) has successfully used isiXhosa and Tshivenda to develop concept literacies in science courses at the University of Cape Town.

Equally, Makalela's (2014a, 2014b) studies report on successes using several African languages as multiple media of learning and teaching where the target language is another African language or English. From these findings, which showed improvements in reading, comprehension and identity development, Makalela (2014a) observed the complexity of input and output juxtapositions in two languages and expanded the crossover of inputs and outputs from multiple languages in the process of meaning making. Here and as described above, this type of African multilingualism, conceptualised as *ubuntu translanguaging*, can best be associated with the African value system of ubuntu where complex interdependences are valued over independences. It is in this context of a porous multilingual system that the notion of discontinuation continuation becomes relevant.

It is instructive to note that translanguaging as a field has received critiques in the recent past. One of these is the unintended consequences of bringing a powerful language such as English into the same classroom as a local African language. They include the view that more powerful languages tend to assimilate the marginalised languages. This view harbours purist notions of language that the minority languages will remain static and immune to evolution. While it is plausible that a powerful language may subsume less powerful ones, leaving less powerful languages in isolation can be equally detrimental to their natural evolution. The classroom space is a third space to renegotiate power and eventually allow for multiple voices in a position of prestige that were historically reserved for dominant languages. Translanguaging provides affordances for the disruption of dominance and the recreation of a negotiated new order.

The second critique of translanguaging is that it is contradictory in that it pushes against boundaries while the concept of language as an isomorphic bounded entity is still used to define its operations. This paradox brought about debates on whether translanguaging is a unitary system or a differentiated system in the speakers' cognitive domains. Otheguy *et al.* (2015, 2017) showed that translanguaging implicates a unitary system especially when speakers are involved in a meaning-making process, while MacSwan's (2017) view is that the languages are differentiated, i.e. multiple languages that stay discrete, even if they are used simultaneously. Makalela (2019) argues that these divergent views can be explained from ubuntu translanguaging where entities are not mutually exclusive as in the 'I' and the 'We'. In this sense, the internal language (I-language) of the speaker follows a unitary system as a repertoire applied in meaning making where speakers are not conscious of the linguistic boundaries. This is a speaker-orientation view. On the other hand, at the moment of speech, differences between languages can be perceived by the hearer alongside the socially named language (E-language) structures. The coexistence of the speaker and hearer viewpoints is what constitutes the translanguaging paradox in the same way that the coexistence and simultaneous separateness of individuality and collectivism are found in the logic of ubuntu.

While all these engagements on translanguaging and ubuntu provide snapshots to understand the complexity of multilingualism, they do not imply that the bottom line should be neglected: monolingual bias in contemporary classrooms. Ubuntu translanguaging thus poses as a construct useful to decolonise one-ness ideology and disrupt monolingualism in the higher education sector. Under the guise of discontinuation continuation, it valorises the cultural competence of multilingual speakers. The following is a description of the study reported in this chapter.

Brief Overview of the Study

This is part of the translanguaging studies undertaken by one of the researchers (Leketi Makalela) in higher education contexts. This particular study focused on using African languages in teaching other African languages and in using African languages in English-medium classes. The linguistic profiles of students included almost all nine official African languages (isiZulu, isiXhosa, isiNdebele, Siswati, Sesotho, Sepedi, Setswana, Xitsonga, Tshivenda), with a few students speaking almost all of the languages. The students approached the researcher individually, asking for mentorship and support with their academic writing development so they could cope in their major subjects. The researcher sought to group them together to reduce meeting times and to treat their issues in a collective space by arranging a once a week lunch-hour tutorial session. By the end of the first quarter of the year, 50 students were attending these informal sessions/tutorials at 13:10–14:00 in a multilingual language laboratory. They came from different fields of specialisation that included maths and science education and language and literacy education. To prepare support, the students were asked to bring samples of their writing from previous assignments and hand these to the instructor in advance of the sessions. The aim of this activity was to identify patterns of writing and areas that might need attention for their development as academic writers.

Multilingual treatment

After reading the assignment samples from each of the students, the instructor asked the students to rewrite the essays in their home languages. The goal of the exercise was to give them a voice so they could focus on the meanings they wanted to convey. Because this was unusual in academic practices, the students experienced some challenges with finding ready-made words to use in languages other than English. They were advised to use their home languages as much as possible and use English (fluidly) to make sense of their writing.

The second part of the project involved students who were learning African languages. As a continuation of the classroom practice, these students were allowed to draw from any of the languages they knew to understand linguistic concepts such as noun class prefixes and cultural nuances around the pragmatics of using African languages as reader-responsible languages. The students were asked to reflect on their use of more than one language in the same exercise and to make comparisons as far as possible with the exercise above. In telling their stories, the students were encouraged to perform multilingual use of the languages (use more than one language to tell their stories). They were then asked to rewrite in more than one language and were encouraged to use any discursive resource they had to get their messages across. This process of meaning making was recorded and analysed using a deductive-inductive thematic approach to guide interpretations and allow for the simultaneous emergence of new themes.

Lessons from Multilingual Tutorials

The results of the study show that the participants had a range of antecedent genres that were drawn from their multilingual encounters and that they were able give space to their discursive discourses in the essays. In the following, we present and discuss specific themes based on the student reflections.

Antecedent genres: 'I do not switch codes'

A number of the respondents showed that they had exposure to different ways of communicating knowledge through languages other than English. In the context of using these languages, the respondents did not know that their languages were mixed, as the following extract illustrates:

Extract 1:
I knew how to communicate very well in all these languages. At times I would borrow words from other languages to maintain a conversation; little did I know I was code-switching. The language which is spoken at home is Setswana and I had my additions: Sesotho, isiZulu, isiXhosa and kasitaal. Uttering a word that made sense and forming conversations with other people, mostly my peers was not an issue, this is because most of us spoke varieties of languages, which we are exposed to in our everyday interactions.

This extract denotes that the respondent has a wide range of antecedent genres developed in languages outside of the language of academic literacy. This respondent spoke up to four languages and a hybrid version of all these referred to as kasitaal (Makalela, 2014). What we read from the student is that she has literacy at least in Setswana – a language she claims is mostly spoken in her household. She also adds that she made up her speech from a range of other languages to make sense of her circumstances. While academic literacy at university deprives her of these usual expressions, the English course has given her space to reflect on her multilinguality and write using all her discursive resources. Worth noting in this extract is that the respondent was not conscious that the languages she used were switched; in other words, she saw a continuum of systems of speech forming a large repertoire. As confirmed by previous studies, instances of language alternation are natural to multilingual speakers, and they do not necessarily represent code-switching (e.g. García, 2009; Makalela, 2018b). Put differently, multilingual speakers do not have codes to switch from one to another; they translanguage.

Blended use of languages

One of the observations from the narrative essays given to the students in this class is their overt and covert use of translingual expressions. Such an intersection of languages brings to the surface their multilingual discourse practices, often not accepted in monolingual academic literacy classes. The following extract is prototypical:

Extract 2

Unlike all my friends, I was born in Johannesburg and did not go visit *ko ma gaeng* during school holidays. The township where I was born and bred, to me it was my homeland. Societies, which consist of eleven official languages, a place where *umakhelwane* can come and ask for anything in the cupboard, which can help, prepare dinner at her house.

Here, the student participant writes about a comparative analysis of a homeland or countryside and semi-urban areas that are referred to as townships. He asserts that he was born in the city and did not visit the homelands; he finds peace in staying where he was born because the neighbourhood is a microcosm of a multilingual country with all 11 official languages spoken in the vicinity. The writer uses three languages and combines their genres within the same paragraph. He shifts from using English when talking about the countryside or homeland, to an equivalent of '*ko magaeng*' [at home] in a variety that represents all three Sotho languages of South Africa: Sepedi, Setswana and Sesotho. He makes another change to isiZulu to refer to neighbour as '*umakhelwane*'.

These interlingual moves in the paragraph are strategic to emphasise a slightly different meaning shade that may not be articulated meaningfully through the English versions that are insisted upon in mainstream higher education writing. Neither the countryside nor homeland represents the idea of locations that were reserved for Black people as their homes. *Ko magaeng* has a 'home' connotation and a history of the apartheid system since the townships were always conceived as temporary living spaces reserved for Black labourers. *Umakhelwane* also goes beyond the English notion of neighbour; it marks a lack of boundaries between homesteads where, in other instances, people had to eat together and share most of what they had. It is a neighbour with a strong sense of community. Because the respondents had a choice to use English equivalents, one sees this as a rhetorical move to emphasise the cultural specifications of the phenomenon of homeland systems and neighbourhood.

Multiple first languages

The results of the analysis showed that the notion of first language is questionable under the complex multilingual and discursive spaces these students live. Extract 3 is revealing:

Extract 3

Most of the languages that I speak *I acquired them* from outside my house, even my older brother did not know as much as I did. This is because I acquired these languages during my period of cognitive development. To me I considered all these languages that I knew as my first languages, because I acquired them through everyday interactions and not through the process of study or schooling, these languages were acquired through subconscious and intuitive process of absorption, and all the vocabulary which was used made me a better Setswana speaker, my interactions made me better and literate with regards to my first language.

The respondent asserts that she acquired her languages simultaneously outside of her home space. Because she learned all her languages outside of school, she considers them all her first languages. The rhetorical move in the first sentence shows the use of a discourse pattern from one of her first languages. In many African languages, topic promotion devices are salient in written forms while in English these tend to be features of oral speech. In 'most of the languages that I spoke *I acquired them* from outside my house', one gets a sense of the acquisition of languages as a prominent topic through syntactic organisation. This shows that the student writer is able to interweave different discourse patterns into a repertoire to communicate her ideas in what is essentially a multilingual literacy overture. Apart from the implicit blend of languages in this extract, having multiple first languages challenges normative language learning theories developed in the West mainly from monolingual orientation, where it is popularly believed that learners needed to be exposed to one language at a time (Brock-Utne, 2009). Here, the notions of first language and mother tongue are not relevant because multilingual language learning did not follow linear models as espoused in these dominant theories.

Multilingual genre overlaps

The study found that the respondents have a flexible use of genres from languages outside of English. In particular, poetic expressions from African languages tended to be used in their essays. This is found in the following sample:

Extract 4

When the time for me to start school arrived, things changed. All the many languages I was used to had to be minimised. I was introduced to English 'the medium of instruction'. At that moment in time I felt as if my home language was side-lined, as if it did not form part of my schooling. There was this time in grade 3 when I asked my teacher '*go reng re sa buise ka Setswana?*' not that I really knew how to read in Setswana but because I understand it, I had the confidence to speak up. English lessons continued and continued, and through this process of study we learned it because we were taught the structure and rules of the language.

The respondent reports that she wanted to have communication in her familiar language to acquire knowledge throughout her basic education experience. This essay shows that she was forced to shift from using many languages to a single medium of instruction. She further observes how such an introduction made her question why her familiar language, Setswana, was not being used as a medium of instruction. As she writes about the question she asked while in Grade 4, she reverts to the use of Setswana in the middle of the English semantic flow. Her next line is a poetic repetition in 'continued and continued' – an expression found in the local Sotho languages. It should be stressed that in this academic essay, the writer freely moves between Setswana and English genres to produce this narration. When the rhetoric move shifts to Setswana, there is an emotional undertone, which can best be expressed in the local language. This overlap of language-specific genres shows that the writer pulls from a wide array of available discourses to communicate the story of distress about using English as the language of learning and teaching. Like most multilingual speakers, the speaker uses a wide array of genres flexibly.

External rhetoric coherence

For second language speakers of English, writing conclusions can be challenging. The priming and cuing feedback sessions with the students enabled them to codemesh and develop conclusion structures that were acceptable. Extract 5 is an example:

Extract 5

In conclusion, language variety is a remarkable fact which reflects societal variety, through communication I improved my language skills and I feel as though my language gives me an identity. When I define who I am, language is a part of it because it plays a big role in all my narrative transitions. In addition, it is known that first language is acquired through everyday interaction and the process of repetition and absorption subconsciously. The second language is learned through the process of study, and we are taught the structure and rules of the language. Lastly, learning our first language is not the same as learning our second language, but the two occur simultaneously.

The writer provides a conclusion in which he avers that language variation is natural in reflecting society. He adds ideas about a first language, identity development and natural ways in which a first language is acquired. This opinion is contrasted with acquiring a second language where rules, structures and grammar are emphasised. Yet, this contrast is not explicit for readers. The final concluding sentence sits at odds with the opening (topic or restatement of the thesis). Here, the writer has acquired conclusion moves to give the essay a sense of finality. However, the internal coherence seems external to the paragraph. The writer uses cohesive devices in phrases such as 'in conclusion' and 'lastly', but the contents of the paragraph do not give a sense of sentence unity and completion.

As we have seen in the above analyses, at least two different rhetorical devices are used in the paragraph. First, the efficiency principle and the maxim of straight to the point are both flouted here. Even though cohesive markers such as 'in conclusion' are used, representation of a coherence structure is external to the paragraph. In other words, readers, as in all reader-responsible languages, figure out meanings by looking not only at the paragraph, but also the contexts outside of it.

Decolonising Multilingualism

The multilingual tutorials supported students' ways of being and sense making in a manner that departs from traditional classroom encounters. The key to the successes expressed was the inclusion of a number of African languages used in the same oral and written interactions. This resonated with the students' cultural competence where use of more than one language is the norm. In particular, the results of the study show that when students' funds of knowledge and linguistic resources are brought into academic engagements, positive literacy development trends are found in the students' discourses. It seems apt to observe that the relevant question is no longer whether African languages can be used in English academic literacies and vice versa, but how effectively these languages can be used simultaneously and strategically to improve multilingual identity construction and enhance epistemic access.

Beyond the overt translingual expressions observed in the data, the study showed that multilingual writers make rhetorical moves drawn from a range of non-conflictual discursive resources. In this study, they used unorthodox strategies such as topic promotion devices that are traceable from Bantu languages and conflated English cohesive devices in conclusions where coherence is external to the paragraph. As in many Bantu languages, which are reader-responsible languages, the paragraph logic of straight to the point and hierarchy of topic sentence and supporting sentences is flouted in favour of a universal and unspecified main topic (Makalela, 2018a). The writers' ability to mesh the rhetorical moves from multilingual literacies depicts multi-competence and a multiple consciousness that underlie their abilities to move between rhetorical organisations of various literacies as and when needed.

When these students are given multilingual spaces to express themselves, they use translingual expressions and shift genres according to the various language systems they know (e.g. isiZulu, Setswana, Sesotho, isiXhosa). They show flexibility and use variants of their genres strategically to emphasise salient points in their narratives. This finding suggests that the pedagogy of multilingual integration is effective in developing academic literacies. Their multilingual languaging activities are, in essence, a performance of their multilingual being. In this connection, it is fitting to state that the hermetic sealing of languages into boxes – as the basic foundational tenet of multilingual education – is not supported in heteroglossic environments as represented by the students who registered for the course.

The results of the study point to the need to decolonise our view of multilingualism in language teaching, in line with the recent scholarship on translanguaging (García, 2009; Hornberger & Link, 2012; Li Wei, 2011). As with other languages in most parts of the world, the traditional view of teaching academic languages as school subjects is based on Eurocentric models and definitions of language, which rely on the territorial inclusion or exclusion of the speakers (Shohamy, 2006). In order to move away from 'linguistic tribes' of the past, as exemplified in the study, the pedagogy of academic literacies can be aligned with the cultural and epistemological conception of multilingual being. As has been stated elsewhere (see Makalela, 2015), the fluid linguistic interface between languages fits in well with the African world view of ubuntu – an African humanism system of belief and a way of life where interdependence is valued over independence. Such interconnectedness is derived from the tale that humans come from the reed and therefore they are inseparable as reflected in the sayings: 'I am because you are' or 'visitor come to my home to complete me'. This view of wholeness can be extended to the relationship between languages as they 'leak' into one another. The use of African languages in an English literacy course typifies an intentional convergence of mutilingual literacies and an effective use of the ubuntu language methodology where the use of literacy from one language is incomplete without other literacies. This people-focused methodology represents an ideological shift in literacy pedagogy from monolingual to multilingual literacies that develop simultaneously.

As shown above, ubuntu translanguaging is premised on two aspects, namely the social practices of the students where their 'multiple voices' come into contact (Bakhtin, 1981) and discontinuous continuation where there is a constant disruption of language and literacy boundaries and simultaneous recreation of new discursive ones (incompletion × interdependence = discontinuous continuities → *ubuntu translanguaging*). Taken together, use of ubuntu translanguaging approaches debunks traditional approaches that treat languages as separate autonomous entities and leverages the cultural competence of the students where use of one language is incomplete without the other.

Conclusion

This chapter described the use of translanguaging as one strategy for decolonising multilingualism in African universities. It focused on the case study of multilingual tutorials that were conducted in a number of African languages outside of the formal classroom structure. Through analysis of student narrative essays, we argued that using more than one language is a cultural competence of students from African language backgrounds. When harnessed in academic discourses that include speaking and writing, ubuntu translanguaging has proved effective not only in improving academic literacy, but also in building confidence and increasing epistemic access. This study established that students of African languages prefer the fluidity of multiple languages used as a resource to use translingual expressions and complex rhetoric moves strategically; that is, to enhance the quality of their writing and to perform a social act where multiple voices come into contact.

Secondly, the study showed that multilingual literacies can be harnessed through flexible use of antecedent genres from languages other than the language of literacy. What Makalela (2015) described as the ubuntu language methodology has liberated the students and enhanced their meta-linguistic awareness that they have multiple first languages. Their experiences of languages in typical multilingual contact zones and in their writing activities for this course represent a state of discontinuous continuation where there is a constant disruption of boundaries and the recreation of new discursive ones (incompletion × interdependence = discontinuation continuation → *ubuntu translanguaging*). It is in this connection that mainstream notions such as mother tongue and first language are seen as divisive tools in tandem with the colonial injunction of divide and rule.

Taken together, the findings of the study suggest that there is a neat fit for a translanguaging approach in academic literacy classrooms and the role of academic literacy instructors to prime and cue the simultaneous development of literacies for academic purpose. This offers African languages opportunities to be used for learning, teaching and research and for students to perform their flexible identities and make full sense of the world around them. There is a need for further exploration of African multilingualism as a decolonising agent and to explore potential fruitful pathways for ubuntu translanguaging to be employed fully in ordinary classrooms in African universities.

Note

(1) Reserves that were created for Black people on the basis of language differences.

References

Amadiume, I. (1987) *Male Daughters, Female Husbands: Gender and Sex in an African Society*. London: Zed Books.
Bakhtin, M.M. (1981) *The Dialogic Imagination. Four Essays* (edited by M. Holquist; trans. C. Emerson and M. Holquist). Austin, TX: University of Texas Press.

Baker, C. (2011) *Foundations of Bilingual Education and Bilingualism* (5th edn). Bristol: Multilingual Matters.
Blommaert, J. (2010) *The Sociolinguistics of Globalization*. Cambridge: Cambridge University Press.
Brock-Utne, B. (2009) The adoption of a Western paradigm in bilingual teaching: Why does it not fit the African situation. In K.K. Prah and B. Brock-Utne (eds) *Multilingualism: An African Advantage, A Paradigm Shift in African Languages of Instruction Policies* (pp. 18–51). Cape Town: CASAS.
Creese, A. and Blackledge, A. (2010) Translanguaging in the bilingual classroom: A pedagogy for learning and teaching? *The Modern Language Journal* 94, 103–115.
Creese, A. and Blackledge, A. (eds) (2018) *The Routledge Handbook of Language and Superdiversity*. London: Routledge.
Cox, R.W. (1996) Civilisations in world political economy. *New Political Economy* 1 (2), 141–156.
Davidson, B. (1992) *The Black Man's Burden: Africa and the Curse of the Nation-State*. London: James Curry.
Department of Education (DoE) (2002) *Language Policy Plan for Higher Education*. Pretoria: Government Printers.
García, O. (2009) *Bilingual Education in the 21st Century: A Global Perspective*. Malden, MA: Wiley/Blackwell.
García, O. (2011) From language garden to sustainable languaging: Bilingual education in a global world. *Perspectives* 34 (1), 5–9.
García, O. and Li Wei (2014) *Translanguaging: Language, Bilingualism and Education*. London: Palgrave Pivot.
Gentil, G. (2011) A biliteracy agenda for genre research. *Journal of Second Language Writing* 20, 6–23.
Heller, M. (2007) Bilingualism as ideology and practice. In M. Heller (ed.) *Bilingualism: A Social Approach* (pp. 1–24). Basingstoke: Palgrave.
Hibbert, L. and Van der Walt, C. (eds) (2014) *Multilingual Universities in South Africa: Reflecting Society in Higher Education*. Bristol: Multilingual Matters.
Hornberger, N. and Link, H. (2012) Translanguaging and transnational literacies in multilingual classrooms: A biliteracy lens. *International Journal of Bilingual Education and Bilingualism* 15, 261–278.
Li Wei (2011) Moment analysis and translanguaging space: Discursive construction of identities by multilingual Chinese youth in Britain. *Journal of Pragmatics* 43, 1222–1235.
Li Wei (2018) Translanguaging as a practical theory of language. *Applied Linguistics* 39 (1), 9–30.
Madiba, M. (2014) Promoting concept literacy through multilingual glossaries: A translanguaging approach. In L. Hibbert and C. van der Walt (eds) *Multilingual Universities in South Africa: Reflecting Society in Higher Education* (pp. 68–87). Bristol: Multilingual Matters.
Makalela, L. (2014a) Teaching indigenous African languages to speakers of other African languages: The effects of translanguaging for multilingual development. In L. Hibbert and C. van der Walt (eds) *Multilingual Universities in South Africa: Reflecting Society in Higher Education* (pp. 88–104). Bristol: Multilingual Matters.
Makalela, L. (2014b) Fluid identity construction in contact language zones: Metacognitive reflections on kasi-taal languaging practices. *International Journal of Bilingual Education and Bilingualism* 17 (6), 668–682.

Makalela, L. (2015) *New Directions in Language and Literacy Education*. Cape Town: CASAS.
Makalela, L. (2018a) Community elders' narrative accounts of ubuntu translanguaging: Learning and teaching in African education. *International Review of Education* 64 (6), 823–843.
Makalela, L. (ed.) (2018b) *Shifting Lenses: Multilanguaging, Decolonisation and Education in the Global South*. Cape Town: Centre for Advanced Studies of African Society (CASAS).
Makalela, L. (2019) Uncovering the universals of ubuntu translanguaging in classroom discourses. *Classroom Discourse* 10 (3–4), 237–251.
Makoni, S. (2003) From misinvention to disinvention of language: Multilingualism and the South African Constitution. In S. Makoni, G. Smithermann, A. Ball and A. Spears (eds) *Black Linguistics: Language, Society and Politics in Africa and the Americas* (pp. 132–149). London/New York: Routledge.
Makoni, S. and Pennycook, A. (eds) (2007) *Disinventing and Reconstituting Languages*. Clevedon: Multilingual Matters.
Matolino, B. and Kwindingwi, W. (2013) The end of ubuntu. *South African Journal of Philosophy* 32 (2), 197–205.
MacSwan, J. (2017) A multilingual perspective on translanguaging. *American Educational Research Journal* 54 (1), 167–201.
Mwaniki, M., van Reenen, D. and Makalela, L. (2018) Advanced language politics in South African higher education post# RhodesMustFall. *Southern African Linguistics and Applied Language Studies* 36, 1, iii–v.
Ndlovu-Gatsheni, S. (2017) The emergence and trajectories of struggles for an 'African University': The case of unfinished business of African Epistemic Decolonisation. *Kronos* 43 (1), 1–27. DOI http://dx.doi.org/10.17159/2309-9585/2017/v43a4
Otheguy, R., García, O. and Reid, W. (2015) Clarifying translanguaging and deconstructing named languages: A perspective from linguistics. *Applied Linguistics Review* 6 (3), 281–307.
Otheguy, R., García, O. and Reid, W. (2017) A translanguaging view of the linguistic system of bilinguals. *Applied Linguistics Review* 10 (4), 625–651.
Raum, O.F. (1993) *Chaga Childhood: A Description of Indigenous Education in an East African Tribe*. Chicago, IL: University of Chicago Press.
Robinson, E., Tian, Z., Martínez, T. and Qarqeen, A. (2018) Teaching for justice: Introducing translanguaging in an undergraduate TESOL course. *Journal of Language and Education* 4 (3), 77–87.
Shohamy, E. (2006) *Language Policy: Hidden Agendas and New Approaches*. London: Routledge.
van Binsbergen, W. (2001) Ubuntu and the globalisation of Southern African thought and society. *Quest: An African Journal of Philosophy* 15 (1/2), 53–89.
Webb, V. and Kembo-Sure (2000) *African Voices: An Introduction to the Language and Linguistics of Africa*. Cape Town: Oxford University Press Southern Africa.

5 Decolonising Multilingualism in National Language Policies

Introduction

The language policy enterprise in postcolonial Africa, and in many other parts of the world that historically were colonial outposts, still proceeds from homogenising standard language ideological frameworks (Ndhlovu, 2015b). Most, if not all, such standard languages currently considered as mother tongues or home languages of students in educational settings are, in fact, colonial impositions that were and continue to be embraced by postcolonial African regimes. We call this 'coloniality of language by stealth', a concept we use as a summary term for describing the ways that colonially invented versions of languages continue to be used as a technology of political control, manipulation and subtle cultural normalisation. This view on language has its roots in colonial modernity, where colonial administrators, aided by early Christian missionaries, embarked on projects of inventing particular identities for native populations that were subsequently conflated with standard African national languages (Brutt-Griffler, 2006; Chimhundu, 1992; Makoni, 1998; Ndhlovu, 2006; Ranger, 1985). The process is still ongoing throughout postcolonial Africa, largely perpetuated through medium of instruction and language education policies that are built around colonially invented languages.

This chapter adds a new angle to conversations on postcolonial African multilingual national language policies. It brings to light those intricate linkages between language policymaking, the interests of politics and the exigencies of fashioning linguistic and cultural uniformity. The argument is that while language policies are generally designed with good intentions, they also have a darker side. They often result in unintended consequences, such as the social, economic and political exclusion or marginalisation of speakers of minority ethnic and reticent languages. The concept of 'coloniality of language' is introduced as an explanatory paradigm for how notions of multilingual national language policy regimes in postcolonial Africa remain colonial.

In discussing contending issues emanating from this legacy of colonial ways of seeing language, the focus is on the dark side of language policy in African contexts. The relation between the Global North and the Global South is problematised by drawing on the idea of coloniality of language. The overall intention is to deploy the analytical framework of decoloniality in fresh and arresting ways that might help us see what we couldn't – or wouldn't – see before in the domain of language education policy.

The chapter brings a critical discussion on postcolonial African language policies, by questioning how contemporary celebratory discourses of diversity – multilingualism, multilingual education, multilingual language policy, additive bilingual education and so on – still reverberate colonial ideologies. Examples are from South Africa and Zimbabwe, with some passing remarks on other comparable countries from the Global South. In line with Ndhlovu and Kamusella (2018), we conclude by suggesting a broadening of the horizon of our conceptualisation of language policies by integrating Southern and decolonial perspectives that draw attention to the *real* language practices of *real* people in *real* life. The goal is to push the envelope beyond the 'norm' of named languages as invented, imposed and controlled by colonialists, and now continued by postcolonial regimes.

On Coloniality of Language

The concept of 'coloniality' originates from the decolonial school of thought. This is a social-theoretical framework pioneered by Latin American and other like-minded thinkers from the Global South, including Walter Mignolo (2000, 2002, 2011, 2017), Aníbal Quijano (1998, 2000), Ramón Grosfoguel (2005, 2006) and Enrique Dussel (1995), among others. It questions the monopoly and universalising tendencies of epistemologies from the Global North and calls for the recognition and mainstreaming of other knowledges and ways of engaging with knowledges. Decolonial theorists, therefore, criticise both the intellectual distortions of Western modernity and the concrete oppression brought by 500 years of colonial domination. Banazak and Ceja (2010) explain the concept of 'coloniality' (which must be clearly distinguished from that of 'colonialism') in the following terms:

> When they use the term 'colonialism' decolonial thinkers are referring to a form of political domination with corresponding institutions; [and] when they use the term 'coloniality' they are referring to something more

important for them, a pattern of comprehensive and deep-reaching power spread throughout the world. In other words, colonialism has been one of the historical experiences constitutive of coloniality; but coloniality is not exhausted in colonialism, as it includes many other experiences and manifestations, which still operate in the present. (Banazak & Ceja, 2010: 115)

The important point here is this: even when the formal process of colonisation has come to an end, there remains a form of power (coloniality) which produces, uses and legitimises differences between societies and forms of knowledge. An additional pertinent point is that although decolonial theory is more broadly associated with scholars from postcolonial societies, the focus of coloniality is in many ways different from that of postcolonial studies. While postcolonial studies have always sought to problematise colonialism as a historical event, coloniality takes a much broader focus that problematises colonial power as a continuum that transcends the colonial era and whose presence continues to influence and affect current social realities, including discourses on language, language education and language policy regimes. Mignolo (2017) introduced the notion of pluriversality as a key argument for calling into question the Euro-modernist concept of universality, which closes off or marginalises ways of thinking and doing that are not grounded in Western cosmology. In the words of Mignolo (2017: x), pluriversality, that is, seeing beyond the West's claim to superiority, 'is the decolonial way of dealing with forms of knowledge and meaning exceeding the limited regulations of epistemology and hermeneutics [through drawing attention to] the entanglement of several cosmologies connected in a power differential'. This power differential constitutes the logic of coloniality that is hidden beneath the discourse and rhetorical narrative of Euro-modernist claims to universality.

Another leading decolonial theorist, Quijano (2000, 2007) provides a taxonomy of 'coloniality' as consisting of four strands, namely: 'coloniality of power', 'coloniality of knowledge', 'coloniality of being' and 'coloniality of nature'. We add to this list the concept of 'coloniality of language', which we use as an explanatory paradigm for how notions of language and language policy regimes in postcolonial Africa remain colonial. We argue that mainstream models of language education – multilingual education, mother tongue education, additive bilingual education – that are widely celebrated in post-apartheid South Africa exemplify the subtle manifestation of 'coloniality of language'. All languages of South Africa accorded official or national language status are semiotic social inventions that serve the colonial purpose of invisibilising other language practices. As was the case during the colonial/apartheid era, those languages that are recognised in bi-/multilingual education programmes inadvertently obscure underlying social and educational inequalities.

It is apparent that the same colonially invented versions of languages are being celebrated as bastions of sociolinguistic justice and equity in the domain of language and literacy education. What a classic and colossal example of history repeating itself! It is now well known that during the colonial and apartheid periods, standard 'African languages', also known as vernacular languages, were invented and then deployed towards sociocultural and political engineering processes that produced skewed versions of local native/indigenous identities (Brutt-Griffler, 2006; Chimhundu, 1992; Ranger, 1989). It is here that the notion of 'coloniality of language' becomes clearly relevant as it reveals in unequivocal terms that there is really nothing new, novel or progressive about current bi-/multilingual or additive bilingual education policies that rest on colonially invented conceptions of language, culture and identity.

What this analysis aims to show is that models of language education in postcolonial Africa thrive on fallacies and misconceptions about the nature and roles of different varieties of language in society – that is, these beliefs are sustained and justified by false assumptions about what certain languages can and cannot be used for in educational and other applied social policy settings. In their critique of the popularisation of the concept of 'additive bilingualism' in educational contexts, Makoni and Pennycook (2007) note what they see as a disconcerting similarity between monolingualism and additive bilingualism in so far as both are founded on notions of language as an 'object'. It is precisely for this reason that we continue to witness hierarchisation of languages in multilingual societies as much as in monolingual ones (Ndhlovu, 2013, 2015b). It is also for this reason that in spite of having a 'multilingual' national language policy framework that prescribes 11 official languages, the entire South African education system continues to be mediated exclusively in English.

The problem with South Africa's multilingual language policy and other similar policies around the world is that they focus on the wrong things while turning a blind eye to those things that, in our view, matter most, namely the diversity of language practices. Conceptually, the standard versions of languages that are currently considered to be the official languages of South Africa (IsiZulu, IsiXhosa, SiSwati, IsiNdebele, Sepedi, Sesotho, Chivhenda, Xitsonga, Setswana, English and Afrikaans) are modernist versions of languages that were embraced by both the apartheid and post-apartheid political systems for the purposes of building social cohesion, political control, manipulation and cultural normalisation (Ndhlovu, 2015a).

Therefore, apart from simply broadening the number of official languages-with-names, postcolonial/post-apartheid language education policies bring no concrete theoretical or practical contributions to the African multilingualism debate. This is because such languages continue to be conceived and imagined as countable ontological objects, the only difference being that this is now happening in the postcolonial era under the watchful eyes of equally hegemonic African political elites. The entire project amounts to repetition without difference insofar as it is bereft of original and innovative thinking about 'languages' beyond the colonially inherited ideologies of language. The current constitution of bi-/multilingual education models and their *modus operandi* in postcolonial African countries is founded on this premise.

African postcolonial language education policies are pre-eminently reinforcement and a carry-over from where the colonial language-based social engineering processes left. In other words, while the objective of promoting standardised language forms during the colonial period was 'marketed as a program of enhancing administrative convenience, the same process is now being popularized as part of a response to the exigencies of "globalisation", "progress" and "modernization" [whatever these mean] in the context of the postcolonial dispensation. However, the common denominator in both cases is that of control, manipulation', subtle cultural oppression and, indeed, coloniality of language by stealth (Ndhlovu, 2009: 144).

This rather uncritical embrace of colonial language ideologies (i.e. that language exists in standard monolithic form) and the almost cultic celebration at the altar of colonial ideologies of language (i.e. that language is there to be used as a tool for cultural normalisation) is an instantiation of 'coloniality of language'. Three crucial questions invoked by this scenario follow: (1) Are there no philosophies of or about language other than those inherited from the Global North?; (2) If they are indeed absent, why are we not able to develop some?; and (3) Why do scholars, governments and social policy experts from the Global South always choose the easy route of adopting those language ideologies and theoretical frameworks originating from the Global North? We address these and other related questions in subsequent sections of this chapter.

Language Policymaking as Coloniality of Language

Regarding the dangers of embracing and imposing some kind of linguistic uniformity on culturally diverse societies, Thompson (1991) cautions that a completely homogeneous language or speech community does not exist in reality: it is an idealisation of a particular set of linguistic practices that have emerged historically and have certain social conditions of existence. This idealisation is the source of what Pierre Bourdieu (1991) calls 'the illusion of linguistic communism'. As Thompson (1991) further points out, by taking a particular set of linguistic practices as a normative model of correct usage, an illusion of a common language is produced that ignores the social-historical conditions that established a particular set of linguistic practices as dominant and legitimate. 'This dominant and legitimate language, this victorious language, is what is commonly taken for granted' (Thompson, 1991: 5). Therefore, the 'idealised language or speech community is an object that has been pre-constructed by a set of social-historical conditions endowing it with the status of the sole legitimate or "official" language of a particular community' (Thompson, 1991: 5).

Most introductory sociolinguistics textbooks have shied away from looking at language and language policies using these critical lenses that bring to light the pitfalls of idealised standard languages. From the pioneering work of Einar Haugen (1972), Joshua Fishman (1968), Charles Ferguson (1959), Ralph Fasold (1984, 1990), Richard Hudson (1996), Ronald Wardaugh (2002) and Bernard Spolsky (1998) to the more recent studies by Florian Coulmas (2013), Janet Holmes (2013) and Enam Al-wer (2011), we see consistent accounts of canonical models of language policies steeped in a rather uncritical glorification of normative language standards. The dominant theme in most of these sociolinguistic textbooks is one of a step-by-step explanation of typologies of language policies in different regions of the world. What is lacking, though, is a very strong and robust critique of the phenomenology of 'language objects', and how they are products of complex ideological processes that empower and disempower different sections of society in equal measure.

While some of these pioneering and more recent studies are critical of the ways in which national language policies sometimes legitimise the social, economic and political disadvantages faced by ethnolinguistic minorities, they have, unfortunately, done so in ways that inadvertently entrench such inequalities. In particular, mainstream sociolinguistics studies have been heavily influenced by Fishman's (1972) typological models of language policies, which are said to correspond to particular types of societies.

Fishman identifies three types of language policy. First is the *modal approach*, which applies to societies that are said to have no overarching linguistic, sociocultural or political past; that is, societies with no 'widely accepted and visibly implemented belief and behavior system of indigenously validated greatness' (Fishman, 1972: 194). The language policy option for these society types is said to be one in which the language of widest communication is selected as a national or official language. Second is the *unimodal approach*, which is said to apply in societies that have long-established sociocultural unities with well-established political boundaries (García & Schiffman, 2006: 38). In this case, a single indigenous or indigenised language is selected as the national language. The *multimodal approach* is third. It is said to pertain to societies that have multiple conflicting or competing 'Great Traditions', thus making it imperative for the nations to aspire to a supra-nationalist goal by developing a language policy that accommodates all competing regional/sub-national identities. Under this model, the outcome is a multilingual language policy regime consisting of regional official languages and a language of widest communication.

All three typologies described clearly indicate that language policies are products of a 'set of deliberate activities systematically designed to organize and develop the language resources of the community' (Fishman, 1973: 24) – otherwise known as language planning. An important point missed by such approaches is that they take for granted the object (language) that is subjected to such planning and policy activities. While Fishman's model is part of the established global orthodoxy in language policies, it betrays the pitfalls of standard language ideological thinking, which has become the subject of recent scholarly criticism. Fishman's typological model seems to gloss over the theoretical and empirical questions on the distinction between 'language as an object' and 'language as capacity', or way of communication. The work of scholars – such as Roy Harris (1987, 1998, 1999, 2006), George Wolf and Nigel Love (1992) and Michael Toolan (1999) – who all argue for an integrationist theory of language and (socio)linguistics, has long demonstrated the unhelpfulness of looking at 'language' as an ontological object – or something that can be subjected to processes of planning and policymaking in unproblematic ways.

Current approaches to language policymaking in postcolonial African countries can be explained in terms of their hegemonic intentions as follows. First, language policies sometimes wrongly consign languages and their associated cultural identities into bifurcated categories of 'superior' and 'inferior', 'useful' and 'less useful' and 'important' and 'unimportant'. This breeds all sorts of injustices, inequities and exclusions, as the fortunes of ethnolinguistic groups and individuals within them become indexically tied to those of the languages they speak (Ndhlovu, 2015a). In multi-ethnic and multilingual African contexts, language policies can determine who has access to schools, who has opportunities for economic advancement, who participates in political decisions, who has access to governmental services and who gets treated fairly by governmental agencies (Brown & Ganguly, 2003). Language policies can determine who gets ahead and who gets left behind. Language policies do, indeed, affect the prospects for ethnic success – for both ethnic groups and the individuals in these groups. Politics, economics, community development, advocacy activities and active participation in all other aspects of life will always remain elusive for the majority as long as they are conducted in languages other than those spoken and easily understood by all sections of society, both local and trans-local. The prevailing conditions in most African countries are such that active citizenship participation and national political deliberations are mediated mainly in standard national and official languages, such as isiZulu, isiXhosa, Setswana, Tshivenda, Sesotho, isiNdebele, ChiShona, Chinyanja, Portuguese, English and Afrikaans (among others). This is exclusionary. For example, participatory democracy requires that the deliberations of legislators be conducted and communicated in languages understood by and accessible to all citizens, including those labelled as minority ethnolinguistic groups.

The second problem about language policies is that they have traditionally proceeded along the route of what has come to be known as the 'standard language ideology'. *Language ideologies* are beliefs that we hold about what constitutes language. Our responses to the question of 'What is language?' explicitly or implicitly betray our language ideologies. On the other hand, the related concept of *ideologies about language* refers to beliefs that we hold about what language is for, or why we need language (Milroy, 2001; Woolard & Schieffelin, 1994). Our responses to the question of 'What are languages used for?' betray our ideologies about language. Both language ideologies and ideologies about language are cultural representations – whether explicit or implicit – of the intersection of language and human beings in a social world. They link language to identity, power, aesthetics, morality and epistemology – and, indeed, to just about everything else we do in life. Ideologies and beliefs about language are also deeply rooted in personal biographies, and in political and educational contexts (Shohamy, 2009). Through such linkages, language ideologies and ideologies about language underpin not only linguistic form and use, but also significant social institutions and fundamental notions of person and community (Woolard & Schieffelin, 1994). Language ideologies and ideologies about language proceed from, and are shaped by, what Mignolo (2000) calls 'locus of enunciation'; that is, our point of departure in looking at the world and everything in it, including how we conceptualise things called 'languages'.

The locus of enunciation of the 'standard language ideology' derives from what Makoni and Pennycook (2007: 143) call the 'census ideology'. Founded on the dual notion of both 'languages' and speakers of those languages being amenable to counting, the census ideology masks the differences in the ways the objects called 'languages' have been conceptualised. Makoni and Pennycook (2007: 143) note that 'it has been widely attested that there is massive disparity between the number of languages that linguists believe exist [the etic or outsider's view] and the number of languages that people report themselves as speaking [the emic or insider's view]'.

The origins of both the standard language ideology and the census ideology of language can be traced back to the emergence of Western modernity. This is tied to the fatalistic claims about universalism and global standards of just about everything that constitutes the modern world system.

Standard language ideologies can, therefore, be said to be part of a global system of hegemony and hierarchies of humanity, whereby the meanings and ideas about languages and what they are meant to do are shaped by dominant modernist world views that tend towards universality and uniformity. In his critique of modernist Euro-American epistemological paradigms and their apparent totalising approaches to the interpretation of social reality, Quijano (2007) cautions:

> It is essential that we continue to investigate and debate the implications of the epistemological paradigm of the relation between the whole and its parts as this relates to socio-historical existence. Eurocentrism has led virtually the whole world to accept the idea that within a totality, the whole has absolute determinant primacy over all of the parts, and that therefore there is one and only one logic that governs behaviour of the whole and all of the parts. The possible variants in the movement of the parts are secondary, as they do not affect the whole and are recognized as particularities within the general rule or logic of the whole to which they belong. (Quijano, 2007: 168)

This quotation clearly captures the homogenising ideology behind standard language forms, often erroneously considered to be constituted by mutually intelligible dialects. Within current imaginings and understandings of postcolonial African cultural identities, all other language forms are and continue to be considered as constituent parts of standard languages. This is a problematic view that stems from modernist ideological thinking about languages. It misses the crucial point that there is no universal concept of language – every cultural group has its own understanding of what constitutes a language. Therefore, the major problem with dominant and universalising theories of language policy, and language and identity, is in their desire to speak for everyone else; yet, beneath such pretentions is the tendency to want to gate keep and monopolise the domain of knowledge production, theory formation and conceptualising the universe. It is this fallacy that this chapter questions and challenges in relation to language policies, languages and their associated political and cultural identities in postcolonial Africa.

Following the rise of standard language ideological frameworks from the Global North, meta-discursive regimes have been constructed to describe languages with significant implications for both 'language' (as a general capacity) and 'languages' (as entities). This means that although it is acknowledged that all humans have language, the way in which both senses of language are understood is constructed through a particular ideological lens that excludes other ways of thinking. These are non-linguistic imperatives that form the basis of language scientists' analyses and evaluations of languages.

In this vein, Makoni and Pennycook (2007) have sought to debunk, in particular, the standard language ideology that underpins dominant understandings of languages, language policies and the discourses that sustain them by pointing out that linguistics does not need to postulate the existence of (standard) languages as part of its theoretical apparatus. They suggest that 'linguistics needs to become the study of how people communicate rather than the scientific study of language … It becomes human linguistics rather than a linguistics of language' (Makoni & Pennycook, 2007: 19). Their overall argument is that the dominant ways of talking about languages (meta-discursive regimes) are part of a process of epistemic (or epistemological) violence that was visited on the speakers of different language forms that were suppressed through modernist and colonial invention and the imposition of standard languages.

'Epistemic violence' is a crucial concept that aligns with the notion of coloniality of language introduced in this chapter. It captures the ways in which the standard language ideology has been applied to the systematic obliteration of other conceptualisations of languages and their associated cultural identities through processes of language policy and planning. As I have argued, the notion of language is more complex and broader than is currently suggested by standard language ideological frameworks. Definitions of language should encompass any or all of the following: dialect continua, cultural practices and identities, discursive practices, traditions, customs, social relationships, connections to the land and nature, religion, spirituality, world views and philosophies, proverbial lore and so on (Ndhlovu, 2013, 2015a). In other words, the concept of language does not have to refer to a noun only; it can be an action word or even a describing word – and all these imperatives should be taken into account when formulating language education policies.

But mainstream language policies seeking to promote additive bilingualism, for example, are founded upon a very specific view of language; a view that takes languages to be 'entities' which, when accessed, will then be beneficial to the speakers. In this regard, additive bilingualism and multilingualism must also be understood as particular ways of thinking about language.

In an edited volume, aptly titled *Dangerous Multilingualism*, Blommaert *et al.* (2012) discuss key themes expressed by the most recent and burgeoning body of sociolinguistics scholarship critical of the 'endangering' nature of mainstream conceptualisations of bilingualism and multilingualism. Pitting the modernist notions of 'order' against 'disorder', 'purity' against 'impurity' and 'normality' against 'abnormality', Blommaert *et al.* (2012: 18) argue that the older tradition of sociolinguistic theorisation saw 'problems with multilingualism ... as problems of (dis) order, and the solutions that emerged out of such analyses rarely brought real benefit to the multilingual subjects to whom they were addressed. The reason for this failure was that sociolinguists of that era tended to overlook the complexity of the phenomenology of multilingualism-on-the-ground'. Blommaert *et al.* (2012: 18) advise that we need to start with our 'feet on the ground from a strong awareness that the phenomenology of language in society has changed, has become more complex and less predictable than we thought it was. We have the advantage over earlier generations of being able to draw on a far more sophisticated battery of sociolinguistic insights and understandings'.

Taking a cue from these insights, I argue that, in its current iteration, the notion of multilingualism and how it is incorporated into language policy frameworks is, indeed, a very dangerous one because it hides more than it reveals. Some of the things that are hidden by seemingly progressive multilingualism discourses include: (i) that the process of enumerating multiple monolithic 'language' objects is underpinned by principles of the standard ideology; and (ii) that like other similar (post)modernist notions – emancipation, multiculturalism, cosmopolitanism, universalism and globalisation – the mainstream conception of multilingualism is part of the global imperial designs constituting the ideological leanings of elite researchers and those in power bent on keeping certain groups out of their areas of interaction (Makoni, 2012). In what I think is the most candid critique of the misleading and disingenuous nature of ideologies that inform mainstream understandings of multilingualism, Makoni (2012) argues that

> [Multilingualism] contains a powerful sense of social romanticism, creating an illusion of equality in a highly asymmetrical world, particularly in contexts characterized by a search for homogenization. (Makoni, 2012: 192–193)

A close look at the epistemological architecture of multilingualism in applied settings (such as multilingual education and multilingual national language policies) reveals that this concept reinforces social class hegemony and privilege by masking endemic inequalities, narrow forms of ethnonationalism and xenophobia.

Conclusion: Way Forward

The primary goals of any meaningful form of education include those of meeting the learning needs and aspirations of individuals; addressing the development needs of society; contributing to the creation, sharing and evaluation of knowledge; and contributing towards the development of enlightened, responsible and constructively critical citizens (Department of Education, 1997). Therefore, in our attempts to mitigate the pervasive effects of the monolingual mindset (Clyne, 2005; Gogolin, 1994) that is prevalent in language classrooms, we need to first of all get the policy settings right. That is, we need to adopt language education policies that are sensitive to the diversity of cultures and language profiles that students bring into the classroom. International research reports on language education policy are replete with case studies on how learners can easily accomplish academic tasks collaboratively when encouraged to draw from multiple linguistic and literacy practices. See, for example, the work of Baker (1996) and Creese and Blackledge (2008) for eloquent theorisation and documentation of hybrid multilingual education practices as well as their benefits. With specific reference to the Australian context, Michael Clyne (2008) has suggested that:

> A way of beating the monolingual mindset might be to have in decision making roles people who were brought up bilingually or who have acquired a high level of bilingualism through the education system, sometimes complemented by travel and/or exposure to other languages in Australia. (Clyne, 2008: 361)

In making this recommendation, Clyne (2008: 361) also cautions that the possibility of beating the 'monolingual mindset' will remain a distant hope because any such efforts are 'largely undermined by the present generation of decision makers obsessed with a monolingual mindset'. This is, indeed, a legitimate concern. However, we would add that what is even more worrisome is the obsession with a narrow and monolingual view of language that we find among both the decision makers and the academic community. As already indicated above, the real substance of the matter is not necessarily about embracing multiple pregiven 'language' objects. Rather, we see the solution to the challenges besetting language education as being located at the sites of policymakers' and academic experts' epistemological and conceptual imaginings of language.

While the desire to have more bilingual or multilingual decision makers is an enviable aspirational goal, the question still remains: What is it that these people will be accommodating in their mindsets? If they only have exposure to multiple named and enumerable things called 'languages', then there is a very slim chance that their decisions will make any difference at all. What these decision makers need to have is openness and a capacity to embrace and formulate language policies that recognise the diversity of language practices, including those communicative practices of Southern communities that fall outside the narrow orbit of standard language ideological frameworks. A foundational principle of the Southern perspective on language education is one about its discourse systems that are 'inherently transdisciplinary, multilingual and multicultural. The choice and use of methods are wide-ranging and eclectic' (Shi-xu, 2014: 362); grounded in local cultural contexts yet still open to global disciplinary dialogue as a way 'to achieve or maintain harmonious relationship with others through attending to others' interests, incorporating differences, avoiding conflicts, balancing powers, etc' (Shi-xu, 2014: 364). These are all useful insights of Southern epistemologies that are in short supply in the hegemonic Northern discourses that currently mediate language education policies.

The African philosophy of ubuntu (meaning 'I am because you are') (Mbigi & Maree, 1997) is one example of a Southern perspective that can help both to broaden the understandings of what counts as language and education, and to simultaneously push back the frontiers of coloniality that are currently embedded in mainstream language education policies. Ubuntu is holistic in its inspirations and emphasises the need to harness the social experiences and world views of African people and align them with successful conceptual frameworks from other parts of the world (Ndhlovu, 2019). In other words, ubuntu does not believe in itself as the only way. Instead, it is an approach that is motivated by the desire to establish rapprochement among the multiple ways in which different societies and civilisations read and interpret the world – including the multiple language practices that ought to have a place in educational policy frameworks.

A significant part of Southern perspectives on language and social policy-making is one of recognising and embracing culturally relevant modes of engaging communities that we serve as educators. Southern perspectives are devoted to finding connections, points of confluence and opportunities for the transfer of methods, pedagogies and concepts, not only among members of academic communities, but also between them and the non-academic communities they serve. A major goal is to develop alternative ways for meeting the practical educational needs of individuals and communities – in ways that mitigate the limitations of conventional approaches such as the interventionist top-down Northern paradigms that tend to overlook the centrality of local community actors. This is about forging collaborative teaching and research agendas with non-academic communities as equal partners, whereby education practitioners and policymakers are willing to learn and co-construct knowledge with community leaders, women, the youth, refugees, migrants – the subaltern so to speak – by listening to their stories, and using such stories to generate concept notes that will inform language education policies. Such an approach is in line with the 'decolonial turn', a trend pursued mainly (but not exclusively) by Latin American, African and other like-minded social scientists from both the Global South and the Global North.

The coloniality of language thesis advanced in this chapter stresses the interdisciplinary and unifying potential of a decolonial epistemology, in particular its applied interests in relation to the cultural mediators of language education policy. It calls for the pluralisation of knowledge production processes in globally inclusive ways that require us to seriously consider contextual particularities and the multidimensional character of educational practices in different societal contexts. This is about integrating praxis, theory, action and reflection in ways that provoke revolutionary thinking about the roles of knowledge and knowledge production in social transformation (Chilisa, 2011; Smith, 2012).

Deploying the analytical framework of 'coloniality of language' holds the promise for overcoming challenges besetting language education policies in postcolonial African contexts. The insights of coloniality of language draw our attention to what Benson (2014) calls a multilingual habitus, which is the direct opposite of a monolingual habitus. A multilingual habitus makes 'the language(s) of teaching and learning explicit'

(Benson, 2014: 293) through the development of appropriate methods, materials and assessments that reflect the social and cultural realities of learners and the communities to which they belong.

Benson (2014) explicates the characteristic features and benefits of a multilingual habitus as follows. First, it allows for the negotiation of language(s) of literacy and interaction among classroom participants. Second, it allows for the design of learning goals and their assessments in terms of the quality and the usefulness of the competences that learners bring to the classroom context, or what others have called 'funds of knowledge' (McIntyre *et al.*, 2001). Third, it provides opportunities for building on children's knowledge and experiences. Fourth, it exposes learners to dominant forms of language at developmentally appropriate levels. Fifth, it promotes the development of a metalinguistic awareness among both teachers and learners as an integral part of language learning. And lastly, while a multilingual habitus values the use of dominant language materials as necessary, it also strongly encourages scaffolding meaning and using methods and other language types appropriate to the learners' needs and experiences. These approaches of the multilingual habitus rely on and promote the use of both fixed and fluid linguistic resources in language education.

When put together, the two notions of coloniality of language and multilingual habitus help us see students' 'funds of knowledge'. This is about harnessing the totality of linguistic resources, communication codes and cultures of learning, and deploying them towards language teaching in multilingual classrooms. Therefore, if we are to successfully circumvent standard language ideologies that underpin current language education policies, we need to revisit those colonial imperatives of language that have usurped and monopolised the domain of language education with the view to opening up spaces for the recognition of alternative, especially Southern, conceptualisations. This is the most important step that we need to take before we can try to address methodological questions around language teaching, language and social justice, language and citizenship participation and so on.

To summarise, this chapter has further extended the promises held by alternative conceptualisations of languages to push the boundaries of the field of educational linguistics. The argument is that language policy and planning research needs to focus not only on the political contexts in which it operates, but also on the nature of the concepts of language that underpin the different options – to question not only the realpolitik, but also the reallinguistik of the 20th century, which appears to be still ensconced in 21st-century academic debates and conversations around this topic. Therefore, when language education policy is seen through the lens of coloniality of language, it should apply a transactive approach to language use whereby language is viewed as an ongoing process of social transaction rather than an institution. As Khubchandani (1997: 37) posits, this will enable us to recognise the 'synergic network of plurilingual language use as a means to inspire trust in cross-cultural settings'. In looking at language from this angle, the intention is to highlight the various ways by which students can find richness and strength from their linguistic capabilities, which will ultimately see them reach their full potential and achieve educational outcomes beneficial to themselves and their communities.

References

Al-wer, E. (2011) *Understanding Sociolinguistics*. Milton Park: Hodder Arnold.
Baker, C. (1996) *Foundations of Bilingual Education and Bilingualism* (2nd edn). Clevedon: Multilingual Matters.
Banazak, G.A. and Ceja, L.R. (2010) The challenge and promise of decolonial thought to biblical interpretation. *Equinoxonline* 113–127.
Benson, C. (2014) Towards adopting a multilingual habitus in educational development. In C. Benson and K. Kosonen (eds) *Language Issues in Comparative Education: Inclusive Teaching and Learning in Non-Dominant Languages and Cultures* (pp. 283–299). Rotterdam/Boston, MA/Taipei: Sense Publishers.
Blommaert, J., Leppänen, S., Pahta, P., Virkkula, T. and Räisänen, T. (eds) (2012) *Dangerous Multilingualism: Northern Perspectives on Order, Purity and Normality*. London: Palgrave Macmillan.
Bourdieu, P. (1991) *Language and Symbolic Power*. Oxford: Polity Press.
Brown, M.E. and Ganguly, S. (2003) *Fighting Words: Language Policy and Ethnic Relations in Asia*. Cambridge, MA/London: The MIT Press.
Brutt-Griffler, J. (2006) Language endangerment, the construction of indigenous languages and world English. In M. Pütz, J.A. Fishman and J.N. Aertselaer (eds) *Along the Routes to Power: Explorations of Empowerment through Language* (pp. 35–54). Berlin/New York: Mouton de Gruyter.
Chilisa, B. (2011) *Indigenous Research Methodologies*. New York: Sage.
Chimhundu, H. (1992) Early missionaries and the ethno-linguistic factor during the invention of tribalism in Zimbabwe. *Journal of African History* 44, 87–109.
Clyne, M.G. (2005) *Australia's Language Potential*. Sydney: UNSW Press.
Clyne, M. (2008) The monolingual mindset as an impediment to the development of plurilingual potential in Australia. *Sociolinguistic Studies* 2 (3), 347–365.
Coulmas, F. (2013) *Sociolinguistics: The Study of Speakers' Choice*. Cambridge: Cambridge University Press.
Creese, A. and Blackledge, A. (2008) *Translanguaging in the Bilingual Classroom: A Pedagogy for Learning and Teaching?* Birmingham: University of Birmingham.
Department of Education (1997) *Education White Paper 3: A Framework for the Transformation of Higher Education*. Pretoria: Republic of South Africa.
Dussel, E. (1995) *The Invention of the Americas* (trans. M.D. Barber). New York: Continuum.

Fasold, R. (1984) *The Sociolinguistics of Society*. Oxford: Blackwell.
Fasold, R. (1990) *The Sociolinguistics of Language*. Oxford: Blackwell.
Ferguson, C.A. (1959) Diglossia. *Word* 15, 325–340.
Fishman, J.A. (1968) Nationality-nationalism and nation-nationalism. In J.A. Fishman, C.A Ferguson and J. Das Gupta (eds) *Language Problems of Developing Nations* (pp. 39–51). New York: John Wiley and Sons.
Fishman, J.A. (ed.) (1972) *Advances in the Sociology of Language II*. The Hague: Mouton.
Fishman, J.A. (1973) Language modernization and planning in comparison with other types of national modernization and planning. *Language in Society* 2, 23–44.
García, O. and Schiffman, H. (2006) Fishmanian sociolinguistics (1949 to the present). In O. García, R. Peltz and H. Schiffman (eds) *Language Loyalty, Continuity and Change: Joshua A. Fishman's Contributions to International Sociolinguistics* (pp. 3–68). Clevedon: Multilingual Matters.
Gogolin, I. (1994) *Der Monolinguale 'Habitus' der Multilingualen Schule*. Münster/New York: Waxman-Verlag.
Grosfoguel, R. (2005) The implications of subaltern epistemologies for global capitalism: Transmodernity, border thinking and global coloniality. In W.I. Robinson and R. Applebaum (eds) *Critical Globalisation Studies* (pp. 283–301). London: Routledge.
Grosfoguel, R. (2006) From postcolonial studies to decolonial studies: Decolonising postcolonial studies: A preface. *Review* 24 (2), 141–143.
Harris, R. (1987) Language as social interaction: Integrationalism versus segregationalism. *Language Sciences* 9 (2), 131–143.
Harris, R. (1998) *Introduction to Integrational Linguistics*. Oxford: Pergamon.
Harris, R. (1999) Integrational linguistics and structuralist legacy. *Language & Communication* 19, 45–68.
Harris, R. (2006) Integrational linguistics and semiology. In K. Brown (ed.) *The Encyclopedia of Language and Linguistics* (2nd edn; Vol. 5; pp. 714–718). Oxford: Elsevier.
Haugen, E. (1972) *The Ecology of Language*. Stanford, CA: Stanford University Press.
Holmes, J. (2013) *An Introduction to Sociolinguistics* (4th edn). London: Pearson Education Ltd.
Hudson, R. (1996) *Sociolinguistics* (2nd edn). Cambridge: Cambridge University Press.
Khubchandani, L. (1997) *Revisualising Boundaries: A Plurilingual Ethos*. New Delhi/London: Sage.
Makoni, S. (1998) African languages as European scripts: The shaping of communal memory. In S. Nuttal and C. Coetzee (eds) *Negotiating the Past: The Making of Memory in South Africa* (pp. 242–248). Oxford: Oxford University Press.
Makoni, S. (2012) A critique of language, languaging and supervernacular. *Muitas Vozes, Ponta Grossa* 1 (2), 189–199.
Makoni, S. and Pennycook, A. (2007) Disinventing and reconstituting languages. In S. Makoni and A. Pennycook (eds) *Disinventing and Reconstituting Languages* (pp. 1–41). Clevedon: Multilingual Matters.
Mbigi, L. and Maree, J. (1997) *Ubuntu: The Spirit of African Transformation Management*. Randburg: Knowledge Resources.
McIntyre, E., Rosebery, A. and González, N. (eds) (2001) *Classroom Diversity: Connecting Curriculum to Students' Lives*. Portsmouth, NH: Heinemann.
Mignolo, W.D. (2000) *Local Histories/Global Designs: Coloniality, Subaltern Knowledges and Border Thinking*. Princeton, NJ: Princeton University Press.
Mignolo, W.D. (2002) Geopolitics of knowledge and the colonial difference. *South Atlantic Quarterly* 101 (1), 57–96.

Mignolo, W.D. (2011) Epistemic disobedience and the decolonial option: A manifesto. *Transmodernity* Fall, 44–66.

Mignolo, W.D. (2017) Foreword. On pluriversality and multipolarity. In B. Reiter (ed.) *Constructing the Pluriverse: The Geopolitics of Knowledge* (pp. ix–xvi). Durham, NC: Duke University Press.

Milroy, J. (2001) Language ideologies and the consequences of standardization. *Journal of Sociolinguistics* 5 (4), 530–555.

Ndhlovu, F. (2006) Gramsci, Doke and the marginalization of the Ndebele language of Zimbabwe. *Journal of Multilingual and Multicultural Development* 27 (4), 302–318.

Ndhlovu, F. (2009) *The Politics of Language and Nation Building in Zimbabwe*. Bern: Peter Lang.

Ndhlovu, F. (2013) Beyond neo-liberal instructional models: Why multilingual instruction matters for South African skills development. *International Journal of Language Studies* 7 (3), 33–58.

Ndhlovu, F. (2015a) *Hegemony and Language Policies in Southern Africa: Identity, Integration, Development*. Newcastle upon Tyne: Cambridge Scholars Publishing.

Ndhlovu, F. (2015b) Ignored lingualism: Another resource for overcoming the monolingual mindset in educational linguistics. *Australian Journal of Linguistics* 35 (4), 398–414.

Ndhlovu, F. (2019) South Africa's social transformation policies: Raciolinguistic ideologies and neoliberal rhetoric. *Journal of Multicultural Discourses* 14 (2), 131–151. Doi: 10.1080/17447143.2019.1592177.

Ndhlovu, F. and Kamusella, T. (2018) Challenging intellectual colonialism: The rarely noticed question of methodological tribalism in language research. In T. Kamusella and F. Ndhlovu (eds) *The Social and Political History of Southern Africa's Languages* (pp. 347–364). Houndmills: Palgrave Macmillan.

Quijano, A. (1998) The colonial nature of power and Latin America's cultural experience. In R. Briceno-Leon and H.R. Sonntag (eds) *Sociology in Latin America (Social Knowledge, Heritage, Challenges, Perspectives)* (pp. 27–38). Proceedings of the Regional Conference of the International Association of Sociology, Caracas/Venezuela.

Quijano, A. (2000) Coloniality of power, ethnocentrism, and Latin America. *Nepantla* 1, 533–580.

Quijano, A. (2007) Coloniality and modernity/rationality. *Cultural Studies* 21 (2–3), 168–178.

Ranger, T.O. (1985) *The Invention of Tribalism in Zimbabwe*. Gweru: Mambo Press.

Ranger, T.O. (1989) Missionaries, migrants and the Manyika: The invention of ethnicity in Zimbabwe. In L. Vail (ed.) *The Creation of Tribalism in Southern Africa* (pp. 118–150). London: James Currey.

Shi-xu (2014) Cultural dialogue with CDA: Cultural discourse studies. *Critical Discourse Studies* 11 (3), 360–369.

Shohamy, E. (2009) Language tests for immigrants: Why language? Why tests? Why citizenship? In G. Hogan-Brun, C. Mar-Molinero and P. Stevenson (eds) *Discourse on Language and Integration: Critical Perspectives on Language Testing Regimes in Europe* (pp. 45–60). Amsterdam/Philadelphia, PA: John Benjamins Publishing Company.

Smith, L.T. (2012) *Decolonizing Methodologies: Research and Indigenous Peoples* (2nd edn). London/New York: Zed Books.

Spolsky, B. (1998) *Sociolinguistics*. Oxford/New York: Oxford University Press.

Thompson, J.B. (1991) Editor's introduction. In P. Bourdieu (ed.) *Language and Symbolic Power* (pp. 1–31). Oxford: Polity Press.

Toolan, M. (1999) Integrationist linguistics in the context of 20th century theories of language: Some connections and projections. *Language & Communication* 19, 97–108.
Wardaugh, R. (2002) *An Introduction to Sociolinguistics* (4th edn). London/New York: Blackwell.
Wolf, G. and Love, N. (1992) Integrational linguistics: An introductory survey. *Proceedings of the XVth International Congress of Linguists* (pp. 313–320; v. 1). Quebec: Presses de l'Universite Laval.
Woolard, K. and Schieffelin, B.B. (1994) Language ideology. *Annual Review of Anthropology* 23, 55–82.

6 African Vehicular Cross-Border Languages, Multilingualism Discourse

Introduction[1]

In the last decade and a half, a meta-linguistic discourse has emerged on the African continent – that of African vehicular cross-border languages (Vcbls). The concept of Vcbls refers to 'languages that are common to two or more states and domains straddling various usages' (ACALAN, 2009: 4). The African Academy of Languages (ACALAN) developed the idea of Vcbls as a strategy for resolving intercultural communication challenges in the context of African regional and continental economic and political integration. The uptake of the concept of Vcbls among relevant academic communities and some education practitioners has been huge. A major reason for the widespread embrace of the notion of Vcbls is the perception that it holds the promise to push back the frontiers of colonially inherited language ideologies that are firmly entrenched in postcolonial African multilingual policy frameworks.

In what follows, we critically engage the underlying assumptions of the proposition that African Vcbls can help overcome colonial philosophies of language. We argue that such a supposition misdirects the African multilingualism debate. We suggest that the perceived utility of Vcbls has to be evaluated against the backdrop of contestations around language definition traditions. Drawing on ideas from decolonial scholarship, we provide a critical analysis of African Vcbls and perceptions about their ability to resolve the anticipated intercultural communication problems of an integrated Africa. In doing so, we bring to the limelight the omissions and blind spots of these projective conclusions about the perceived potential of Vcbls by interrogating dominant, neoliberal and Euro-modernist ideologies that inform such assumptions about multilingualism.

Critique of VCBL Concept and Discourse

ACALAN's (2009) proposition of the concept of African VCBLs appears to be on a collision course with a plurilingualistic view of African integration. African VCBLs are conceived in a manner that does not set them apart from African national languages that are now well known for being the worst killer languages in postcolonial Africa. Almost all 12 VCBLs prioritised by ACALAN are the national languages of at least two African nation-states: Chichewa/Chinyanja is the national language of Malawi and Zambia; Setswana is the sole national language of Botswana, and 1 of the 11 official languages of South Africa; KiSwahili is the official national language of Tanzania, and is one of the national languages of Kenya; and both Arabic and Beberé are the *de facto* national languages of most North African nation-states.

This simply means that the prioritisation of these VCBLs amounts to change without difference. The same hegemonic languages that were used for administrative convenience and for fashioning 'imagined' uniform identities by both the colonial and postcolonial African nation-state would continue to be appropriated for similar purposes by a trans-national African state. The only two things that have changed are (i) the naming of this category of languages, which changes from 'national language' to 'vehicular cross-border language'; and (ii) the expansion of the spatial jurisdiction of each of the selected languages – that is, from national boundaries to trans-national/regional boundaries. In other words, the terminology of 'vehicular cross-border language' is another metaphor for territorial conquest by current African national languages that gives them more political clout.

The ACALAN (2011) December Quarterly Newsletter indicates that VCBL commissions have been established for all the selected VCBLs, with the exception of modern standard Arabic and Berbére. The language commissions are charged with the responsibility of spearheading and coordinating the harmonisation of writing systems for the selected VCBLs, as well as organising regional training and capacity-building workshops in areas of language standardisation and other related corpus planning activities. The Chichewa/Chinyanja and Setswana language commissions held their first workshop on the harmonisation of these VCBLs in Gaborone, Botswana, 29–30 May 2011 (ACALAN, 2011). In October of the same year, ACALAN organised a capacity-building workshop for the Cinyanja/Chichewa, Mandenkan and Somali VCBL commissions in Lusaka, Zambia. These workshops sought to

Create a common ground for the harmonisation of the activities of the Vehicular Cross-border Language Commissions in relation to the development and promotion of African languages in general and the vehicular cross-border languages in particular. (1) Build the capacity of the Vehicular Cross-border Language Commissions for optimal performance and define strategies for advocacy, project management, monitoring and evaluation as well as fund raising. (2) Prepare and adopt a draft binding and working document on the functioning of the Vehicular Cross-border Language Commissions. (ACALAN, 2011: 17)

It is important to recall that the choice of African VCBLs was mainly motivated by the desire to circumvent the use of ex-colonial languages (such as English, French and Portuguese), which are perceived to be incapable of adequately representing a truly African world view due to their status as 'foreign', ex-colonial languages. By virtue of their African indigenous language status, VCBLs are perceived as being better positioned to serve the desired goals of the African integration project in a manner that promotes the flourishing of multilingualism across the continent. However, it must be noted that the methodological and conceptual processes of promoting and propagating VCBLs constitute wholesale mimicry of the same hierarchisation processes that pushed ex-colonial languages and other African national languages to the hegemonic positions they currently occupy.

What the above description of the work of VCBL commissions shows is that the elevation of VCBLs into languages of African integration follows precisely the same route that rendered standard African national languages objects of subtle cultural oppression for which they are now notoriously well known (Ndhlovu, 2015). The methodology that underpins the operational procedures of the VCBL commissions is purely colonial; it is driven by monolingual language definition traditions that see languages as isomorphic forms that should always be subjected to rigorous corpus planning activities (development of standard grammars and orthographies) if they are to be deployed in such important domains as economic and political integration.

Another important point is ACALAN's enumeration of 12 VCBLs. This misdirects and misrepresents the notion of multilingualism in the sense that the counting of multiple standardised languages equates to what others have called 'multiple monolingualisms' (Ndhlovu, 2014); 'parallel monolingualism' (Heller, 1999); 'bilingualism through monolingualism' (Fishman, 1967); or 'separate bilingualism' (Creese & Blackledge, 2008). The phenomenon of 'multiple monolingualisms' is about the side-by-side coexistence of multiple languages in which the majority of people do not engage in cross-linguistic interactions because they are not proficient in each other's languages (Ndhlovu, 2014). This means that the existence of many languages in a community or society does not necessarily translate into a working knowledge of several languages or proficiency skills in multiple languages. What such an understanding of multilingualism is missing is that the issue is not so much about the 'number' of language 'objects' recognised and accommodated into the African integration project, as it is about how such entities are conceptualised (Ndhlovu, 2013). As Ndhlovu (2015) argues, multilingualism must be understood as something that encompasses multiple and diverse views on dialects, language forms and other communicative modes, including symbolic, metaphorical and discursive ones.

Seen in this light, the concept of VCBLs tends to misdirect African multilingualism because it provides a misinformed and misleading solution to the intercultural communication challenges of an integrated Africa. ACALAN's adoption of the enumerative model of multilingualism thus runs parallel to the broader thesis of socially realistic multilingualism that we advance in this project. As we have already indicated in Chapters 1 and 2, most standard African languages are imposed colonial inventions, which were later embraced by postcolonial African regimes for political control, manipulation and cultural normalisation. All other language forms were, and continue to be, considered constituent parts of standard languages. This idea dates back to the colonial period where the role of early Christian missionaries in aiding colonial administrators in the project of inventing standard African national languages is well documented in the relevant literature.[2]

Focusing on 'language' as a problematic concept, Pennycook (2008) provides a compelling argument on the historical evolution of standard 'languages' and how they have come to be simplistically accepted as underpinning pillars for multilingual policy frameworks. Pennycook looks at the historical and contemporary interests behind the long construction of things called 'languages' and asks in whose interests we continue to divide and categorise 'languages' into these named entities. In unpacking this paradox, Pennycook (2008) argues:

> Nearly all language-names have had to be invented by Europeans [and] are founded on words which have received English citizenship [...] while others are based on existing names of countries and nationalities. While it is interesting at one level to observe simply that the names for these entities were invented, the point of greater significance is that these were

not just new names for extant objects (language pre-existed naming), but rather the invention and naming of new objects. The naming performatively called languages into being. (Pennycook, 2008: 19–21)

This means that 'language-things' were called into existence, named and then speakers were recruited through such institutions as schools, universities and churches. The African VCBLs discourse follows hard on the heels of this logic. There is copious literature indicating that African languages now elevated to the status of VCBLs have a checkered and tainted historical association with these colonial and postcolonial projects of subtle cultural oppression, and other forms of everyday language-based marginalisation. With specific reference to Chichewa (one of the VCBLs for Southern Africa), Themba Moyo (2002) gives a detailed analysis of how the promotion and propagation of this language by the first president of postcolonial Malawi, Kamuzu Banda, and his Malawi Congress Party resulted in the demise of multilingualism in the country. Moyo demonstrates how, on 21 September 1968, the Chewa dialect of Chinyanja, which happened to be Kamuzu Banda's dialect, was elevated to become the only national language of Malawi:

> The Chewa dialect of Chinyanja was now promoted and became a symbol of national language. The language was decreed as the sole national language for mass communication on the radio and printed media. It also came to symbolize his [Banda's] project of national unification and integration, linguistically and culturally. This was at the expense of seven other indigenous languages. (Moyo, 2002: 265)

As can be seen from this quotation, Chichewa, which was primarily part of the Chinyanja dialect continua, was elevated to a national language because it was the president's own dialect. To elaborate on this point, Moyo (2002: 265) says 'with the elevation of the Chichewa dialect to a national language came the rise of the Chewa [people] to political power, while the political power of other groups declined'. As a result, Chewa values came to be exalted as supreme over the languages, cultures and traditions of other ethnic groups. In Malawi, class interests eventually came to affect social, linguistic, economic and political imbalances at the national level. Here, we see the replication of colonial habits and practices of domination, control and the exercise of power through the invention of languages of command (see Chapter 1 for more on this).

In their most recent book titled *Innovations and Challenges in Applied Linguistics from the Global South*, Pennycook and Makoni

(2020) push the envelope even further by pointing the laser light to questions of ontology. With a specific focus on research in applied linguistics, they question the discipline's foundation on traditional science within the Eurocentric perspective: the central themes of rationality, linearity, development and disembodiment of science. A serious concern for Pennycook and Makoni (2020: 79) is how 'the colonial linguistic project and its applied linguistics offshoot produced a vision of language that had little to do with how people understood language locally'. This is an extension of Makoni and Pennycook's (2007) earlier argument to disinvent and reconstitute languages; and a reiteration of Pennycook's 2010 thesis on language as local practice.

Arguably, national languages, of which VCBLs are an integral part, can be seen as semiotic social inventions used to make other language practices invisible by projecting an impression of uniformity in the midst of social, cultural, political and linguistic diversity. In other words, as Ndhlovu (2013b, 2015) has suggested, the idea of a standard national language serves to invisibilise and diminish the value of multiple language forms and expressions that fall outside the normatively constructed standard forms. It is the same national languages invented during the heyday of colonial and postcolonial nation-state formation processes that are projected as the best vehicles for an integrated yet multilingual Africa. This is a classic and colossal example of history repeating itself. Here, decolonial theory becomes a useful explanatory paradigm that helps us see that there is really nothing new, novel or progressive about the idea behind the commissioning of African VCBLs. What is it that the idea of VCBLs brings to the table of ideas about languages and philosophies of languages? Apart from merely expanding the geographical extent of the selected standard languages beyond the confines of individual nation-states, the notion of VCBLs brings no concrete theoretical or empirical contributions to the African multilingualism and identitarian discourse. Just like the African national languages that came before them, VCBLs are constituted and imagined as countable ontological objects, the only difference being that the geographical area for VCBLs is much wider. The entire project amounts to repetition without difference – it is bereft of an original and innovative rethink of what is meant by 'language' beyond modernist versions of languages as enumerable monolithic forms (Ndhlovu, 2013b). Both the constitution of VCBLs and the *modus operandi* of VCBL commissions are founded on this false premise.

In a seminal work on abyssal lines, abyssal thinking and ecologies of knowledge, de Sousa Santos (2007) says

The colonies provided a model of radical exclusion that prevails on modern Western thinking and practice today as it did during the colonial cycle. Today as then, both the creation and the negation of the other side of the line [the marginalized and invisibilized] is constitutive of hegemonic principles and practices. Today as then, the impossibility of co-presence between the two sides of the line runs supreme. (de Sousa Santos, 2007: 10)

Drawing on these ideas, we argue that the intersection of language and African integration is a complicated and multifaceted issue that interweaves colonial processes of manipulation and control as well as postcolonial and post-national (Soysal, 1994) political goals of skewed nation building, cross-cultural integration and identity formation. The current post-national African nation-building enterprise (marketed as continental integration) is pre-eminently a reinforcement and carry-over from where the colonial and postcolonial language-based social engineering processes left. In other words, while the objective of promoting standard language forms (national languages) during the colonial and postcolonial periods was 'marketed as a program of enhancing administrative convenience, the same process is now being popularized as part of a response to the exigencies of "globalization", "progress" and "modernization" (whatever these mean) in the context of the post-national dispensation. However, the common denominator in all three cases is that of control, manipulation, subtle cultural oppression and, indeed, linguistic imperialism' (Ndhlovu, 2009b: 144).

Decolonial scholarship helps illuminate this rather uncritical embrace of modernist language ideologies (that is, that language exists in standard monolithic form) and the almost cultic celebration at the altar of colonial ideologies of language (that is, that language is there to be used as a weapon of cultural normalisation). Some of the crucial questions to arise include the following: Are there no philosophies of language and multilingualism other than those inherited from the Global North? If they are indeed absent, why are we not able to develop some? Why do scholars, governments and social policy experts from the Global South always choose the easy route of adopting language ideologies and theoretical frameworks originating from the Global North? As we argue throughout this book, languages do not necessarily have to exist as ontological entities in the world, and neither do they emerge from or represent a fixed real environment. This view on language exposes the tensions, contradictions and falsehoods underpinning dominant narratives about multilingualism sustained by standard language ideologies.

In advancing this argument, we share the views expressed in some of the most recent scholarly debates and conversations in the fields of linguistics and applied linguistics critical of dominant meta-discourses on language in society (see e.g. Blommaert *et al.*, 2012; Mahboob & Knight, 2008; Ndhlovu, 2013b, 2014; Pennycook, 2010). These scholars have poignantly suggested the need to rethink, question, challenge and problematise orthodox understandings of 'language'. The 2008 volume, *Questioning Linguistics*, edited by Mahboob and Knight, is one such example of work that takes a critical look at the discursive construction and imagination of 'languages'. This book originated from research presentations given at the First International Free Linguistics Conference held at the University of Sydney in October 2007. In short, *Questioning Linguistics* invites us to critique the language assumptions that we often take as facts, and to find alternative ways of understanding how individuals and communities conceptualise the diversity of language practices they encounter on a daily basis.

Overall, the argument of all the contributions in *Questioning Linguistics* is that 'those parameters and boundaries that have grown out of the linguistics discipline, creating oppositions rather than complementarities, have obscured the way that linguists pursue their endeavors towards language' (Mahboob & Knight, 2008: 4), including the discourse and praxis of multilingualism. Mahboob and Knight (2008: 15) further argue that 'a deeper understanding of languages is only possible if we look beyond the versions of "languages" constructed by experts and engage with different traditions, understandings, and approaches to linguistics'. We see this as an explicit call for language experts to explore and engage with other conceptualisations of 'language' – and by implication, multilingualism – to address the manifold language-related needs and challenges, such as those of intercultural communication in African economic and political integration.

Multilingualism and the Idea of Africa

The other glaring issue ignored or inadequately captured by the African VCBLs discourse is the idea of 'Africa'. This is, no doubt, a very old but still relevant question that has been raised and discussed extensively by leading international scholars of African studies.[3] In their current iteration, mainstream academic discourses on VCBLs adopt a limiting and limited idea of Africa, focusing mainly on the physical landmass consisting of 54 nation-states, plus the surrounding island nations and polities. Such a conceptualisation of Africa narrows and misdirects complex issues of multilingual African identities, steering them in the direction of conservative, neoliberal thinking reflected in the current notion of VCBLs. Imaginings of the idea of Africa and of cross-border languages with an exclusive focus on the cartographic landmass called 'Africa' do not provide space for multiple trans-language practices and communicative modes of the peoples and polities that the integration project seeks to bring together (Ndhlovu, 2015; Ndhlovu & Kamusella, 2018).

Africa and African identities are often defined on the basis of numerous taxonomies, including religious, ecological, ethnic, biological, linguistic, geographical and historical ones. Noting that 'Africa does not end on Africa's shores', Mazrui (2005: 81) says the way Africa is defined has been *a product of its interaction with other civilisations, including Islam and the impact of the West*. While this is partly the case, such a view of Africa only tells half of the story. The other half is this: there have always been African indigenous understandings of Africa and being African that have a long historical trajectory dating back to periods prior to contact with other civilisations. To help explicate this, we may as well draw on Marco Jacqemet's (2005: 5) notion of transidiomatic identities that 'describes the communicative practices of transnational groups that interact using different languages and communicative codes simultaneously present in a range of channels, both local and distant'. This shades some useful insights for a better and more nuanced understanding of how Africa and African identities have evolved and how they continue to be discursively constructed. The approach of transidiomatic practices is a useful framework that redirects our focus on tolerant, accommodative and recombinant identities based on multi-present, multilingual, de-territorialised and decentred sociopolitical relations (Jacqemet, 2005: 6). Unlike mainstream definitions that underwrite essentialised linguistic identities emphasising cultural insularity, the transidiomatic perspective is akin to Homi Bhabha's (1994) notion of constitutive hybridity.

There is, therefore, a compelling need for us to build on and extend the idea of being and becoming African into new directions of emerging scholarly and social policy research. These should centre on multilingual citizenship (Stroud, 2018) to provide fresh insights into understandings of African economic integration. Briefly defined, multilingual citizenship entails the recognition, active support and promotion of the actual use of most language forms, dialects and communication modes used by citizens as part of their individual and collective identities (Blackledge, 2005). The concept of multilingual citizenship is increasingly becoming an established conceptual framework widely used in international research to inform social policy on identity, participation, social cohesion and cross-cultural understanding. Examples of such studies include Blackledge (2005), Hogan-Brun et al. (2009), McNamara (2009) and Shohamy (2009). These studies have shown how crucial it is to consider competing identity narratives to understand who is accepted as being in or out of multilingual communities. This is in the context of concerns over social justice for speakers of different languages who may be unable to gain access to membership of normative national identity narratives in different regions or parts of the world (Blackledge, 2005). With specific reference to the United Kingdom, Blackledge (2005: 32) suggests 'there is often a dynamic tension between identities asserted and chosen by self, and identities asserted and chosen for the individual by state, nation or institution'. This observation is applicable to the current African situation in which the African Union (through ACALAN) seeks to impose VCBLs as prime markers of individual and group identities, thereby ignoring the complex social formations of African polities.

Another recent body of work (see e.g. Coleman, 2008; Coleman & Rowe, 2005; Collin, 2009; Ndhlovu, 2009a, 2010; Ward, 2008) suggests that personal experiences increasingly shape the way most people in multilingual societies make sense of, and develop strategies for managing competing ideas, identity options, histories and language resources. For instance, despite all the odds against them (such as monolingual ideologies of language policies, and the temptation to cling onto homogenising national linguistic and cultural identities), African migrant and diaspora communities continue to see themselves as connected to the idea of being African. In a study on patterns of language use among the African-Australian diaspora community, Ndhlovu (2010) found that the surveyed group expressed positive attitudes towards their ethnic languages.

> Exigencies of group socio-cultural cohesion within migrant communities of shared linguistic backgrounds and the desire to maintain strong connections with native homeland [were cited as] the main motivations for positive attitudes towards ethnic languages. (Ndhlovu, 2010: 296)

Thus, in the broader context of the realities of global migration and cross-border movements of human populations, individual and group agency ensures that different African linguistic identities continue to thrive alongside other language and cultural identities far away from geographical 'Africa'. One lingering question that begs for answers is this: To what extent does the idea of African integration mediated through

African VCBLs promise to take into account and accommodate these competing and contending versions of being and becoming African?

Conclusion

When considered from a non-critical perspective, the concept of VCBLs would appear to be a new, attractive, innovative and Africa-centred approach to solving the intercultural communication challenges associated with economic and political integration projects. Because they are widely used across different borders of existing African nation-states, VCBLs seem to be the natural successors to those national languages that were instrumental in fashioning hegemonic national identities during both the imperial and post-imperial epochs. However, as we have shown throughout this chapter, African linguistic and cultural diversities are too complex to be accommodated within a selection of 12 monolithic language forms modelled after the Euro-modernist philosophies of language. Drawing on insights from decolonial thought, the chapter has challenged Eurocentric language ideologies that inform the idea of VCBLs. What the decolonial epistemic perspective reveals is that we need to think beyond the traditional modernist paradigms and conceptualisations of 'languages'. We also need to take a closer look at what dominant views on multilingualism can and cannot do.

The present iteration of VCBLs is too limited and limiting both in scope and in content for this category of languages to be used in a manner that addresses the anticipated intercultural communication challenges of an integrated Africa. In the final analysis, this chapter concludes that the architects of African integration need to de-link from colonial matrices of power and think differently about these issues – think in ways that are consistent with the multiversity of African polities that communicate in multiple, non-standardised language forms and other multimodal communication channels – or what we also call languages of the people (see Chapter 9). Such a paradigm shift will help us avoid misdirecting the African multilingualism debate, and lead to the acknowledgement, recognition and accommodation of multiple ways of knowing, doing, reading and interpreting the world into the African integration agenda.

Notes

(1) Some of the material in this chapter is a significantly revised version of Ndhlovu (2013b).
(2) See e.g. the work of Brutt-Griffler (2006), Chimhundu (1992), Makoni (1998), Mufwene (2001, 2002), Ndhlovu (2006, 2007, 2009b) and Ranger (1985).
(3) See e.g. the works of Mudimbe (1988), Mazrui (2005) and Zelelza (2006).

References

ACALAN (2009) Report on ACALAN's synthesis conference on national policies on the role of cross border languages and the place of less diffused languages in Africa. Addis Ababa, Ethiopia. See https://www.yumpu.com/en/document/read/4517488/report-of-the-synthesis-conference-au-acalan-website (accessed 19 March 2021).

ACALAN (2011) AU/ACALAN Quarterly Newsletter, December. Koulouba, Mali. See https://archives.au.int/bitstream/handle/123456789/1624/Synthesis_Recomendations_E.pdf?sequence=1&isAllowed=y (accessed 19 March 2021).

Bhabha, H.K. (1994) *The Location of Culture*. London: Routledge.

Blackledge, A. (2005) *Discourse and Power in a Multilingual World*. Amsterdam/Philadelphia, PA: John Benjamins Publishing Company.

Blommaert, J., Leppänen, S., Räisänen, T., and Pahta, P. (eds) (2012) *Dangerous Multilingualism: Northern Perspectives on Order, Purity and Normality*. London: Palgrave Macmillan.

Brutt-Griffler, J. (2006) Language endangerment, the construction of indigenous languages and World English. In M. Pütz, J.A. Fishman and J.N. Aertselaer (eds) *Along the Routes to Power: Explorations of Empowerment through Language* (pp. 35–54). Berlin/New York: Mouton de Gruyter.

Chimhundu, H. (1992) Early missionaries and the ethnolinguistic factor during the invention of tribalism in Zimbabwe. *Journal of African History* 44, 87–109.

Coleman, S. (2008) Doing IT for themselves: Management versus autonomy in youth e-citizenship. In W.L. Bennett (ed.) *Civic Life Online: Learning how Digital Media can Engage Youth* (pp. 189–206). Cambridge, MA: The MIT Press.

Coleman, S. and Rowe, C. (2005) *Remixing Citizenship: Democracy and Young People's Use of the Internet*. London: Carnegie Young People Initiative.

Collin, P. (2009) The making of good citizens: Participation policies, the internet and youth political identities in Australia and the United Kingdom. Unpublished PhD thesis, University of Sydney.

Creese, A. and Blackledge, A. (2011) Separate and flexible bilingualism in complementary schools: Multiple language practices in interrelationship. *Journal of Pragmatics* 43 (5), 1196–1208.

De Sousa Santos, B. (2007) Beyond abyssal thinking: From global lines to ecologies of knowledge. *Review* 15 (1), 1–66.

Fishman, J.A. (1967) Bilingualism with and without Diglossia; Diglossia with and without Bilingualism. In Li Wei (ed.) *The Bilingualism Reader* (pp. 8189). London: Routledge.

Heller, M. (1999) *Linguistic Minorities and Modernity: A Sociolinguistic Ethnography*. London: Longman.

Hogan-Brun, G., Mar-Molinero, C. and Stevenson, P. (eds) (2009) *Discourse on Language and Integration: Critical Perspectives on Language Testing Regimes in Europe*. Amsterdam/Philadelphia, PA: John Benjamins Publishing Company.

Jacqemet, M. (2005) Transidiomatic practices: Language and power in the age of globalization. *Language and Communication* 25 (3), 257–277.

Mahboob, A. and Knight, N. (eds) (2008) *Questioning Linguistics*. Newcastle upon Tyne: Cambridge Scholars Publishing.

Makoni, S. (1998) African languages as European scripts: The shaping of communal memory. In S. Nuttal and C. Coetzee (eds) *Negotiating the Past: The Making of Memory in South Africa* (pp. 242–248). Oxford: Oxford University Press.

Makoni, S. and Pennycook, A. (2007) Disinventing and reconstituting languages. In S. Makoni and A. Pennycook (eds) *Disinventing and Reconstituting Languages* (pp. 1–41). Clevedon: Multilingual Matters.

Mazrui, A.A. (2005) The re-invention of Africa: Edward Said, V.Y. Mudimbe and beyond. *Research in African Literatures* 36 (3), 68–82.

McNamara, T. (2009) Language tests and social policy: A commentary. In G. Hogan-Brun, C. Mar-Molinero and P. Stevenson (eds) *Discourse on Language and Integration: Critical Perspectives on Language Testing Regimes in Europe* (pp. 153–164). Amsterdam/Philadelphia, PA: John Benjamins Publishing Company.

Moyo, T. (2002) Language politics and national identity in Malawi. *South African Journal of African Languages* 4, 262–272.

Mudimbe, V.Y. (1988) *The Invention of Africa*. Bloomington, NC: Indiana University Press.

Mufwene, S. (2001) *The Ecology of Language Evolution*. Cambridge: Cambridge University Press.

Mufwene, S. (2002) Colonisation, globalisation, and the future of languages in the twenty-first century. *International Journal of Multicultural Societies* 4 (2), 165–197.

Ndhlovu, F. (2006) Gramsci, Doke and the politics of language marginalization in Zimbabwe. *Journal of Multilingual and Multicultural Development* 27 (4), 305–318.

Ndhlovu, F. (2007) Historicizing the socio-politics of Shona language hegemony in Zimbabwe. *Lwati Journal of Contemporary Research* 4, 295–313.

Ndhlovu, F. (2009a) The limitations of language and nationality as prime markers of African diaspora identities in the state of Victoria. *African Identities* 7 (1), 17–32.

Ndhlovu, F. (2009b) *The Politics of Language and Nation Building in Zimbabwe*. Oxford/Bern: Peter Lang AG.

Ndhlovu, F. (2010) Belonging and attitudes towards ethnic languages among African migrants in Australia. *Australian Journal of Linguistics* 30 (2), 283–305.

Ndhlovu, F. (2013a) Cross-border languages in Southern African economic and political integration. *African Studies* 72 (1), 19–40.

Ndhlovu, F. (2013b) How the idea of vehicular cross-border languages misdirects multilingualism in the African integration debate: A decolonial epistemic perspective. *Africanus* 43 (2), 13–33.

Ndhlovu, F. (2014) *Becoming an African Diaspora in Australia: Language, Culture, Identity*. Houndmills: Palgrave Macmillan.

Ndhlovu, F. (2015) *Hegemony and Language Policies in Southern Africa: Identity, Integration, Development*. Newcastle upon Tyne: Cambridge Scholars Publishing.

Ndhlovu, F. and Kamusella, T. (2018) Challenging intellectual colonialism: The rarely noticed question of methodological tribalism in language research. In T. Kamusella and F. Ndhlovu (eds) *The Social and Political History of the Languages of Southern Africa* (pp. 347–364). London: Palgrave Macmillan.

Pennycook, A. (2008) Language-free linguistics and linguistics-free languages. In A. Mahboob and N. Knight (eds) *Questioning Linguistics* (pp. 18–31). Newcastle upon Tyne: Cambridge Scholars Publishing.

Pennycook, A. (2010) *Language as a Local Practice*. London/New York: Routledge.

Pennycook, A. and Makoni, S. (2020) *Innovations and Challenges in Applied Linguistics from the Global South*. London/New York: Routledge.

Ranger, T.O. (1985) *The Invention of Tribalism in Zimbabwe*. Gweru: Mambo Press.

Shohamy, E. (2009) Language tests for immigrants: Why language? Why tests? Why citizenship? In G. Hogan-Brun, C. Mar-Molinero and P. Stevenson (eds) *Discourse* on *Language and Integration: Critical Perspectives on Language Testing Regimes in Europe* (pp. 45–60). Amsterdam/Philadelphia, PA: John Benjamins Publishing Company.

Soysal, Y. (1994) *Limits of Citizenship: Migrants and Postnational Membership in Europe.* Chicago, IL: Chicago University Press.

Stroud, C. (2018) Linguistic citizenship. In L. Lim, C. Stroud and L. Wee (eds) *The Multilingual Citizen: Towards a Politics of Language for Agency and Change* (pp. 17–39). Bristol: Multilingual Matters.

Ward, J.R. (2008) *Youth, Citizenship and Online Political Communication.* Amsterdam: Amsterdam School of Communications Research.

Zeleza, P.T. (2006) The inventions of African identities and languages: The discursive and developmental implications. Selected Proceedings of the 36th Conference on African Linguistics (pp. 14–26). Somerville, MA: Cascadilla Proceedings Project.

7 African Multilingualism, Immigrants, Diasporas

Introduction

In this chapter, we explore the prospects for re-theorising African multilingualism by drawing on the language practices of African migrants and diasporas. We use narrative ethnographic data from African migrant communities in rural and regional Australia to argue the need to look closely at the communicative practices of mobile people in order to sharpen our understanding of multilingualism. At the heart of the chapter is the question: What can we learn about multilingualism from the language practices, mobilities and social and cultural experiences of migrants and diasporas? The argument we advance is built around the mobility paradigm, an approach that seeks to include the historic movement of people with the contemporary importance of individuals' contributions to society. The mobility paradigm focuses on 'novel ways of theorising how people, objects, and ideas travel, by looking at social phenomena through the lens of movement' (Salazar *et al.*, 2017: 2).

In what follows, we leverage the mobility paradigm to draw attention to the small details of living with languages that may contain the potential to develop or question big theories (Strathern, 2004: xx), such as those that inform mainstream understandings of multilingualism. Additionally, we introduce the notion of denizen and the promises it holds for alternative understandings of multilingualism in ways that accord with the mobilities of Africans from diverse linguistic, social and cultural backgrounds. Following this framework of analysis, we provide a laser-like focus on African migrants' comments and take on things (no matter how insignificant they might seem on the surface), in order to apprehend underlying and collective discourses. In paying particular attention to people's mobilities, movements, encounters, exchanges and mixtures, the chapter brings the voices and perspectives of immigrants and diasporas into the multilingualism debate. We conclude that developing new, meaningful and broad-based theorisations of multilingualism entails meticulously weaving together the stories of research participants and researchers' mindful reflection on them.

Background: The African Story in Australia

The number of Australians born in Africa has grown extremely rapidly, from a very small base, over the last two and half decades. Different cohorts of African immigrants have arrived, including humanitarian and refugee entrants as well as economic migrants (Ndhlovu, 2011, 2013, 2014). Australian Bureau of Statistics (ABS) (2012, 2017) census data indicates that the number of people born in Africa rose from about 338,000 in 2011 to 380,000 in 2016, representing an increase of 12.4% within a period of five years. The major countries of birth are South Africa, Egypt, Zimbabwe, Sudan, Mauritius, Kenya, Ethiopia, Somalia, Zambia, Ghana, Nigeria, Sierra Leone, Liberia, Rwanda, Burundi and Eritrea (Australian Bureau of Statistics, 2012; Jakubowicz, 2010; Ndhlovu, 2014). Most Australians born in Africa come from multilingual communities and bring with them a rich repertoire of homeland languages and additional ones acquired in transit during their migration journeys.

The received view on refugees, migrants, diasporas and other displaced people (hereafter 'denizens') is that they constitute a disadvantaged social group – disadvantaged economically, socially, politically, linguistically and in many other ways. Such a reading of 'denizens' ignores the prospects, opportunities and spheres of possibility that belie the temporal experiences of multilingual migrants. In much of this chapter, we use the concepts of 'denizenship' and 'marginality' to suggest fruitful ways that might inform alternative understandings of the phenomenology of multilingualism in immigrant and diasporic contexts. The specific focus is on how the psychosocial distribution of multiple linguistic usages by African denizens and their mapping onto everyday interactional processes can enrich theories of multilingualism. The overall intention is to capture previously undescribed language practices of individuals and groups, their linkages with life stories, migration histories and temporal experiences, and how these constitute spheres of possibility for how to talk about the multilinguality of African multilingualism in relation to migration and mobility. This is important because as people move, they reconstitute and repackage the resources they carry – both material and non-material – in the process of building new social relations in their new and continuously evolving milieu.

Denizens, Creativity, Multilingualism

Thomas Hammar (1990: 15) introduced the term 'denizen' to describe the unique and rather ambiguous situation of people 'who are foreign citizens with a legal and permanent resident status'; that is, people with a legal status that is more than that of a foreigner but less than that of a citizen. In much of the citizenship and migration studies literature, the term denizen is often used to refer to 'foreign citizens who have been allowed to enter a state's territory [but] are usually not allowed to stay on without restrictions' (Hammar, 1990: 12). Thus, the classical view of denizens considers them foreigners who reside in another country and 'enjoy neither political rights nor a complete equality of social rights' (Castles & Davidson, 2000: 95). However, Hammar's more detailed explanation of the notion of denizen revealed that the traditional definition of who is a foreigner and who is a citizen has become untenable, as it does not correspond easily with the actual situation on the ground.

In many immigration countries, great numbers of foreign citizens have established intense and close relations with their host country. Some have lived there most of their lives. Some may even have been born there to parents of foreign citizenship. They may have grown up in that country and gone to school there. They may be absolutely fluent in the language, which may be their mother tongue. They may own property in the host country and some may be influential businesspeople or professionals, while others may hold other high positions. However, for various reasons, they have remained foreign citizens, and perhaps also prefer to retain their original citizenship (Hammar, 1990).

African denizens in Australia are an extremely diverse group, reflecting the linguistic, cultural, ethnic and political diversity of the African continent as well as their different immigration trajectories, histories and life journeys. Before final settlement in Australia, most African denizens lived in at least two countries for significant periods of time, during which they picked up other languages, cultures and life experiences that broadened their already significant levels of diversity (Ndhlovu, 2013, 2014). Their cultures, identities and language practices are far more complex than is often suggested in Australian academic studies (Marlowe et al., 2013; Musgrave & Hajek, 2010) and political and public/media discourses. Like most emerging migrant communities in Australia, African denizens are often described in terms of their perceived lack of (or limited) English language proficiency, and how this supposedly diminishes their chances of living good-quality lives. The emphasis that government and non-government agencies put on the 510 hours of Adult

Migrant English Language Programme (AMEP) lessons is one example of the tendency to prioritise English language skills over proficiency in other languages. This emphasis overlooks the different cultural, linguistic and experiential capabilities of members of migrant communities.

While there is no doubt that English is a useful language for African denizens in Australia, the data we present and analyse in this chapter suggests that not everything in the everyday lives of migrant communities is done (well) using the English language. African denizens have an overlay of other categories of languages and language types that include African cross-border languages, refugee journey languages, small ethnic languages and symbolic languages such as discursive and cultural practices. These linguistic resources are rarely considered from a perspective that focuses on how multiple language types and practices enrich and strengthen the abilities of groups and individuals. Recognising such levels of language and cultural diversity would help us better understand the community's capacities and the depth of established social networks among multilingual African denizens, which are used to support each other and also reach out to other non-African background communities.

A working knowledge of many languages is an important skill that enables African denizens to get by, broaden their social networks and make sense of life in their new environments. This suggests that there are plenty of opportunities and prospects for the emergence of new and creative ways of deploying multilingual resources in a manner that sidesteps reified perceptions about the language practices of immigrants and diasporas (Ndhlovu, 2018). It is out of such linguistic usages that we can draw new insights for generating alternative theories of socially realistic multilingualism: those theories that emerge out of and speak to people's everyday realities of living with languages. The main argument is that the past experiences of African denizens – whether they be experiences of conflict, war, hunger, political persecution, displacement and/or loss of property, along with their associated emotional, social and economic consequences – should not prevent us from seeing the capabilities and the 'spheres of possibility' (the prospects and opportunities of intra- and cross-cultural networking that are facilitated by the ability to speak multiple languages in remote rural and regional areas of Australia) that lie beneath these tragic events.

As will be indicated in the data and analysis section, African denizens have the freedom to creatively use language varieties that are not widely recognised in the national language policies of their African countries of origin. Language varieties such as pidgins and creoles enable African denizens to broaden their circles of social networks at different sites of interaction, with significant positive impacts on the quality of life for both individuals and communities. All of these cultural and linguistic resources are crucial 'spheres of possibility' that need to be looked at from a positive perspective in order to offer fruitful insight into how the capabilities and experiences of denizens might enrich current theories of multilingualism.

Marginality and Multilingualism

The concept of marginality is generally used to refer to zones and forms of exclusion, disadvantage and vulnerability (Anderson & Larsen, 1998; Bodwin, 2001; Davis, 2003; Gurung & Kollmair, 2005). In this chapter, we adopt a more positive view of marginality and consider it a sphere of possibility, transformation and new beginnings (Seshadri-Crooks, 1995; Viljoen, 1998). Seen from this perspective, the margin is a privileged place for writing one's identity, history, cultural values, desires and fears and not a space of victimhood and exclusion. We co-articulate the notion of marginality with that of denizenship to broaden our understanding of complex, mixed and criss-crossing language practices that are characteristic of most immigrant communities around the world.

African denizens who took part in the study that forms the core of this chapter exhibit almost all of the vulnerability indicators that have been identified by the literature as being the hallmark of denizenship. Such vulnerability indicators include immigration history, country of origin, length of residence in the new country, level of dependence on social welfare and charity, language skills and level of education (Benton, 2014). As indicated in the introduction, African immigration to Australia is relatively recent. This means that, although they may have been naturalised into Australian citizens (or at the very least hold permanent residence visas), most African denizens have limited established social networks, employment opportunities or other special connections when compared to more established Australian citizens of European and Asian backgrounds. However, as we show below, African denizens have enormous linguistic and cultural capabilities that can be deployed towards circumventing the challenges that come with the identified vulnerability indicators of being marginal. Here, we extend the concept of denizenship beyond its traditional meaning of being vulnerable to domination and disadvantage. We use it to describe denizens' capabilities to utilise their multiple linguistic and cultural resources as well as other life skills and experiences acquired during migration journeys to generate creative communicative practices that fall outside current framings of multilingualism.

This is a germane and revealing line of argument with significant implications for our understanding of African denizens and their linguistic repertoires. We are talking here about people who occupy a marginal space within the Australian immigrant context. Their cultures are deemed marginal when compared to dominant Anglo-Saxon cultural norms and their languages are considered marginal and less favourable compared to English, which is perceived as the main language of access, participation and engagement in the necessary social transactions of everyday life. The linguistic repertoires of migrants reveal that the languages of African denizens exist on the fringes or periphery of the broader Australian language map. However, such location of African denizens and their languages in this seemingly powerless and negligible space does not necessarily mean they are unimportant and, therefore, exposed to the whims of the centre, where categories of relevance are laid down, decreed and enacted. Rather, the margin that they occupy is a zone where categories and systems of relevance become deconstructed, where the power to control and dictate meaning becomes irrelevant and where power is questioned and no longer applies automatically or self-evidently (Viljoen, 1998). This means that the margin is a site for transformation, (re)creating, brainstorming and charting the way forward. In the words of Seshadri-Crooks (1995: 59), the margin is a space of agitation, subversion and theoretical innovation – the condition of possibility – the 'unthought and unsaid that makes a positive knowing possible'. Viljoen (1998) extends further the idea of the margin, noting that it contains the elements of the good life and is a site of freedom, fecundity and a point from which the world can be surveyed intellectually. This means that the margin is a privileged position; a space where new ideas are formed, trialled and then disseminated.

In the next section, we consider the cultural identities, linguistic repertoires and temporal experiences of African denizens to gauge their potential for epistemic reconstitution of the multilingualism discourse. While there is no doubt that many African denizens in Australia were forced out of their countries of origin by conflict, war, persecution and/or other forms of oppression, domination and/or abuse, we argue the need to move beyond the exclusive focus on the negative aspects of their experiences. We suggest that we need to think through and look positively at the wealth of linguistic, cultural and other experiential resources accumulated by African denizens along the convoluted refugee journeys that ultimately brought them to Australia. The premise of this line of argument is that the lives of African denizens did not freeze or come to a halt at the time they fled their countries of origin, only to pick up again upon their permanent settlement in Australia.

As we show in the data and analysis section, the linguistic and cultural skills that African denizens gained during the course of their asylum and refugee journeys have now become a permanent and defining feature of who they are (linguistically and culturally) and how they live their lives in Australia. These capabilities remain the least understood and under-theorised in multilingualism research, as most previous studies and social policy frameworks in this area have adopted deficit-led approaches that consider the profiles and life experiences of migrants and denizens as characterised merely by conditions of lack, disadvantage and vulnerability.

Overview of Methods and Data

The data that supports our argument was collected through focus groups and one-on-one interviews with African denizens originally from three regions of the African continent: the Horn of Africa, East-Central Africa and West Africa. Specific countries of origin included Ethiopia, Eritrea, Somalia and Sudan, the Democratic Republic of Congo, Rwanda, Burundi, Kenya, Sierra Leone, Liberia, Ivory Coast, Guinea, Ghana and Nigeria. Focus groups were organised using the criterion of region of origin in Africa, in order to facilitate the comparison of patterns of response both within groups and across groups with different historical, linguistic and cultural experiences.

All participants were recruited from the New South Wales regional areas of the Mid North Coast (Coffs Harbour), the Hunter Valley (Newcastle) and the Riverina (Wagga Wagga). In order to ensure representativeness in relation to ethnic and linguistic diversity within the target population, 60 people (20 from each of the three research sites) were initially contacted and requested to participate. However, by the end of the study, 36 people had been interviewed, with this number determined by theoretic saturation and the availability of people to participate in the study. Both male and female participants aged 18 years and over who had lived in Australia for at least two years were included in the sample.

Participants were asked to narrate personal stories about their migration journeys, highlighting their linguistic repertoires and language experiences. In order to safeguard participants' anonymity, every interviewed person was allocated a name code derived from the research site in which they were interviewed (NC = Newcastle; WG = Wagga Wagga; CH = Coffs Harbour) followed by a number; that is, NC1, WG4, CH9, etc. All interviews were carried out in English since it is one of the languages spoken by all of the people included in the sample and because the study did not aim to do a linguistic analysis of the participants' speech. Rather, the goal was to ascertain the extent to which participants' language experiences and practices can provide new insights, which might enrich the current project of searching for alternative conceptualisations of multilingualism.

The study found that most African denizens in regional Australia use multiple and complex linguistic resources in different contexts and with different people. African migrant languages such as Swahili, Kriol, Arabic and Amharic, which are spoken across the national borders of more than two African countries, were found to be an important means of facilitating social networking and community building by people originally from the same regions in Africa. For example, Kriol (and its variants) is a common language for people from the West African nations of Liberia, Sierra Leone, Ghana, Nigeria, Gambia and Cameroon. Similarly, Swahili is a common language for most people from Kenya, Tanzania, Uganda, Burundi, South Sudan and the DRC. A second category of languages is that of small ethnic languages spoken mainly at the family level, where they function as a means for intergenerational transmission of close-knit family ties and cultural practices. This picture of language mapping was found to be enriched even further by the use of a third category of languages – those acquired along the refugee journey, in countries of first, second or third asylum. For instance, some people who migrated as refugees from the DRC, Rwanda and Burundi reported a working knowledge of the Shona and Chinyanja languages of Zimbabwe and Zambia, respectively. These participants had stayed in refugee camps in Harare (Zimbabwe) and Lusaka (Zambia) for periods ranging from six to nine years and had picked up Shona and Nyanja as additional languages while there.

Another category of language types is that of discursive and cultural practices. These are various symbolic and pragmatic ways of communicating that are not expressed in verbal terms but that constitute a particular language type with wider implications for the epistemic reconstitution of the multilingualism discourse. Discursive languages were evident from the stories and tales that African denizens indicated they narrate to their children, and in unspoken and other symbolic gestures, memories and desires.

Prospects for Epistemic Reconstitution of Multilingualism

In this section, we introduce the language map of African denizens that challenges two commonly held beliefs and perceptions about linguistic usages in immigrant and diasporic contexts. The first is the common-sense assumption that English language proficiency holds *the* key to living successful and fulfilling lives in Australia. The second is the perception that migrant languages have no greater role than that of being repositories of migrant cultures and traditions and as a medium to connect with 'people back home'. Figure 7.1 attempts to visualise the level of complexity characterising the linguistic cartographies of African denizens and their usages in regional Australia. In the next few paragraphs, we discuss different categories of languages (represented in Figure 7.1) to illustrate the ways in which linguistic repertoires are mapped onto the everyday interactional processes of African denizens.

First are varieties of English, namely Australian English and African Englishes. There are two scale levels at which the different varieties of English operate among African migrant communities. The obvious one relates to the *de facto* official status of Australian English, whereby this language assumes the unrivalled role of lingua franca within and across different communities. English occupies the realm of bridging capital, enabling people from different cultural and linguistic backgrounds to connect with one another and perform all the necessary social transactions that transcend their immediate friendships and family circles. Out-group

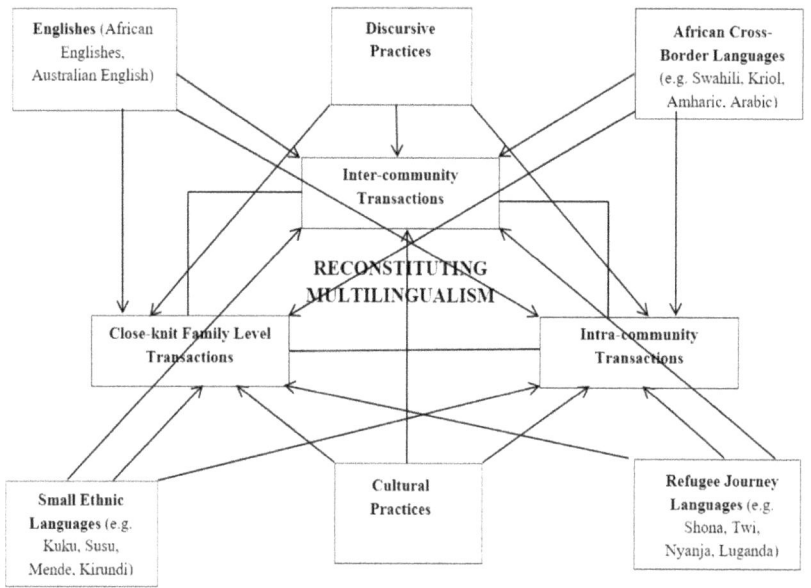

Figure 7.1 Possibility for epistemic reconstitution of multilingualism[1]

social networking is crucial for active and productive participation in employment and other socioeconomic activities and this is facilitated by a working knowledge of the lingua franca, which is Australian English in this case. As it is the default language of widest communication in domains such as employment and education, Australian English can determine who has access to schools, who has opportunities for economic advancement, who participates in political decisions, who has access to government services and who gets treated fairly by government agencies (Brown & Ganguly, 2003). In short, Australian English language skills can affect the prospects of success for ethnic groups and for individuals in these groups. It was in recognition of the pragmatic and symbolic functions of Australian English that study participants overwhelmingly concurred with the predominant view that this language occupies an important space in social transactions at inter- and intra-community levels.

The second scale level is in relation to other varieties of English (especially African Englishes) as the main languages of intergenerational communication between marginal African parents and their children. This dimension was raised by almost every interviewed parent as somewhat of a concern revolving around generational differences in linguistic repertoires and the compromises that parents have embraced to circumvent the ensuing intercultural communication problems at the family level. As studies on language acquisition have long demonstrated (see e.g. Baker, 1992; Carreira, 2005; Norris-Holt, 2001), it is generally expected that the process of learning a new language and the ability to use it with a near-native level of proficiency will be fairly easy among young children and youth. For adults, it is a different story altogether and the consequence of this is clearly captured in the submission from WG1, who arrived in Australia in 2003 as a refugee from Sudan via Cairo, Egypt.

WG1 is a single mother who indicated she speaks Kuku (a variety of Bari) and Arabic, and has a working knowledge of English. She narrated in the following terms her experiences with the tenuous act of balancing her language abilities with those of her five children, who now have near-native English language skills:

> [...] the language I think; because like my young one, he can speak English very well but sometimes when he speak and I don't understand what he is saying, and when I speak he doesn't understand what I mean, I think that's the difficult decision... I don't know what can be done because for us, I don't know... we pushing our self to learn the English yeah... also because we are trying our best for the kids also to understand the English and my language, their language. (WG1)

Although the acquisition of English language skills is generally seen as desirable to facilitate interaction between African denizens and other Australian communities, the sentiments expressed in the above transcript suggest that there are additional motivations that further complicate the language maps of these people. The desire to close communication gaps between immigrant parents and their young children is projected as one of the key pragmatic motivations for parents to push themselves very hard to acquire communication skills in Australian English, the main language of their children. What we see here are overlapping spaces for Australian English and African Englishes, thus pointing to the possibility of a theory of multilingualism that takes into account varieties of English. This is to say, Australian societal conditions coupled with complex migration journeys and the linguistic repertoires of African denizens constitute a unique set of circumstances requiring us to reopen debates and questions around multilingual Englishes. If a theory of multilingual Englishes is possible, what would it look like in the linguistic landscape of postcolonial settler societies such as Australia? Would it be possible to imagine Australia's AMEP in multilingual terms through the positive evaluation and recognition of African and other immigrant varieties of English?

Seeking answers to these questions would enable us to challenge predominant assumptions about language and multilingualism in immigrant contexts. The current mainstream view in Australia (and other comparable contexts) considers multilingualism as mostly about the recognition of migrant languages (excluding varieties of English). What this has done is to pull apart the complex language resources of immigrants and silo them into hierarchised boxes of context of usage. For example, the family setting is perceived to constitute a bastion for intergenerational transmission of heritage languages among migrant communities, while English (in whatever form or variety) belongs in formal domains outside of the family sphere. However, the findings of this study contest this reductionist and overgeneralised view. The study found that the family is yet another site for contestation, negotiation and re-evaluation of languages and language practices. The family has, indeed, become an arena that carries a rhetorical function as a surrogate barometer for language use wherein some languages and language practices are validated (Australian English in this instance) while others are silenced or diminished (specifically migrant heritage languages such as Kuku and Arabic in the case of WG1). All of this points to the emergence of previously unpredicted linguistic cartographies that contest and defy dominant assumptions about the multilingualism and language practices of African denizens and other migrant communities in Australia.

The foregoing line of argument and analysis was attested to by 20-year-old NC6 who arrived in Australia in 2005 as a refugee from Uganda. While her parents were originally from Sudan, NC6 was born and spent her early childhood years in Uganda until she migrated to Australia at the age of 13. In addition to English, NC6 reported that she has some knowledge of Maadi and Luganda, both being indigenous languages of Uganda. This is what she had to say regarding the use of languages between African denizen parents and their children:

> Let the parents go to school too and learn how to speak a little bit of English, which will help them and also when the kids come back from school they can just speak their normal language at home. (NC6)

This is an explicit call for broadening and (re)constituting the ways we theorise multilingualism such that the (re)negotiated language abilities of individuals, families and communities become part of the matrix. The main point highlighted in this excerpt considers a two-way process whereby both the parents and the children put effort into learning each other's languages. However, as has already been noted, because Australian English has more sociopolitical clout than migrant languages, and because the process of learning a new language is much easier for young people, the scales are obviously tipped against parents who have to put a lot more effort into redrawing their own language maps. As for the children, there appears to be very little or no motivation at all for them to learn the languages spoken by their parents, given that English (in its various forms) is increasingly becoming the predominant home language for most migrant families and communities (Ndhlovu, 2014). Nevertheless, the co-existence of multiple varieties of English within the Australian linguistic ecology presents a compelling case for us to rethink and reconfigure theories of multilingualism in ways that accord with mundane language practices and experiences of denizens.

There is no doubt that multilingual English is useful among African denizens in Australia, as is the case in other comparable immigrant communities around the world. The only lingering conundrum is about how to imagine social and educational policies in ways that pitch English as a multilingual medium that people from differing backgrounds use differently to read and interpret social experiences. Debates around the benefits of English language skills among migrant communities are too well known to rehearse (see e.g. the work of Crystal, 2006; Davies, 1991; Graddol, 2006; Ndhlovu, 2011).

Nevertheless, the utility of (monolingual) English tends to be overplayed, with most supporting arguments, such as the communicative currency and language of widest communication theses (Ndhlovu, 2009), telling us only part of the story. The other part is this: not everything in the everyday lives of migrant communities is done (well) using the normative standard variety of English. This leads us to other categories of languages and language types, namely African cross-border languages, refugee journey languages, small ethnic languages and symbolic languages such as discursive and cultural practices. In the paragraphs that follow, we discuss these language types and how they are mapped onto the identities and interactional processes of the people who use them.

Let us consider African cross-border languages first. As already indicated in Chapter 6, cross-border languages are 'languages that are common to two or more states and domains straddling various usages' (ACALAN, 2009: 4).[2] The concept of cross-border languages is concretised by reference to both the history of African national borders, which were arbitrarily drawn during the 18th-century European scramble for Africa, and by the general nature of the African language ecology. The latter is characterised by the existence of many languages that cross the borders of multiple countries (see Barro, 2010; Ndhlovu, 2013; Prah, 2009).

The cross-border languages that featured prominently in this study are Kiswahili and Arabic. Their significance was highlighted by participants sampled from all three research sites. NC2 underscored the importance of cross-border languages as essential social capital for overcoming ethnolinguistic fragmentation, thus leading to the formation of strong and viable pan-African denizen communities in Australia.

> It is true that it is important that we have to speak our dialect. I think the major problem here is that Africa itself is fragmented; we have so many tribes, so many ethnic groups, divided [...] for example, take Sudan alone, there are about 400 dialects in Sudan, massive 400. But if there were, like ... only one language from West Africa, and one from Eastern Central Africa, like Swahili, it would have been fantastic. Like now nearly 20–30% of people, Africans in Newcastle are Swahili speakers, either from Congo, Kenya, from East and Central Africa, which brings people closer together. (NC2)

NC2's comments highlight how the need to interact within a narrow circle of friends/relatives and to also engage cross-culturally gives rise to language maps characterised by the co-existence of different language types within the same psychosocial spaces. This observation was evident in the responses of many participants, who emphasised in particular the increased role of Kiswahili in forging cross-cultural and cross-linguistic ties among people who originally came from different African countries. Narrating her experiences with how Kiswahili enables her to network easily within and across different African communities in Wagga Wagga, WG8 stated:

> Kiswahili is big, Kiswahili you can speak with Congolese, you can speak with Rwanda. Swahili is common, you know, even some people from Sudan, they speak Kiswahili, even Kenya, even Uganda. So I have different friends who speak Kiswahili, so I use Kiswahili most of the time. Even Tanzanians I speak with them Kiswahili most of the time. I think I have more friends in Kiswahili language than Kirundi. (WG8)

WG8 was born in Burundi and here she mentions five other national groups that she easily identifies with on account of her knowledge of Kiswahili. This is a clear example of how African cross-border languages occupy an important space in the entire discourse of multilingualism in relation to transnational identity formation and community building among people who would otherwise be seen as belonging to different national identity categories. Furthermore, cross-border languages were reported as being especially useful among speakers of small languages, whose ethnic groups are not well represented within the wider African community in Australia. Cross-border languages enable such people to connect with other African denizens, thereby reducing the incidence of social isolation and overreliance on service providers for basic needs. The problems associated with social isolation for minority groups with no working knowledge of either English or any one of the African cross-border languages were summed up by NC7:

> They get their way around through service providers; if they have bills, they have issues that are complicated, they go to service providers. Service providers in turn use the telephone interpreting service to get things sorted for them. They have been doing this for over years and years. Secondly, these are people who just flock around their own communities only. From their friends to members from the same community, that is all you will find them. They don't go; they don't mix with other people from outside. Even with other African communities, they don't mix. So they just flock around their own communities. (NC7)

However, as the example of WG8, cited above, shows, having a working knowledge of an African cross-border language is a useful skill that can help people from small ethnolinguistic groups avoid social isolation by building cross-linguistic friendships and relationships that enable them to live independent and fulfilling lives. This is one of the benefits of looking at margins and marginality as zones of transformation and creativity. It helps us reframe theories of multilingualism in ways that speak to people's everyday experiences of living with multiple language resources.

An important lesson we learn from the language practices of African migrants and diasporas is that mainstream theories of multilingualism constructed from a position of social privilege need the perspective of the margin to gain the larger view of the everyday lifeways of people living with multiple language types. Looking at multilingualism from the margin does matter because it is at the margins 'where the majority of the world's people live, where most of the world's cultures have flourished, and where most economic activity occurs' (Connell, 2014: 217). Therefore, although the mainstream view from the metropole or the centre dominates the arena of knowledge production and theorisation, a marginal perspective gives us the larger view – a world-centred view that draws attention to what happens within the atoms of society.

Further analysis of participants' stories shows that the linguistic cartographies of African denizens clearly constitute spheres of possibility for people who belong to small ethnolinguistic groups. Having a cross-border language as part of one's linguistic repertoire is, indeed, another site for new beginnings that enables the building of new and wider social networks. Therefore, unlike bureaucratic approaches that tend to reify and literally view multilingualism in terms of discrete languages tied to nationality, alternative speaker-based approaches consider language boundaries as fluid, porous and capable of contracting and expanding depending on the dynamics of spatial and virtual scales of social interaction.

When WG8 says she has more friends in the Kiswahili language community (as opposed to her ethnic Kirundi community), she clearly projects a typical African denizen identity – characterised by the complex use of transnational language varieties – which transcends the limitations of nation-state-centric imaginings of multilingualism. Cross-border languages are thus envisaged as meeting points and bridges into all forms of cross-community and cross-cultural engagements among African denizens. The significance of cross-border languages resides in their ability to create cultural links and linguistic unity that go beyond the identity categories born out of political maps and national borders. Therefore, in African diasporic contexts, the cross-border language phenomenon provides new and empirically grounded lenses for theorising multilingualism in a manner that takes into account the everyday multilingual and discursive practices, as well as the histories, of both individuals and groups. A consideration of the ways in which cross-border languages are strategically deployed to achieve the best social outcomes for individuals and communities indicates that there is much to be gained from a multidimensional conception of language diversity by moving beyond country of origin as either the unit of analysis or the sole object of study (Glick-Schiller et al., 2006). The breadth and depth of diversity associated with cross-cultural interactional processes mediated by the use of African cross-border languages surpass the reach of monolingual approaches. This means that theories about people's past experiences have significant application in the study of multi-group relations in contemporary societies characterised by unprecedented and complex forms of diversity. It is for this reason that in reframing the discourse and praxis of multilingualism, we have to appreciate the coalescence of factors that condition people's choices as to who they network with and in what medium.

The research participants' narratives of their identities, linguistic repertoires and life stories analysed above suggest that African denizen identities and language practices do not proceed in a straight, unbroken line from some fixed, single point of origin. Rather, they are framed and shaped by multiple vectors and axes of similarity, continuity, difference and rupture, all simultaneously operative in dialogic relationship (Ndhlovu, 2013). In other words, difference persists in and alongside continuity, in which boundaries of difference are continually being repositioned in relation to different points of reference (Hall, 1990). This is how we should look at the linguistic cartographies of African denizens, seeing them not as fixed or complete markers of identity but rather as reflexive categories whose usages swing unsteadily between the poles of contingency and essentialism in a manner that reflects the temporalities of African denizens' lived experiences (Ndhlovu, 2013, 2014).

Another point worth noting here is one relating to the predominant mention of Kriol among participants originally from West Africa, who saw it as one language that straddles several borders – mental and physical – as well as domains of usage in their region of origin and a significant point of reference for their identity imaginings in immigrant contexts. For people from countries such as Sierra Leone, Liberia, Ghana, Nigeria and Guinea, Kriol (and its variant, pidgin English) is an important cross-border language that enables them to connect and forge new identities and social networks among themselves. Responding to a question on what she thought was the place of each of the five languages she claimed to have a working knowledge of, WG4 particularly emphasised the importance of Kriol and its variant pidgin English:

> We have like six to eight families here from my country that we can speak the same language, some can speak different dialects because of the ethnic group, but we all speak the Pidgin English, the Kriol, so we communicate in that most of the time. Even when we meet in gatherings, with all the people we still communicate in Kriol. [People from] Sierra Leone, Liberia, speak that Kriol, Ghana, speak that Kriol, but just theirs are different versions but when they speak their Pidgin English we can understand them. They have different names how they call theirs, we call it Kriol, they have got different names. Like the Liberians they call it Pidgin English, but it's the same Kriol, it's like borrowed English ... Most times when we meet in gatherings like parties or any social gatherings, we speak that Kriol more to one another, we only turn into English if we have like white people there that we want to tell them what we are saying. (WG4)

Again, we see here language maps that overlap and transcend nation-state-centric approaches to multilingualism. The above observation on the role and place of Kriol was corroborated by other participants interviewed in all three research sites. For instance, when asked about the language varieties that are widely used in community meetings of West African people in Coffs Harbour, CH1 was quick to say:

> Pidgin English, the Kriol and Pidgin English is the best one that people can express themselves ... someone who is in his forties or fifties, just expresses themselves speaking the Pidgin or the Kriol. At least with that you can best express yourself. (CH1)

The above excerpts are important submissions that point to how new transnational identity categories and new linguistic cartographies are evolving among African denizen communities through the widespread use of language varieties that are not highly regarded in multilingual policy frameworks back in Africa. Like other emergent languages all over the world, Kriol does not have a prestigious official status within the language policy regimes of those African nation-states in which it is spoken, as it is seen as a variety that is incomplete, broken, corrupt and not worthy of serious attention (see e.g. Bickerton, 1976; Holm, 2000; Kouwenberg & Singler, 2008; Siegel, 2008). Isabelle Léglise (2019: 253) has recently reminded us about how a number of studies and research reports on languages and cultures in contact tend to initially presuppose the existence of isolated linguistic and cultural communities to investigate, and then follow this with a description of the consequences of contact between them. The limitation of such an approach is that it perpetuates erroneous assumptions about creoles and pidgins as incomplete and inferior varieties. As Léglise (2019) further argues, in the context of the Global South, the concepts of language, language contact, code-switching and so on are particularly inadequate due to the multiplicity of language practices that defy the logics of segregationist approaches. Léglise's (2019) approach is in line with arguments advanced by scholars who study language from the Harrisian or integrationist perspective (Harris, 1987, 1998, 1999, 2006). From an integrationist perspective, languages are considered integrated systems and not separate self-contained entities. Scholars working under the banner of Southern epistemologies have revived the integrationist approach to language by drawing attention to the promises it holds for decolonising the field of applied linguistics. Sinfree Makoni (2020) has recently edited a collection of chapters on this theme titled *Integrationism and Southern Theory*, with key contributions by Pable (2020) and Fang (2020), among others.

Therefore, although negative attitudes towards non-standardised language varieties might still be prevalent, some rapid changes are taking place, particularly among marginal communities that continue to draw the attention of relevant scholarly communities to the significance of creoles and pidgins as an integral part of transient postmodern identities. The stories elicited from members of the African denizen community originally from West Africa suggest that creoles and pidgins are, in fact, not wrong versions of other languages. Rather, they are the real languages of the people[3] whose socio-pragmatic functions are shaped and mediated by the everyday interactional and communicative needs of their speakers. Here, we see language varieties that have traditionally not been highly regarded on the African continent assuming an important role as an overriding medium of communication and a marker of group identity among African denizen communities in Australia. This is not because Kriol has suddenly found a space in the centre. Rather, this is the positive outcome of being in the marginal space – the periphery – that zone of undecidability which simultaneously constitutes a favourable environment for self-actualisation and creativity.

The widespread use of Kriol does indeed reflect the transnational, constantly evolving, emergent and incomplete nature of the linguistic and cultural identities of contemporary African denizen communities. Therefore, the cultural and linguistic landscape of African denizens in

Australia is a sphere of possibility; a zone of opportunity to freely use language varieties that are not highly regarded in their countries of origin. This supports the proposition that margins are, in fact, privileged zones for questioning and challenging hegemonic impositions (such as notions of multilingualism that are based on standard language ideologies). African denizens in Australia are immune from and beyond the reach of the hegemonic national language policies of West African states that constrict and curtail the use of creoles and pidgins. Such are the benefits of occupying a marginal space: African denizens are now able to express their genuineness and authenticity with very little or no hindrance at all. People occupying the centre both in countries of origin and in Australia do not have access to this privilege. So, in short, being on the margin does not always mean being in limbo; it sometimes means being in a privileged place for writing one's identity, for self-assertion, for creativity and for doing things the way you like. Existing on the margins is, in fact, a liberating experience for African denizens, one that frees them from the shackles of linguistic and cultural normalisation, at least for as long as they are not yet fully 'integrated' into the monolingual mindset that is endemic in Australia.

Small ethnic or heritage languages (e.g. Kuku, Mende, Kirundi and Maadi) constitute yet another category of languages that are an essential part of African denizen multilingual identity. Although they might appear to be less significant when compared to the widely used cross-border languages and varieties of English, small ethnic languages were highly regarded by the sampled members of the African denizen community, who consider such languages to be the most important symbols of who they are as a people. Most parents, in particular, indicated that they strongly encourage their children to practice speaking heritage languages in order to ensure they can communicate with grandparents and other relatives who do not normally speak English. They projected the maintenance of or desire to continue using heritage languages as something that is directly connected to prospects of 'going back home' in the future. This line of thinking was evident in a submission by WG11, who shared similar sentiments to those of WG10:

> I don't want my child to grow up to a stage where all she knows is I am African because I can tell by my colour. But she should be able to identify by customs, belief systems. Even if she doesn't really even believe it, she knows it by head knowledge – I know where I come from, where my people come from, these things are not done, this is not done, you can't say this here, you can't do this. Some day we hope to take them home,

one day. They wouldn't be total strangers when they get back home because they can easily identify, when people speak they can understand, they know how to relate to the elderly back home. (WG10)

Cultural competence is crucial for successful communication with families and friends who stayed behind in countries of origin. Therefore, for example, WG11 considers it only prudent for African diasporas intending to go back home to continue developing these skills even among their young children. This is a sphere of the possibility of building social cohesion among African denizens and cultural understandings across different generations both within Australia and in countries of origin.

Conclusion

In this chapter, we have suggested a much broader conception of multilingualism based on the language practices of African denizens. We have shown that taking into account prior cultural experiences, migration journeys and linguistic practices can enhance the capabilities of African denizens in Australia. The suggested framework considers language maps or linguistic cartographies of African denizens as consisting of various types or forms of languages that include varieties of Englishes, refugee journey languages, African cross-border languages, small ethnic or minority languages, cultural and discursive practices and so on. The overall mapping of the linguistic repertoires of African denizens also takes into account past and present communication needs with friends and relatives in countries of origin; cultural and linguistic experiences accumulated along refugee journeys; and the exigencies of present and future-oriented relationships and social networks in Australia. The quality of life for African denizens moving into the future is not just about interacting with other people within the confines of Australian national borders. Rather, for the future of these people to be open, space must be open too (Massey, 2005). This means conceptualisations of the linguistic cartographies of multilingual communities and individuals must sufficiently capture and articulate the transnational frames needed to comprehend the cultural identities, language practices and capabilities of denizens resident in predominantly immigrant societies such as Australia. Overall, the data presented and analysed in this chapter presents a strong case for rethinking the phenomenology of multilingualism in terms of functionality; or how individual speakers and communities deploy their language resources to achieve specific goals. Such a project must anchor on looking at all language resources as being in minor relation to one another. This kind of approach would write context specificity into the multilingualism discourse; and thus push back the posture of mainstream discourses that erroneously see multilingualism as a generic, universal and context-free phenomenon.

Notes

(1) This language map of African denizens was adapted from the language nesting model (Ndhlovu, 2014), which was developed from the same dataset reported in this chapter.
(2) ACALAN is an acronym for the African Academy of Languages, an arm of the Social Affairs Commission of the African Union (AU) which is charged with the responsibility of developing and providing expert advice on language policy matters for the AU.
(3) The concept 'languages of the people' is discussed in detail in Chapter 9.

References

ACALAN (2009) Report on ACALAN's synthesis conference on national policies on the role of cross-border languages and the place of less diffused languages in Africa. Addis Ababa, Ethiopia. See https://www.yumpu.com/en/document/read/4517488/report-of-the-synthesis-conference-au-acalan-website (accessed 19 March 2021).
Anderson, J. and Larsen, J.E. (1998) Gender, poverty and empowerment. *Critical Social Science Policy* 18 (2), 241–258.
Australian Bureau of Statistics (2012) *2011 Census of Population and Housing*. Canberra: Australian Bureau of Statistics.
Australian Bureau of Statistics (2017) *Census of Population and Housing*. Canberra: Australian Bureau of Statistics.
Baker, C. (1992) *Attitudes and Languages*. Clevedon: Multilingual Matters.
Barro, M. (2010) Trans-nationalizing the African public sphere: What role for transborder languages? *African Development* 35 (1 & 2), 55–70.
Benton, M. (2014) The problem of denizenship: A non-domination framework. *Critical Review of International Social and Political Philosophy* 17 (1), 46–69.
Bickerton, D. (1976) Pidgin and creole studies. *Annual Review of Anthropology* 5, 169–193.
Bodwin, P. (2001) Marginality and cultural intimacy in a transnational Haitian community. Occasional paper number 91. Department of Anthropology, University of Wisconsin-Milwaukee, Milwaukee, WI.
Brown, M. and Ganguly, S. (eds) (2003) *Fighting Words: Language Policy and Ethnic Relations in Asia*. Cambridge, MA: The MIT Press.
Carreira, J.M. (2005) New framework of intrinsic/extrinsic and integrative/instrumental motivation in second language acquisition. *The Keiai Journal of International Studies* 16, 39–64.
Castles, S. and Davidson, A. (2000) *Citizenship and Migration: Globalization and the Politics of Belonging*. London: Macmillan Press Limited.
Connell, R. (2014) Margin becoming centre: For a world-centred rethinking of masculinities. *NORMA: International Journal of Masculinities Studies* 9 (4), 217–231.
Crystal, D. (2006) English world-wide. In R. Hogg and D. Denison (eds) *A History of the English Language* (pp. 422–445). Cambridge: Cambridge University Press.

Davis, B. (2003) Marginality in a pluralistic society. *Eye on Psi Chi* 2 (1), 1–4.
Davies, A. (1991) *The Native Speaker in Applied Linguistics*. Edinburgh: Edinburgh University Press.
Fang, X. (2020) The semiological implications of knowledge-ideologies: A Harrisian reflection. In S. Makoni (ed.) *Integrationism and Southern Theories*. London/New York: Routledge.
Glick-Schiller, N., Caglar, A. and Gulbrandsen, T.C. (2006) Beyond the ethnic lens: Locality, globality and born-again incorporation. *American Ethnologist* 33 (4), 612–633.
Graddol, D. (2006) *English Next*. London: The British Council.
Gurung, G. and Kollmair, M. (2005) Marginality: Concepts and their limitations. IP6 working paper number 4. Department of Geography, University of Zurich, Switzerland.
Hall, S. (1990) Cultural identity and diaspora. In J. Rutherford (ed) *Community, Culture, Difference* (pp. 222–237). London: Lawrence and Wishart.
Hammar, T. (1990) *Democracy and the Nation State*. Aldershot: Gower Publishing Press.
Harris, R. (1987) Language as social interaction: Integrationalism versus segregationalism. *Language Sciences* 9 (2), 131–143.
Harris, R. (1998) *Introduction to Integrational Linguistics*. Oxford: Pergamon.
Harris, R. (1999) Integrational linguistics and structuralist Legacy. *Language & Communication* 19, 45–68.
Harris, R. (2006) Integrational linguistics and semiology. In K. Brown (ed.) *The Encyclopedia of Language and Linguistics* (2nd edn; Vol. 5; pp. 714–718). Oxford: Elsevier.
Holm, J.A. (2000) *An Introduction to Pidgins and Creoles*. Cambridge: Cambridge University Press.
Jakubowicz, A. (2010) Australia's migration policies: African dimensions. Background paper for *African Australians: A Review of Human Rights and Social Inclusion Issues*. Canberra: Australian Human Rights Commission. See https://andrewjakubowicz.com/publications/australia%E2%80%99s-migration-policies-african-dimensions/ (accessed, 19 March 2021).
Kouwenberg, S. and Singler, J.V. (eds) (2008) *The Handbook of Pidgin and Creole Studies*. Oxford: Wiley-Blackwell.
Léglise, I. (2019) Multilingualism and heterogeneous language practices: New research areas and issues in the Global South. *Language et Société, Maison des Sciences de L'homme*, Hal-02065599.
Makoni, S. (ed) (2020) *Integrationism and Southern Theories*. London and New York: Routledge.
Marlowe, J., Harris, A. and Lyons, T. (eds) (2013) *South Sudanese Diaspora in Australia and New Zealand: Reconciling the Past with the Present*. Cambridge: Cambridge Scholars Publishing.
Massey, D. (2005) *For Space*. London: Sage.
Musgrave, S. and Hajek, J. (2010) Sudanese languages in Melbourne: Linguistic demography and language maintenance. In Y. Treis and R. De Busser (eds) *Selected Papers from the 2009 Conference of the Australian Linguistic Society* (pp. 1–17). Melbourne: Australian Linguistic Society. See http://www.als.asn.au.
Ndhlovu, F. (2009) *The Politics of Language and Nation Building in Zimbabwe*. Oxford and Bern: Peter Lang AG.
Ndhlovu, F. (2011) No to everything British but their language: Re-thinking English language and politics in Zimbabwe (2000–2008). *Language, Society and Culture* 33, 108–119.

Ndhlovu, F. (2013) Cross-border languages in southern African economic and political integration. *African Studies* 72 (1), 19–40.
Ndhlovu, F. (2014) *Becoming an African Diaspora in Australia: Language, Culture, Identity*. London: Palgrave Macmillan.
Ndhlovu, F. (2018) *Language, Vernacular Discourse and Nationalisms: Uncovering the Myths of Transnational Worlds*. Houndmills: Palgrave Macmillan.
Norris-Holt, J. (2001) Motivation as a contributing factor in second language acquisition. *The Internet TESL Journal* VII, 6. See http://teslj.org/ (accessed 2 October 2014).
Pable, A. (2020) Three critical perspectives on the ontology of 'language'. In S. Makoni (ed.) *Integrationism and Southern Theories*. London/New York: Routledge.
Prah, K.K. (2009) The burden of English in Africa: From colonialism to neo-colonialism. Keynote address delivered at the International Conference: Mapping Africa in the English-Speaking World, University of Botswana, 2–4 June.
Seshadri-Crooks, K. (1995) At the margins of postcolonial studies. *Ariel: Review of International English Literature* 26 (3), 47–71.
Salazar, N.B., Elliot, A. and Roger, N. (2017) Studying mobilities: Theoretical notes and methodological queries. In N.B. Salazar, A. Elliot and N. Roger (eds) *Methodologies of Mobility: Ethnography of Experiment* (pp. 1–24). New York and Oxford: Berghahn.
Siegel, J. (2008) *The Emergence of Pidgin and Creole Languages*. New York: Oxford University Press.
Strathern, M. (2004) *Partial Connections*. Lanham: Rowman & Littlefield Publishers.
Viljoen, H. (1998) Marginalia on marginality. *Alternation* 5 (2), 10–22.

8 Multilingualism from Below: Languaging with a Seven Year Old

Introduction

Much of what informs current methodological approaches to multilingualism research derives from the logics of the (post)positivist tradition that have assumed the hegemonic posture of universal relevance. Dominant research paradigms that follow positivist 'scientific' principles ignore the diversity of ways of reading and interpreting social experience – that there are multiple and equally valid and legitimate ways of doing the research. In this chapter, we review the autoethnographic method and the promises it holds for alternative trajectories in multilingualism research. The chapter tells and analyses a story that is based on Finex's casual and unplanned encounter with Omphile, a seven-year-old boy, in Johannesburg, South Africa. Omphile and Finex interacted using communicative practices that confirmed the anti-conventional theories of multilingualism posited in this book.

The story also challenged the methods that support empirical observations of mainstream multilingualism research. It pushes the conversation in the direction of how language works in everyday real life. A major line of argument we advance is one about the promises that autoethnographic approaches hold for researching multilingualism in ways that sidestep the language and methods of the positivist 'scientific' tradition. We suggest that in the same way that contemporary sociolinguistics theorisations remind us about how communication is not limited to determinate languages or codes, research does not have to be limited to controlled, systematic scientific methods. The framework of autoethnography we review is one example of a praxis that is anti-methodological and thus in line with many of the anti-foundational premises of the entire book.

Framing the Problem

Scholars of sociolinguistics and allied disciplines have made quite commendable theoretical and conceptual progress when it comes to challenging linguistic normativity and those frameworks that have crystallised into some kind of traditional orthodoxy in language research. Such progress is attested by the burgeoning of theorisations around language as process, dating back to the 1970s and 1980s' work of Einar Haugen, Lachman Khubchandani, John J. Gumperz and Howard Giles. By the 1990s, the cacophony of voices following this line of critique had grown, with Khubchandani (1997: 14) proposing what he called 'plurality of consciousness' and 'communication ethos', which are about consideration of how individual language users have 'day-to-day, moment-to-moment successes that make language transactive, functional and alive'. This was a call to shift the locus of enunciation and see language as an ongoing process of social transaction and not something that is located in an institution.

Such critique of conventional understandings of language has continued to gather momentum in recent times with the emergence of quite contemporary theories such as 'transidiomatic practice' (Jacquemet, 2005), 'polylanguaging' (Jørgensen, 2008, 2010) and 'codemeshing' (Canagarajah, 2011). 'Translanguaging' (García, 2009; García & Li Wei, 2014; García & Kleyn, 2016) and 'metrolingualism' (Pennycook & Otsuji, 2015) are the latest additions to the long list of contemporary sociolinguistic theorisations. These theories echo Blommaert et al.'s (2012: 18) advice on the need to start with our 'feet on the ground from a strong awareness that the phenomenology of language in society has changed, has become more complex and less predictable than we thought was'. A crucial foundational premise shared by these theoretical frameworks is their call for unbounding language from its position as an object of study and situating it in the sociocultural complexity that surrounds speakers' 'real language use' (Ndhlovu, 2015).

What also unites the majority of followers of this scholarly tradition – in a rather negative way – is their reliance on conventional research methodologies that are limited to controlled scientific experiments: oral interviews, surveys, focus groups, participant observations and so on. This chapter argues that notwithstanding commendable theoretical and conceptual innovations that have been made, there is a gap that is yet to be filled in contemporary sociolinguistics research. This is about doing research using methodologies that are consistent with the anti-foundational stance of emerging theories such as translanguaging.

Current conventional scientific methods and the language they use remain rarely challenged or – at the very least – sufficiently problematised. This invites several questions centring on the ways sociolinguists continue to be wedded to conventional methodologies in language research.

If we recognise that the phenomenology of language is very complex and that the ways human beings communicate eschew any easy generalisations:

- Why do we still do research using the same conventional methods that are used to investigate languages as ordered and enumerable objects?
- How realistic is it for new philosophies of language to claim they are pushing scholarship forward in a new direction when their theoretical suppositions are supported by data generated through conventional research methods? How do we do ethnographic social science research in ways that allow us to capture the complex relations between society and communication resources?
- In other words, can we really claim to be theorising in unconventional ways when our methodologies remain conventional?

We address these questions by narrating and analysing a story about Finex's casual and unplanned encounter with Omphile, a seven-year-old boy whose communicative practices prompted us to think more critically about widely used methods in social science research.

The arguments we advance are in line with the frameworks of autoethnography, a type of 'narrative research that entails a double narrative process, one that includes the narratives generated by those participating in the research, and one that represents the voice of the researcher as narrator of those narratives' (Kyratzis & Green, 1997, cited in Méndez, 2013: 280). Additionally, the central themes of the analysis align with debates around reflexivity in ethnomethodology (Colombo, 2003; Czyzewski, 1994; Watson, 2005) and approaches of conversational analysis (CA) that elucidate basic aspects of human sociality that reside in talk (Atkinson & Heritage, 1984; Heritage, 1995; Mazeland, 2006). We discuss autoethnography in greater detail in a later section with an eye on prospects and possibilities for enriching translanguaging research methodologies. In the same section, we also make some passing remarks on the relevant theoretical and methodological insights of reflexivity and CA to support the argument that the things we know so foundationally about multilingualism are not as straightforward as they are thought to be. But first, let us go to the story of Finex's encounter with Omphile, which we tell in first-person narrative with Finex as the narrator.

Encounter with Translingual Omphile

In August 2016, I attended the Third International Conference on Language and Literacy Education that was organised and hosted by Leketi (second author) at the Wits School of Education, Witwatersrand University, South Africa. In the afternoon of Day 2, there were three parallel sessions themed 'Translanguaging Lesson Demonstrations'. Although I had a very keen interest in seeing what a translanguaging lesson would look like, I was underwhelmed by the translanguaging lesson demonstrations that were no different in form and content from the traditional bilingual or dual medium of instruction approaches. The translanguaging lesson demonstrations reinforced a view of languages as fixed and bounded objects that are separate from each other, supposedly because the presenters' misunderstood translanguaging pedagogy. Owing to my frustration over the 'translanguaging lesson' demonstrators' limited understanding of what the theory and praxis of translanguaging is all about, I decided to slip out of the conference venue and took a short walk around the Parktown Campus of Wits University. I then sat on a chair in one of the campus courtyards, reading the conference programme and reflecting on how some scholars were missing the crucial message of translanguaging theory. Little did I know that this was, in fact, going to be an opportunity for me to witness conversational practices that would prompt us to analyse contradictions between contemporary sociolinguistics theories (including theories of multilingualism) and the methods used to collect data that support such theoretical positions.

While sitting on the chair, I saw this little boy coming from the other end of the campus kicking a soccer ball and seemingly unbothered by the few cars that drove past. As he got closer to me, he slowed his pace of walking and kicking the ball. He then stopped and greeted me using the honorific Setswana/Sepedi greeting *'Dumelang'* (literally: plural form for 'hello') to which I replied using the singular form *'Dumela, ukae?'* (literally: singular form for 'hello, how are you?').

The rest of our conversation, in multiple languages that we both moved in and out of or mixed, subconsciously, went as follows (M = me; O = Omphile):

M: (speaking in isiZulu) *'Ungubani igama lakho?'* (What is your name?)
O: (with a little smile): *'Omphile'*.
M: (speaking in isiZulu) *'Kutheni udlala wedwa?'* (Why are you playing alone?)

O: (speaking in isiZulu) *'Anginaye ubhuti noma usisi. Ngihlala nogogo'* (I do not have any brother or sister that I can play with. I live with my grandmother).
O: (this time around mixing isiZulu and Setswana expressions) *'Wena awunaye umosimane?'* (Don't you have a son?)
M: (mixing isiZulu and English expressions): *'Nginaye but umkhulu kakhulu, unaseventeen'* (I do have a son but he is big, he is seventeen).
O: (looking at me with a sullen face and gasping a sigh of great disappointment) *'Ah! ngibe ngisithi ungangami, ngifuna adlale nami'* (Oh, no! I thought he was of my age, I would have wanted him to play with me).[1]

Based on this last statement, I came to realise that my new-found friend, Omphile, really wanted someone with whom to play. So, I offered to kick the soccer ball with him, which he jumped at with a lot of excitement and declared from the start (again using a mixture of expressions from isiZulu, Setswana, Sepedi and English) that he was going to beat me. So, we quickly identified some temporary goal posts and started kicking the ball. After about five minutes of play, he had scored three goals while I had zero. Each time he scored he would jump up and down in excitement, declaring in mixed expressions from isiZulu, Sepedi, Setswana and English that he was a very good soccer player and that I was never going to beat him. It was, indeed, a lot of fun until after I temporarily caught up with him by scoring three goals, thus making it a draw.

We continued playing, with Omphile really determined to prove that he was unbeatable. He eventually scored two more goals, which was a very big win for him. I kept on trying hard but I could not catch up with him. So, in the end I gave up; he still wanted to keep on playing but I had to go back to the conference venue. In order to bring the game to an end, I admitted that he was the winner and gave him a few coins as a way of conceding defeat. The soccer game eventually came to an end after 20–25 minutes of play.

So, what is the point of this story? It is not so much about me meeting a seven-year-old boy and playing soccer with him. Three things are significant here: (i) the dynamic of our interaction, the ways in which we negotiated and deployed our respective linguistic systems; (ii) the methodological implications of my empirical observations that were not based on pre-planned approaches of the scientific method; and (iii) the implications of the observed linguistic usages for fruitful pathways of enriching current theories of multilingualism. It is evident that the interaction I had with Omphile and the attendant language practices confirmed both the theoretical suppositions and empirical observations of previous sociolinguistics scholarship described in the first section of this chapter. The soccer game itself was, in many ways, a form of language; an integral part of the discourse and praxis of communication in naturally occurring environments.

As the literature on CA has posited, single acts are parts of larger, structurally organised entities, also known as sequences (Schegloff, 2006). The most basic and quite important sequences consist of actions performed by one interactant, which invite particular types of further actions performed by another interactant, and so on. The actions can be vocal (as in question–answer, greeting–greeting, invitation–acceptance/declination) or performative (as in gestures or partaking in an activity of mutual interest) (Schegloff, 2006). My interaction with Omphile consisted of all of these. Furthermore, consistent with the suppositions of reflexivity, the soccer game in particular was a constituent part of the communicative practice we describe here and, therefore, elaborates the circumstances of our interaction and conversation while simultaneously being elaborated by them (Watson, 2005: 7).

An equally important point that is at the core of this story is one about how my empirical observations were made outside the orbit of mainstream social science methodologies – thus tying in with the tenets of the anti-conventional agenda. I did not go out with a pre-planned research idea built around a scientific experimental design that sought to address some preconceived research questions. Neither Omphile nor I, at any point, attempted to raise the question about which named language(s) each one of us could speak well as a way of establishing common ground (Enfield, 2008; Goffman, 1981) in our interaction. We did not even bother to find out whether there was any named language that we had in common. From the very start of our conversation, we tapped into our respective linguistic systems that emerged naturally and spontaneously during the course of our interaction. Although my knowledge of Setswana and Sepedi is quite limited, I did not alert Omphile to this when he passed a greeting in these languages. Neither did I ask him about his level of knowledge of both isiZulu and English, the other two languages that contributed to the linguistic systems that we used throughout the course of our interaction.

Another notable point is one about the blurring or porosity of language boundaries that was evident in my conversation with Omphile. We both crossed effortlessly – and even disregarded – the supposed language boundaries as we used linguistic resources available to us in rather seamless and fluid ways. This laid to rest notions of linguistic purism whereby languages are perceived as distinctly bounded entities that are to be used in particular ways. Though named languages are real and exist in societies that have coined names for them, 'they do not necessarily overlap with the linguistic systems of individual speakers' (García & Kleyn, 2016: 10). This is precisely what we see in my conversation with Omphile. The linguistic usages and interactional processes between Omphile and me are a clear example of what living with many language resources looks like in real life. But in what ways does the story of my encounter with Omphile both confirm and challenge theoretical suppositions of contemporary sociolinguistic theorisations? And what does this story tell us about how to do research on language and communication in ways that enable us to observe and report on casual naturally occurring conversational data that escapes the attention of conventional scientific methods? We address these and related questions in the rest of this chapter.

An Appraisal of Translanguaging and Allied Theories

Translanguaging is one of the most recent theories of language and communication that seek to contribute a more nuanced conceptualisation of how real people communicate in everyday real life. A common definition of translanguaging is one provided by García and Kleyn (2016):

> [T]ranslanguaging refers to the deployment of speakers' full linguistic repertoire, which does not in any way correspond to the socially and politically defined boundaries of named languages. (García & Kleyn, 2016: 14)

García and Kleyn further suggest a bifurcated view of translanguaging – the *weak version* and the *strong version*. The weak version of translanguaging is one that supports named language boundaries, and yet calls for the softening of these boundaries. This view, which follows hard on the heels of traditional sociolinguistic notions of 'code-switching' and 'code-mixing', is associated with the work of Suresh Canagarajah (2011) on 'codemeshing' and Jim Cummins' (1979, 2007) 'interdependence hypothesis' and 'transfer theories'. On the other hand, the strong version of translanguaging, which I also subscribe to, posits that bilingual people do not speak languages, but rather use their repertoire of linguistic features selectively. Seen from a translanguaging perspective, 'language' is not something that a speaker simply 'has', but a repeated and expansive system of communicative practices in which he or she continuously engages (Canagarajah, 2011; García, 2009; García & Li Wei,

2014; Li Wei & Zhu, 2013). Translanguaging thus becomes a summary term that should be taken in the sense of 'transcending' or going beyond the two or more named languages of bi-/multilinguals (García & Kleyn, 2016: 10). In this regard, it converges with other quite contemporary scholarly conversations that promote and value language as local practice (Pennycook, 2010); languages as creative linguistic practices (Otsuji & Pennycook, 2010); languages as plurilingual multimodal communication resources (Piccardo, 2013); and languages as communicative resources (Blommaert, 2010). The main argument of these studies is that boundaries between languages are somewhat temporal, porous and irrelevant if we consider the dynamic, unpredictable and spontaneous ways by which people use language as a social practice (Ndhlovu, 2015). This body of work begins the movement away from didactic thinking about language and how human beings communicate. However, the key point here is that although translanguaging and similar theories challenge linguistic normativity and push the debate on language theorisation towards an anti-foundational direction, they still rely on the traditional scientific method of data collection. Attempts to transcend conventional scientific methods in most translanguaging reports have remained somewhat tentative and parsimonious as most such studies continue to rely on focus groups, oral interviews and ethnographies (in the traditional sense of 'researcher as impartial observer').

As the relevant body of literature dating back to the early 1970s has clearly demonstrated, the idea of language as object is a modernist and colonial invention that does not capture the complex communicative practices of the majority of people around the world (see e.g. Giles, 1984; Gumperz, 1982; Haugen, 1972; Khubchandani, 1997). Here is how Haugen (1972: 325) expressed his frustration with mainstream sociolinguistics theorisations: 'The concept of language as a rigid, monolithic structure is false, even if it has proved to be a useful fiction in the development of linguistics. It is the kind of simplification that is necessary at a certain stage of a science, but which can now be replaced by more sophisticated models'. This line of argument has been pursued further in more recent times by scholars such as Jan Blommaert (2010), Sinfree Makoni and Alastair Pennycook (2007), Lesley Milroy (2001) and many others.

These scholars argue that the emergence of modern linguistics as a social science at the dawn of the 20th century was prompted by fundamental questions around the relationship of language, thought and cognition, and how human beings interact with one another and with their immediate environment. Some well-known pioneering thinkers such as Ferdinand de Saussure, Leonard Bloomfield, Noam Chomsky and those who followed their tradition of linguistics tried to address these issues in their work. However, they did so from a segregationist/colonial perspective, which has come to be known as orthodox/mainstream linguistics. Segregationists treat 'language and languages as objects existing in their own right, independently of other varieties of communication' (Harris, 1987: 131). Such insistence on the study of language structure rather than the study of linguistic communities or communities of practice is consistent with the approaches of colonial linguistics that sought to homogenise what were otherwise disparate communities to facilitate colonial domination and control (Brutt-Griffler, 2006; Errington, 2008; Makoni, 1998; Ndhlovu, 2010).

Therefore, the rise of the translanguaging school of thought is a welcome development not because it is a novelty but rather because it has to be seen as symptomatic of homecoming by academics and education practitioners. It signals a reawakening and a reconnection with the foundational questions of language in society – those basic questions around how human beings communicate. The renewed interest in understanding the complex communicative practices of plurilingual and translingual individuals is essentially about bringing back to mainstream academic conversations an important issue that had been overlooked and marginalised following the rise of modernist theories of language that have erroneously come to be seen as if they were of a 'natural kind'. So, essentially, translanguaging is about going back to basics.

The majority of scholars who have exercised their minds on the theory and praxis of translanguaging have done so in the context of educational linguistics – in language education classroom contexts, second language acquisition, bilingual education, teaching English as a second language (TESOL) education and so on (see e.g. Canagarajah, 2011, 2013; Creese & Blackledge, 2010; Cummins, 1979, 2007; García, 2009; García & Li Wei, 2014; Hornberger & Link, 2012). The flourishing of translanguaging theorisation in educational settings is perfectly understandable given that the roots of this theory actually lie in Cen Williams' (1994) doctoral thesis that explored opportunities presented by the presence of bilingual children in Welsh school classrooms (García & Kleyn, 2016). Some other scholars have, however, theorised and tested the applied interests of translanguaging in out-of-classroom contexts. For example, Li Wei (2011) and Li Wei and Zhu (2013) use the insights of translanguaging theory to investigate the transnational identities and ideologies of Chinese university students in the UK. Li Wei and Zhu (2013: 516) use narrative data and ethnographic observations of British-born Chinese students (whose parents came from China, Taiwan, Hong Kong and Singapore) to 'explore issues such as their socio-cultural identification processes, the interactions between their linguistic and political ideologies, their multilingual practices and what they have learned from being part of this new [transnational] social space'. Li Wei and Zhu (2013) conclude by highlighting the promises of translanguaging theory in the context of identity studies. They point out that the 'translanguaging approach has the capacity to demonstrate how multilayered social, linguistic and community practices and reflections yield multipleness in identity construction'. The story of my encounter with Omphile described above adds another dimension to the theory and praxis of translanguaging, that of communicative translanguaging. What we see from the moments of interaction between Omphile and myself are instantiations of linguistic boundary crossing that take place in spontaneous and unplanned social encounters in the community. The communicative strand of translanguaging (as opposed to those found in educational and transnational identity formation arenas) is located within and mediated by a different set of conversational circumstances that call for humility, empathy, accommodation and the need for interactants to concede space for each other's linguistic systems.

However, notwithstanding these different contextual applications, all translanguaging theorists are united on one thing, which is this: in translanguaging, named languages do exist only insofar as they have social reality and not linguistic reality. There is very little, if anything at all, that is linguistic about named languages (García & Kleyn, 2016). From a translanguaging perspective, the linguistic is located within the communicative systems of individual speakers who have the capacity to appropriately leverage their repertoires in ways that enable them to perform according to social norms while simultaneously not being constrained by such norms. Thus, in spite of their differing contexts of applied interests, translanguaging theorists are united on the fact that linguistic resources or knowledge of multiple languages are part of a single language system that an individual uses to create meaning and accomplish goals (Daniel & Pacheco, 2015).

So far so good – but a glaring problem still remains: to what extent has this body of quite contemporary scholarship pushed the boundaries of sociolinguistics research towards a new methodological direction that encourages the use of yet to be proven and anti-foundational methods?

Colonialism and Contending Methodological Issues

The tenuous foundation of logical positivism continues to exert an enormous influence on the social sciences (Baronov, 2004), including sociolinguistics. It seems that much of the burgeoning scholarship of this tradition is yet to break free from the conventional scientific method. There is a tendency to do very little or no analysis of the underlying assumptions and beliefs that form the ideological presuppositions of the widely used systematic research tools of the positivist tradition such as questionnaires, surveys, oral interviews, focus groups and participant observations. These are often treated as if they were ideologically neutral and objective, yet, as we know, they emerged out of specific contextual and cultural conditions in the Global North. The content and *modus operandi* of conventional methods are predominantly shaped by colonial understandings of what constitutes valid and legitimate knowledge (Ndhlovu, 2017). The universalising tendencies of the conventional scientific method are regularly imposed on all societies (including those in the Global South) without due regard for contextual particularities. A major problem with adopting these conventional scientific methods holus bolus is that they also shape the nature of our research questions, what we look for or overlook in our data sets and, ultimately, our answers to such questions.

Four geopolitical assumptions that underpin the architecture of conventional methods have been suggested in the relevant social science literature (Connell, 2007; Nustad, 2004; Peet, 1997). First is the claim to universality whereby the very idea of mainstream research methods involves talking about universals and generalisations as if the whole world was a homogeneous continuum. The fatalistic assumption of this claim is that 'all societies are knowable in the same way and from the same point of view' (Connell, 2007: 44). The second assumption is that of reading from the centre – the construction of a social world read through the eyes of the metropole and not through an analysis of the metropole's action on the rest of the world. What conventional scientific approaches overlook is the fact that the experiences of cultures and societies from other parts of the world cannot be fully understood through the use of methods that arose out of a colonial metropolitan reading of the world (Ndhlovu, 2017). The third problem with conventional scientific methods is how they are underpinned by what Connell (2007) calls 'gestures of exclusion'. This is about the total absence or marginalisation of methodologies and theoretical frameworks from the non-Western and formerly colonised world in metropolitan texts on research. In those exceptional instances where material culture and ideas from these other parts of the world are acknowledged, they are rarely considered as part of the mainstream dialogue on research theory and method. Riding on the back of colonial ethnography and social anthropological frameworks emphasising the modern/premodern distinction, the method of 'science' renders the cultures and thought processes from the Global South irrelevant and treats them as belonging to a world that has been surpassed (Connell, 2007; Ndhlovu, 2017). This leads us to the fourth contour, which has been termed 'grand erasure'. The point here is that when empirical knowledge and theorisation about humanity more generally are seen as coming solely from metropolitan society (where the roots of conventional research methods lie), the immediate effect 'is erasure of the experience[s] of the majority of human kind from the foundations of social thought' (Connell, 2007: 46).

All of the above question the claims of objectivity and neutrality that are often said to be the hallmarks of most of these scientific methods. For this reason, some humanities and social science scholars from across a range of disciplines have consistently called for breaking free from the conventional scientific method. They include scholars who work under the banners of Southern Theory (Comaroff & Comaroff, 2011; Connell, 2007); decolonial epistemology (Maldonado-Torres, 2007; Mignolo, 2002, 2011; and many others); and decolonising indigenous methodologies (Chilisa, 2011; Smith, 2012). Linda Smith (2012: i–xiv) in particular raises four pertinent points that undergird my line of argument:

- That we need to develop 'counter-practices of research' relevant to the agenda of disrupting the current hegemonic rules of the research game.
- That we need to articulate research practices that arise out of the specificities of the epistemology and methodology rooted in people's cultural experiences.
- That stories of research, examples of projects, critical examination and mindful reflection must be woven together to make meaningful and practical designs.
- That we need new ways of knowing and discovering, and new ways to think about research in order to demonstrate the possibilities of re-imagining research as an activity that can be pursued outside the narrow box of the scientific experimental design.

This is about integrating praxis, theory, action and reflection in ways that provoke revolutionary thinking about the roles of knowledge and knowledge production in social transformation. These methodological issues are not explicitly addressed in the frameworks of most contemporary sociolinguistic theories. I see this as a missed opportunity to integrate new and alternative methods more fully into language research. Therefore, I argue that in spite of their anti-conventional and anti-foundational stance, most researchers who have embraced contemporary theories of language (such as translanguaging), still submit to the use of the 'scientific method of enquiry'.

As I have already said in the introduction to this chapter, earlier and present generations of sociolinguists have made major advances in terms of generating new theoretical frameworks that challenge normativity and purism in language research. However, I do not think that it is good enough for us to simply come up with new conceptual frameworks that are not complemented by equally innovative methodological paradigms. I am guilty of this omission myself insofar as I have proffered new sociolinguistics theories such as 'the language nesting model' (Ndhlovu, 2013) and 'ignored lingualism' (Ndhlovu, 2015) that are not supported by fresh and anti-foundational methodologies. If we are indeed serious about pursuing this type of intellectual endeavour, we need to formulate counter-methods of scientific enquiry that are consistent with the anti-foundational premises of contemporary social science theories. In addition to the much broader humanities and social science scholarship cited above, some leading international applied linguists and sociolinguists such as Li Wei (2011), Li Wei and Zhu (2013) and Pennycook and Emi Otsuji (2010, 2015) have articulated with greater clarity the call for methodological innovations in language research. Taking after Heller's (2011) notion of critical ethnographic sociolinguistics, Pennycook and Otsuji (2015: 20) posit that we need to study contextually (ethnographically) the social use of language (sociolinguistics) with an eye to understanding the relations of social differentiation and inequality. In discussing the methods that underpin their theory of 'metrolingualism', Pennycook and Otsuji suggest the following about what we need to do in language research:

> Ethnographic research [should] not only be about the gathering of data in specific contexts, the note-taking, the recording, the questioning, the observing, nor is it only about the writing, the attempts to capture what is going on, to describe the bustle of the market, the hectic work in the restaurant or kitchen, the interactions over lunch in a construction site. It is also about the conversations, the developing understandings as we sit and talk about the market gardens, watch conical hats in the fields and the plane flying overhead and try to make sense of all this. (Pennycook & Otsuji, 2015: 44)

Drawing on their ethnographic work in metropolitan areas in Australia and Japan, Pennycook and Otsuji (2015: 88) describe how the methodologies they used have sought to capture the 'throwtogetherness of linguistic resources – across space and through different interactions and observing how resources come and go in one place – in order to relate physical activities of work, the social and historical trajectories of participants, the organisation of space and the language resources at play in particular places'. Along the same vein, Li Wei (2011: 1224) pioneered the innovative method of moment analysis that is based on the idea that reflections of the critical moments often result in fundamental learning that enables individuals and groups to uncover or create knowledge from their own experiences for improving their future actions. Li Wei applied the method of *moment analysis* to a study that used a combination of observation of multilingual practices and metalanguage commentaries by three Chinese youths in Britain. He says 'metalanguaging data can be collected through conversations, individual or group interviews, journals and autobiographies' (Li Wei, 2011: 1225). Although *moment analysis* seems to retain some footprints of the conventional scientific method, it takes a rather different turn by focusing on 'moments' of interaction. Thus, the data collection processes and procedures of *moment analysis* do not necessarily follow the sequential, systematic, directed and controlled approaches of the conventional scientific tradition.

This is precisely the methodological direction that the story of my encounter with Omphile is taking us. The next section builds on and extends the methodological innovations of this previous body of work by reviewing the framework of autoethnography as a possible explanatory paradigm for my empirical observations in the story I narrated above. Though it has been widely applied in other social science disciplines, autoethnography is rarely used as a method in language research. Next, I describe the insights of this approach and spotlight the promises it holds for a more innovative methodology of doing language research in ways that are in line with the anti-foundational stance of contemporary sociolinguistics theories.

The Case for Autoethnography in Multilingualism Research

The origins of autoethnography are traced to the 1980s, what Holt (2003: 18) calls the 'crisis of representation' period because this was a time when researchers were concerned about formalising qualitative research to be as 'rigorous' as quantitative research. It was also that point in history when qualitative researchers found themselves using diverse research strategies that were borrowed from the quantitative paradigm (Méndez, 2013). Autoethnography, therefore, emerged in response to this challenge and to increasing 'calls to place greater emphasis on the ways in which the ethnographer interacts with the culture being researched' (Holt, 2003: 18). Steven Pace (2012: 4) says that the earliest uses of the term 'autoethnography' are found in a 1979 essay by cultural anthropologist Hayano who made a case for self-observation in traditional ethnographic research.

In recent times, the term 'autoethnography' has come to be associated with the work of Carolyn Ellis (2004, 2007, 2009) and Arthur Bochner (1997, 2000, 2001, 2002). By way of definition, Ellis and Bochner (2000: 739) say autoethnography is 'an autobiographical genre of writing and research that displays multiple layers of consciousness, connecting the personal to the cultural'. In a later publication, Ellis *et al.* (2011) elaborate further on this definition, noting that autoethnography expands and opens up a wider lens on the world in a manner that eschews rigid definitions of what constitutes meaningful and useful research. They posit that the autoethnographic approach 'helps us understand how the kinds of people we claim, or are perceived to be, influence interpretations of what we study, how we study it and what we say about our topic' (Ellis *et al.*, 2011: 2). In their *Handbook of Autoethnography*, Jones *et al.* (2013) provide an extended explanation of what autoethnography as method entails.[2]

Autoethnography as method is about using unconventional ways of doing and presenting research. Some such non-conventional ways include the use of conversational styles of presentation that make the narration engaging and emotionally rich. As Ellis *et al.* (2011: 3) further advises '"Telling" is a writing style that works with "showing" in that it provides readers some distance from the events described so that they might think about the events in a more abstract way. Adding some "telling" to a story that "shows" is an efficient way to convey information needed to appreciate what is going on, and a way to communicate information that does not necessitate the immediacy of dialogue and sensuous engagement'. What this essentially means is that autoethnography provides room for the researcher/writer to use first-person to tell a story. This is especially powerful when the writer tells in an intimate way a story he or she observed or an interaction he or she participated in. It is precisely for this reason that I see the story of my encounter with Omphile as a good example of autoethnographic praxis in language research. Some of the subtleties of my interaction with Omphile that I have presented in this chapter might have been missed were it not for the first-person narrative style that enabled me to 'tell' and 'show' my eyewitness account in my own words. The first-person narrative technique provided me with the opportunity to tell the story as I experienced it without waiting for others to express what I, as a researcher-participant really wanted to be known and understood (Richards, 2008). To summarise, it is worth quoting Anderson (2006: 388) who says 'the definitive feature of autoethnography is this value-added quality of not only truthfully rendering the social world under investigation but also transcending that world through broader generalisation'.

The main contours of autoethnography that set it apart from the procedures of mainstream experimental research designs are six-fold.

- The author of an autoethnographic research report usually writes in the first-person style, thus making himself or herself an integral part of the object of research.
- Writing autoethnographically allows for the researcher's life to be studied along the lives of other participants in a reflexive connection. The researcher engages in analytic reflexivity, demonstrating an awareness of the reciprocal influence between himself or herself, the setting and other participants (Chang, 2008). It is here that autoethnography aligns with the views of scholars who follow the tradition of reflexivity, which expresses 'the inextricability of ordinary descriptions (such as typifications of persons, actions or situations) from the circumstances they describe, [whereby] the description and the circumstances are reciprocally-elaborative' (Watson, 2005: 7).
- The accessibility of an autoethnographic writing style helps position the reader as an involved participant in the dialogue, rather than as a passive receiver (Pace, 2012).
- Autoethnography enables the researcher to demonstrate commitment to theoretical analysis while simultaneously capturing (in an accessible style of writing) what is going on in individual lives or sociocultural environments (Ellis, 2004).
- The richness of autoethnography is found in those realities that emerge from the interaction between the self and its own experiences that reflect the cultural and social context in which those events took place (Méndez, 2013: 284). On this point, the auto-ethnographic approach compares quite favourably with CA, which 'studies the organization of talk as situated, socially organized sets of practices ... as interactional structures that both shape the context in which they operate and enable its interactionally coordinated progression' (Mazeland, 2006: 156). As in autoethnography, the main focus in CA is on systematic practices such as overlap positioning and overlap

resolution, collaborative turn construction and the role of gaze, gesture and body positioning (Lerner, 1996; Mazeland, 2006; Schegloff, 2000).
• The subjective interpretations that may arise from personal narratives oppose the positivist view of research which aims at presenting an 'objective' account of the truth. The personal and emotional involvement of the researcher in autoethnography thus counter-balances the rather distant and perceived 'objective' role of the researcher in a positivist stance (Méndez, 2013: 284).

Therefore, the distinct benefit of the autoethnographic method is that in addition to reporting about other participants, it also makes the researcher/narrator part of the research story. It engenders collaboration between the researcher-as-participant and other participants, thus levelling the power imbalances that characterise most conventional social science methods. In the context of my story with Omphile, autoethnography clearly doubles as a method for generating empirical observations about our interaction, and as a framework for presenting the story and making sense out of it. The autoethnographic approach enabled me to construct a narrative that sidesteps the language of conventional ways of doing and thinking about research.

Like all other methods or conceptual frameworks, autoethnography has had its fair share of criticisms. Three such criticisms follow. First, autoethnography has been dismissed on perceptions of being insufficiently rigorous, theoretical, too aesthetic and emotional (Delamont, 2009). Second, those scholars following the autoethnographic approach have been accused of doing too little fieldwork, observing too few cultural members and not spending enough time with different others (Anderson, 2006). The third criticism levelled against autoethnography is about how the researcher uses personal experience, hence supposedly biased data that does not fulfil scholarly obligations of hypothesising, analysing and theorising (Ellis, 2009; Madison, 2006). While these criticisms are welcome, we see them as biased because they evaluate the utility of autoethnography using the standards of the scientific experimental method. Autoethnography does not subscribe to the procedures and processes of conventional approaches. It is a totally different methodology that seeks to inaugurate 'an-other logic', 'an-other language' and 'an-other way' of doing research that has the potential to make fruitful contributions to social science research, which is currently in the clutches of hegemonic conventionalism.

We argue that it is, in fact, these perceived limitations of autoethnography that hold the promise for doing research in ways that are in line with quite contemporary anti-foundational social science frameworks such as translanguaging, metrolingualism and many others. The conceptual and methodological premises of autoethnography open a window for social scientists to ask big questions of small data (Salazar *et al.*, 2017), which clearly sets them apart from the conventional scientific method that is largely preoccupied with big data. Therefore, although research methodologies that are driven by big data are useful in certain contexts, they also tend to hide more than they reveal – in some contexts – hence the need for approaches such as autoethnography that help us see the big picture out of small data. This way, we get to see and learn more about the minute but quite significant human interest stories that often remain hidden in the masses of big data.

Conclusion

In this chapter, we sought to extend the application of the insights of autoethnography by deploying them to explain the nature of human communication and linguistic usages in unplanned naturally occurring encounters. We have done this by locating the discussion within contemporary scholarly debates in sociolinguistics and related frameworks of reflexivity and CA. There are at least four important points that can be gleaned from the story described and analysed in the chapter. First, the moments of interaction and conversation that Omphile and Finex had from the very first point of contact through the mini-soccer game disprove – in very clear and unequivocal terms – popular assumptions about the need to first establish the existence of a common code with our interlocutors prior to initiating a conversation. In naturally occurring human communication, the boundaries of named languages can be crossed without much recourse to deliberate bridging processes such as translation and interpretation. And, in the process of crossing language boundaries, we also simultaneously cross social boundaries and social distances. This creates opportunities for us to enter and experience each other's life-worlds, thus paving the way for the establishment of common ground, ultimately leading to effective communication and mutual understanding.

Second, the willingness to participate in a common practice paves the way for effective communication even in those instances where we encounter less familiar languages. The conversation between Omphile and Finex applied a transactive approach to language use whereby the deployment of their respective linguistic systems was an ongoing process of social transaction. This enabled them to recognise the 'synergic network of plurilingual language use as a means to inspire trust in cross-cultural settings' (Khubchandani, 1997: 37) as they played the mini-soccer game as if they were old friends. Therefore, what this story tells us is that speakers need ways of negotiating difference and converging on practices of mutual interest rather than negotiating codes. Such strategies of managing and accommodating linguistic difference without necessarily resorting to standard language ideological approaches teach us that communication always works (not in spite of) but because of the rampant diversity of language practices (Ndhlovu, 2015: 410).

The third take-home message is one about the centrality of humility, empathy and willingness to come down to the level of our interlocutors in establishing the common ground needed for effective communication to occur in multilingual contexts. Although Omphile and Finex had never met before, they were able to establish a very good rapport and sustain their conversation not on the basis of a common linguistic code. Rather, their successful and productive interaction was sustained by our mutual willingness to accommodate each other's linguistic systems and social interests. They were both ready and willing to participate in a common social practice – the mini-soccer match – which eventually saw them exist as a small community of practice with shared interests. Throughout the interaction, their linguistic practices tended to fluctuate depending on individual and collective evaluations of how the communication process was going (Ndhlovu, 2018). Finex, in particular, expanded and contracted his linguistic system at various stages during the interaction as a way to accommodate the developing linguistic system of a seven year old. The overall outcome was that both Omphile and Finex felt very comfortable in communicating and playing with each other.

The fourth point is this: although the conventional scientific method of positivism remains entrenched as the established way of doing research due to its perceived objectivity and neutrality, it has a dark side. The things that we know foundationally about the conventional method of science (research questions, research design, sampling techniques and so on) are neither objective nor neutral. They are laden with subjective ideological presuppositions, assumptions and beliefs tied to contextual particularities and cultural specificities of those regions of the world from where they originate (Ndhlovu, 2021). In particular, the very close and intimate association of the positivist tradition of scientific enquiry with the rise and spread of colonial modernity means that we need to rethink many of its common-sense assumptions. We need to rethink, for example, the supposed universal relevance of established approaches to multilingualism research. The majority of them originated from the locality and particularism of the social and cultural conditions of the Global North, and then generalised to all other societies – through colonial and other imperial processes – as if the whole world was a homogeneous continuum. Overall, the dynamic of linguistic usages that we have 'shown' and 'told' in the story of Finex's interaction with Omphile would have been missed if the scientific method that emphasises conventionalism and systematicity had been followed. What we learn from the story narrated and analysed in this chapter is that an autoethnographic praxis of multilingualism research that is anti-establishment is possible – after all. It is possible to develop innovative methodologies that allow us to be specifically attentive to the small details of everyday life that present opportunities to ask big questions of small data.

Notes

(1) We only identify different languages by their names as a way to help the reader follow the story. This does not mean that we subscribe to the view that recognises named and identifiable 'languages' as being the most legitimate means of human communication. Rather, we see 'languages-with-a-name' as part of more complex linguistic systems that we deploy strategically – individually and collectively – to facilitate our social interactions.

(2) 'Autoethnography is not simply a way of knowing about the world; it has become a way of being in the world, one that requires living consciously, emotionally, reflexively. It asks that we not only examine our lives but also consider how and why we think, act, and feel as we do. Autoethnography requires that we observe ourselves observing, that we interrogate what we think and believe, and that we challenge our own assumptions, asking over and over if we have penetrated as many layers of our own defences, fears, and insecurities ... And in the process, it seeks a story where authors ultimately write themselves [into the narrative]' (Jones *et al.*, 2013: 10).

References

Anderson, L. (2006) Analytic autoethnography. *Journal of Contemporary Ethnography* 35 (4), 373–395.

Atkinson, J.M. and Heritage, J. (eds) (1984) *Structures of Social Action: Studies in Conversation Analysis*. Cambridge: Cambridge University Press.

Baronov, D. (2004) Navigating the hidden assumptions of the introductory research methods text. *Radical Pedagogy* 1–6.

Blommaert, J. (2010) *The Sociolinguistics of Globalization*. Cambridge: Cambridge University Press.

Blommaert, J., Leppänen, S., Pahta, P. and Räisänen, T. (eds) (2012) *Dangerous Multilingualism: Northern Perspectives on Order, Purity and Normality*. London: Palgrave Macmillan.

Bochner, A.P. (1997) It's about time: Narrative and the divided self. *Qualitative Inquiry* 3 (4), 418–438.

Bochner, A.P. (2000) Criteria against ourselves. *Qualitative Inquiry* 6 (2), 266–272.
Bochner, A.P. (2001) Narrative's virtues. *Qualitative Inquiry* 7 (2), 131–157.
Bochner, A.P. (2002) Perspectives on inquiry III: The moral of stories. In M.L. Knapp and J.A. Daly (eds) *Handbook of Interpersonal Communication* (pp. 73–101, 3rd edn). Thousand Oaks, CA: Sage.
Brutt-Griffler, J. (2006) Language endangerment, the construction of indigenous languages and World English. In M. Pütz, J.A. Fishman and J.N. Aertselaer (eds) *Along the Routes to Power: Explorations of Empowerment through Language* (pp. 35–54). Berlin/New York: Mouton de Gruyter.
Canagarajah, S. (2011) Codemeshing in academic writing: Identifying teachable strategies of translanguaging. *The Modern Language Journal* 95 (3), 401–417.
Canagarajah, S. (2013) *Translingual Practice: Global Englishes and Cosmopolitan Relations*. London/New York: Routledge.
Chang, H. (2008) *Autoethnography as Method*. Walnut Creek, CA: Left Coast Press.
Chilisa, B. (2011) *Indigenous Research Methodologies*. New York: Sage.
Colombo, M. (2003) Reflexivity and narratives in action research: A discursive approach. *Forum: Qualitative Social Research* 4 (2). See http://www.qualitative-research.net/index.php/fqs/article/view/718/1554.
Comaroff, J. and Comaroff, J.L. (2011) *Theory from the South: Or, how Euro-America is Evolving toward Africa (The Radical Imagination)*. New York: Paradigm Publishers.
Connell, R. (2007) *Southern Theory: The Global Dynamics of Knowledge in Social Science*. Crows Nest: Allen & Unwin.
Creese, A. and Blackledge, A. (2010) Translanguaging in the bilingual classroom: A pedagogy for learning and teaching? *Modern Language Journal* 94, 103–115.
Cummins, J. (1979) Linguistic interdependence and the educational development of bilingual children. *Review of Educational Research* 49, 222–251.
Cummins, J. (2007) Rethinking monolingual instructional strategies in multilingual classrooms. *The Canadian Journal of Applied Linguistics* 10 (2), 221–240.
Czyzewski, M. (1994) Reflexivity of actors versus reflexivity of accounts. *Theory, Culture and Society* 11, 161–168.
Daniel, S.M. and Pacheco, M.B. (2015) Translanguaging practices and perspectives of four multilingual teens. *Journal of Adolescent and Adult Literacy* 59 (6), 653–663.
Delamont, S. (2009) The only honest thing: Autoethnography, reflexivity and small crises in fieldwork. *Ethnography and Education* 4 (1), 51–63.
Ellis, C. (2004) *The Ethnographic I: A Methodological Novel about Autoethnography*. Walnut Creek, CA: AltaMira Press.
Ellis, C. (2007) Telling secrets, revealing lives: Relational ethics in research with intimate others. *Qualitative Enquiry* 13, 3–29.
Ellis, C. (2009) Telling tales on neighbours: Ethics in two voices. *International Review of Qualitative Research* 2 (1), 3–28.
Ellis, C. and Bochner, A.P. (2000) Autoethnography, personal narrative, reflexivity: Researcher as subject. In N.K. Denzin and Y.S. Lincoln (eds) *Handbook of Qualitative Research* (pp. 733–768). Thousand Oaks, CA: Sage.
Ellis, C., Adams, T.E. and Bouchner, A.P. (2011) Autoethnography: An overview. *Forum: Qualitative Social Research* 21 (1), 1–19.
Enfield, N.J. (2008) Common ground as a resource for social affiliation. In I. Kecskes and J.L. Mey (eds) *Intention, Common Ground and the Egocentric Speaker-Hearer* (pp. 223–254). Berlin/New York: Mouton de Gruyter.

Errington, J. (2008) *Linguistics in a Colonial World: A Story of Language, Meaning, and Power*. Oxford: Blackwell.
García, O. (2009) *Bilingual Education in the 21st Century: A Global Perspective*. Malden, MA/Oxford: Wiley Blackwell.
García, O. and Li Wei (2014) *Translanguaging: Language, Bilingualism and Education*. Basingstoke: Palgrave Macmillan.
García, O. and Kleyn, T. (2016) Translanguaging theory in education. In O. García and T. Kleyn (eds) *Translanguaging with Multilingual Students: Learning from Classroom Moments* (pp. 9–33). New York/London: Routledge.
Giles, H. (1984) The dynamics of speech accommodation. *International Journal of the Sociology of Language* 46, 49–70.
Goffman, E. (1981) *Forms of Talk*. Philadelphia, PA: University of Pennsylvania Press.
Gumperz, J.J. (1982) *Language and Social Identity*. Cambridge: Cambridge University Press.
Harris, R. (1987) Language as social interaction: Integrationalism versus segregationalism. *Language Sciences* 9 (2), 131–143.
Haugen, E. (1972) *The Ecology of Language*. Stanford, CA: Stanford University Press.
Heller, M. (2011) *Paths to Post-Nationalism: A Critical Ethnography of Language and Identity*. Oxford: Oxford University Press.
Heritage, J. (1995) Conversation analysis: Methodological aspects. In U. Quasthof (ed.) *Aspects of Oral Communication* (pp. 391–418). Berlin/New York: Walter de Gruyter.
Holt, N.L. (2003) Representation, legitimation and autoethnography: An autoethnographic writing story. *International Journal of Qualitative Methods* 2, 18–28.
Hornberger, N.H. and Link, H. (2012) Translanguaging and transnational literacies in multilingual classrooms: A bilingual lens. *International Journal of Bilingual Education and Bilingualism* 15 (3), 261–278.
Jacquemet, M. (2005) Transidiomatic practices: Language and power in the age of globalization. *Language & Communication* 25 (3), 257–277.
Jones, S.H., Adams, T.E. and Ellis, C. (eds) (2013) *Handbook of Autoethnography*. Walnut Creek, CA: Left Coast Press, Inc.
Jørgensen, J.N. (2008) Poly-lingual languaging around and among children and adolescents. *International Journal of Multilingualism* 5 (3), 161–176.
Jørgensen, J.N. (2010) Languaging. Nine years of poly-lingual development of young Turkish-Danish grade school students, vol. I-II. *Copenhagen Studies in Bilingualism, the Køge Series, vol. K15-K16*. Copenhagen: University of Copenhagen.
Khubchandani, L. (1997) *Revisualising Boundaries: A Plurilingual Ethos*. New Delhi/London: Sage.
Kyratzis, A., and Green, J. (1997) Jointly constructed narratives in classrooms: Co-construction of friendship and community through language. *Teaching and Teacher Education* 13, 17–37.
Lerner, G. (1996) On the 'semi-permeable' character of grammatical units in conversation: Conditional entry into the turn space of another speaker. In E. Ochs, E. Schegloff and S. Thompson (eds) *Grammar in Interaction* (pp. 238–276). Cambridge: Cambridge University Press.
Li Wei (2011) Moment analysis and translanguaging space: Discursive construction of identities by multilingual Chinese youth in Britain. *Journal of Pragmatics* 43, 1222–1235.
Li Wei and Zhu, H. (2013) Translanguaging identities: Creating transnational space through flexible multilingual practices amongst Chinese university students in the UK. *Applied Linguistics* 34 (5), 516–535.

Madison, D.S. (2006) The dialogic performative in critical ethnography. *Text and Performance Quarterly* 26 (4), 320–324.
Makoni, S. (1998) African languages as European scripts: The shaping of communal memory. In S. Nuttall and C. Coetzee (eds) *Negating the Past: The Making of Memory in South Africa* (pp. 242–248). Oxford: Oxford University Press.
Makoni, S. and Pennycook, A. (eds) (2007) *Disinventing and Reconstituting Languages.* Clevedon: Multilingual Matters.
Maldonado-Torres, N. (2007) On the coloniality of being and the geopolitics of knowledge: Modernity, empire, coloniality. *City* 8 (1), 1–33.
Mazeland, H. (2006) Conversation analysis. *Encyclopedia of Language and Linguistics* 3, 153–162.
Méndez, M. (2013) Autoethnography as a research method: Advantages, limitations and criticisms. *Colombia Applied Linguistics Journal* 15 (2), 279–287.
Mignolo, W.D. (2002) Geopolitics of knowledge and the colonial difference. *South Atlantic Quarterly* 101 (1), 57–96.
Mignolo, W.D. (2011) Epistemic disobedience and the decolonial option: A manifesto. *Transmodernity* 1 (2), 44–66.
Milroy, J. (2001) Language ideologies and the consequences of standardization. *Journal of Sociolinguistics* 5 (4), 530–555.
Ndhlovu, F. (2010) Language politics in postcolonial Africa revisited: Minority agency and language imposition. *Language Matters* 41 (2), 21–38.
Ndhlovu, F. (2013) Language nesting, superdiversity and African diasporas in regional Australia. *Australian Journal of Linguistics* 33 (4), 426–448.
Ndhlovu, F. (2015) Ignored lingualism: Another resource for overcoming the monolingual mindset in language education policy. *Australian Journal of Linguistics* 35 (4), 398–414.
Ndhlovu, F. (2017) Southern development discourse for Southern Africa: Linguistic and cultural imperatives. *Journal of Multicultural Discourses* 12 (2), 89–109. Doi: 10.1080/17447143.2016.1277733.
Ndhlovu, F. (2018) Omphile and his soccer ball: Colonialism, methodology, translanguaging research. *Multilingual Margins* 5 (2), 5–22.
Ndhlovu, F. (2021) Decolonising sociolinguistics research: Methodological turn-around next? *International Journal of the Sociology of Language* 267–268, 193–201. DOI https://doi.org/10.1515/ijsl-2020-0063
Nustad, K.G. (2004) The development discourse in the multilateral system. In M. Bøås and D. McNeill (eds) *Global Institutions and Development: Framing the World?* (pp. 13–23). London: Routledge.
Otsuji, E. and Pennycook, A. (2010) Metrolingualism: Fixity, fluidity and language in flux. *International Journal of Multilingualism* 7, 240–254.
Pace, S. (2012) Writing the self into research: Using grounded theory analytic strategies in autoethnography. *TEXT Journal* 13, 1–15.
Peet, R. (1997) Social theory, postmodernism, and the critique of development. In G. Benko and U. Strohmayer (eds) *Space and Social Theory: Interpreting Modernity and Postmodernity* (pp. 72–87). Oxford: Blackwell.
Pennycook, A. (2010) *Language as a Local Practice.* London/New York: Routledge.
Pennycook, A. and Otsuji, E. (2015) *Metrolingualism: Language in the City.* New York: Routledge.
Piccardo, E. (2013) Plurilingualism and curriculum design: Toward a synergic vision. *TESOL Quarterly* 47, 600–614.

Richards, R. (2008) Writing the othered self: Autoethnography and the problem of objectification in writing about illness and disability. *Qualitative Health Research* 1, 1717–1728.
Salazar, N.B., Elliot, A. and Norum, R. (eds) (2017) Introduction. In N.B. Salazar, A. Elliot and R. Norum (eds) *Methodologies of Mobility: Ethnography of Experiment* (pp. 1–24). New York/Oxford: Berghahn.
Schegloff, E. (2000) Overlapping talk and the organization of turn-taking for conversation. *Language in Society* 29, 1–63.
Schegloff, E.A. (2006) Interaction: The infrastructure for social institutions, the natural ecological niche for language and the arena in which culture is enacted. In N.J. Enfield and S.C. Levinson (eds) *The Roots of Human Sociality: Culture, Cognition and Interaction* (pp. 70–96). New York: Berg.
Smith, L.T. (2012) *Decolonizing Methodologies: Research and Indigenous Peoples* (2nd edn). London/New York: Zed Books.
Watson, R. (2005) Reflexivity, description and the analysis of social settings. *Ciências Sociais Unisinos* 41 (1), 5–10.
Williams, C. (1994) Arfarniad o Ddulliau Dysgu ac Addysgu yng Nghyd-destun Addysg Uwchradd Ddwyieithog [An evaluation of teaching and learning methods in the context of bilingual secondary education]. Unpublished doctoral thesis, University of Wales, Bangor.

9 Recentring Silenced Lingualisms and Voices

Introduction

Would a framework for socially realistic multilingualism be possible and what would its applications to language and literacy education look like? In this concluding chapter, we present a case for advancing Africa-centred conceptions of multilingualism. Tying together narrative stories about the language practices of diverse African communities analysed in the preceding pages of the book, the chapter argues that a more complex and broader conception of African multilingualism is possible – after all. It is one that is grounded in local cultural contextual particularities including the following: dialect continua, cultural practices and identities, discursive practices, linguistic frontiers, social relationships and interconnections, among others. Such mapping of African conceptions of multilingualism takes into account the past and present communication practices of local communities, among themselves and with outsiders; the cultural and linguistic experiences of African migrants and refugees; and the exigencies of present and future-oriented relationships and social networks within continental Africa and in the diaspora.

The communication needs and social transactional activities of Africans (whether on the continent or in the diaspora) are not limited to interacting with people within the confines of their own communities. Rather, they transcend the social and cultural boundaries of communities and nation-states in ways that accord with the current realities of an interconnected world. For this reason, African conceptions of multilingualism posited in this chapter try to capture and articulate transnational frames needed to comprehend the cultural identities and language practices of a world that is characterised by complex modes of interconnections and diversities.

Decolonisation and Imperative for Epistemological Turn-Around

While the language now exists for us to talk about the possibility of other forms of knowledge apart from hegemonic monolingual models, the struggle for legitimacy in the eyes of the academy continues (Smith, 2012). A major challenge we are still facing in humanities and social science research is one around what we would call methodological stasis. We have been able to break new ground theoretically in some aspects of multilingualism research, allowing ourselves to conceptualise research in unconventional ways that transcend the positivist Euro-modernist 'scientific' tradition. However, although a number of scholars have drawn our attention to the endless possibilities of theorising and conceptualising in ways other than mainstream approaches, a gaping hole remains on the epistemological side of things. Arguably, we are still stuck with those conventional ways of knowing that are associated with monolingual frameworks that we are trying to unsettle – and to work against, as it were. As decolonial theorist Walter Mignolo (2011) has advised, we must step away from inherited Eurocentric habits through delinking from colonial legacies.

We would like to suggest that the methodologies that inform our approaches to the analysis of multilingual policies in educational and other social settings originate from what others have called 'colonial linguistics' (Errington, 2001, 2008; Fardon & Furniss, 1994; Makoni, 1998, 2003; Severo, 2016). Early missionaries and other colonial academics who pioneered language (and by extension multilingualism) research in sub-Saharan Africa followed Euro-modernist imperial methodologies. Such methods and assumptions about the nature of language underpin the way we currently collect, document, analyse and disseminate data on multilingualism. We would further argue that as relevant academic communities, we have thus far made commendable strides when it comes to challenging colonially inherited theories and concepts.

However, we are yet to do the same when it comes to methodologies. The majority of sociolinguists and applied linguists still see mainstream multilingualism research methodologies as if they were self-evident things of a natural kind that are forever relevant and applicable in every context in similar ways (Ndhlovu, 2021). We have to remember though that these methods – the qualitative/quantitative paradigm, the survey, the questionnaire, the case study and so on – originated from observations made in specific sociocultural contexts and conditions that are different from those that obtain in communities of the Global South. As a way to start a new conversation around these matters, we argue that struggles for epistemic and cognitive justice are won and lost on the methodology battlefield. There is a compelling need for us to 'undo the dirty history of conventional Euro-modernist methodologies because they emerged as the handmaiden of colonialism and imperialism' (Ndhlovu, 2021: 197). Under the aegis of colonial scholarship, 'research' into language and associated meta-discourses became a critical part of the imperial colonial project. As Sabelo Ndlovu-Gatsheni (2019) argues:

> Our present crisis is that we continue to use re-search methods that are not fundamentally different from before. The critique of methodology is interpreted as being anti-research itself ... Consequently, methodology has become straightjacket that every researcher has to wear if they are to discover knowledge. This blocks all attempts to know differently. It has become a disciplinary tool that makes it difficult for new knowledge to be discovered and generated. (Ndlovu-Gatsheni, 2019: 3)

Those scholars who try to exercise epistemic disobedience are disciplined into an existing methodology, thus draining them of their profundity. This is especially the case if such scholars are speaking from the South.

For these reasons, we share decolonial theorists' and indigenous researchers' advice about the need for us to be seized with the task of establishing what it means to ask and investigate our own research questions using our own methodologies and conceptual frames. The ultimate goal is to contribute fruitful pathways for our own ways of knowing, being and doing research. The need for us to delink from the Western imperial logic of doing research and conceptualising multilingualism is a must and not an option. We need a language to explore spaces and modes of living with languages that do not exist in the spaces of the current research tradition but that do exist in our communities.

We would even go further and suggest that the burden of Euro-modernist imperial methodologies is part of the reason we find ourselves going round and round in circles jumping onto the bandwagon of supposedly new, novel and innovative theories and conceptual frameworks churned out from the Global North *ad infinitum*. We suggest that we need a different set of narratives on how to carry out research; narratives that emphasise the role and power of scholars speaking from Southern and decolonial perspectives to not only theorise but also develop and own the methodologies they use to elicit empirical data that supports their theoretical suppositions. As decolonial theorists and indigenous scholars have suggested, we need to push the agenda of epistemic reconstitution (Mignolo, 2011; Smith, 2012). This is to say we need a different set of locally grounded and culturally relevant grammars and vocabularies for eliciting empirical data to support the suppositions and arguments we advance in our academic and policy conversations on multilingualism.

In this vein, we see national multilingual policy prescriptions across different African nation-states and territories as being in many ways aligned with the ongoing project of decolonisation on the African continent. However, we are also alert to the fact that simply including multiple African languages in national language policy documents will never be equal to the task of decolonisation and social transformation at hand. Decolonisation must involve more than just 'settlements' (Smith, 2012) to address the effects of historic epistemic wrongs and injustices. Rather, a decentring of the dominant (methodological) voice is required. Such a process calls for an increase in other voices speaking from different methodological postures that are yet to be tried and tested. We need to do this because decoloniality is neither a mission nor a manifesto, but an option (Mignolo, 2020). The power of decoloniality rests in the introduction of options, pluralities, interconnections and incompleteness (Nyamnjoh, 2015). And when we introduce one option, it effectively means everything becomes an option. This is at the core of a project that aims to decolonise multilingualism in the Global South.

A related and equally important body of work that is worth drawing upon in our efforts to chart alternative explanatory frames for multilingualism is that of the mobility paradigm (Novoa, 2015; Salazar *et al.*, 2017; Sheller & Urry, 2006). The mobility paradigm seeks to include the historic movement of people with the contemporary importance of individuals' contributions to society. It focuses on 'novel ways of theorising how people, objects, and ideas travel, by looking at social phenomena through the lens of movement' (Salazar *et al.*, 2017: 2) – in both the literal and metaphorical senses. Also known as the 'mobility turn', the mobility paradigm calls researchers' attention to the importance of 'being there', 'moving along' and 'riding along' in order to capture the mobilities of research participants *in situ* (Novoa, 2015: 100). It encourages researchers to be specifically attentive to the small details of everyday life that may contain the potential to develop or question big and established paradigms (Strathern, 2004: xx). This entails registering and documenting most of the informants' comments and take on things (no matter how insignificant they might seem on the surface), in order to apprehend underlying and collective discourses. The imperative is about adopting methodologies that will enable us to pay particular attention to people's mobilities, movements, experiences, encounters, exchanges and mixtures – what Clifford (1997: 8) called 'fieldwork as travel practice'.

In the context of multilingualism research, a major benefit of the mobility paradigm would be that of mitigating the limitations of current conventional approaches, which tend to overlook complex diversities that are embedded in supposedly 'standard' and uniform languages. Forging collaborative research with non-academic communities as equal partners is one way to apply the insights of the mobility paradigm in multilingualism research. Against this backdrop, we present below a set of alternative pathways for reframing the multilingualism discourse that we hope will enrich existing approaches.

Languages of the People, Socially Realistic Multilingualism

We return to the crucial question that we posed earlier in this book. Could the notion of 'multilingualism' in Africa be disconnected from societal language practices and expectations? If this were indeed to be the case, what must we do? We admit that we do not have a definite answer to this question as doing so would be no different from adopting the positivist tradition of 'certainties' that we are questioning in this book. Having said this, we would suggest that in our efforts to map out alternative approaches to multilingualism and multilingual policy frameworks, we need to start with our feet firmly on the ground; from a position that embraces what we call socially realistic understandings of multilingualism. In what follows, we propose a five-point alternative trajectory built around notions of 'language of the people', 'socially realistic multilingualism' (Winford, 2003); 'disinvention and reconstitution of languages' (Makoni, 2003; Makoni & Pennycook, 2007); 'ignored lingualism' (Ndhlovu, 2015b); and the Nhlapo/Alexander harmonisation option. In particular, we reiterate the importance of revisiting the political and ideological significance of Jacob Nhlapo's proposal in the 1940s and 1950s to harmonise Nguni and Sotho languages; and the subsequent efforts by Neville Alexander in the 1980s to resuscitate Nhlapo's proposal. Additionally, we review more recent efforts by other African sociolinguists to bring back to centre stage the harmonisation project.

First is the concept of *language of the people* as opposed to language of the state. As we indicated in our critique of colonial linguistics (see Chapters 1 and 2), African languages (that supposedly account for African multilingualism) are analogous to artificial territorial/nation-state borders imposed under the aegis of colonial imperialism. The language-things that form the basis for our conversations, discourses and policy prescriptions on multilingual education are not the real languages of the people. In this regard, we argue that such types of languages fall within the remit of what Ngugi Wa Thiong'o (2009) calls 'linguistic encirclement'. Ngugi introduced the concept of 'linguistic encirclement' to describe how Africans were colonised and territorialised through the deployment of European languages, thus giving rise to alien nomenclature such as Francophone Africa, Anglophone Africa, Lusophone Africa, all being identifications and definitions informed by imposed languages. Here, we extend the notion of linguistic encirclement to cover colonial projects that produced particular types of 'indigenous African languages' that were and continue to be used as mechanism for consigning Africans into language-based categories or hierarchies of humanity. Such processes proceeded through what has been characterised as 'command over language' that resulted in the production of 'languages of command' (Brutt-Griffler, 2006; Cohn, 1996). Subsequently, these language types were used to encircle Africans at the zones of colonial encounters. Here is how Wa Thiong'o elaborates notions of linguistic encirclement, command over language and languages of command:

> So wherever you look at modern colonialism, the acquisition of the language of the colonizer was based on the death of the languages of the colonized. African languages were weaponized against Africans. Language was a weapon of war ... Language was a very important element in both the conquest and maintenance of colonial rule, because it was likely to bind the minds of the middle class. (Wa Thiong'o, 1981: 9)

The significant point here is that over and above such languages as English, French and Portuguese that came to Africa as imperial languages, a new category of 'indigenous African languages' was produced. Standard African languages such as IsiZulu, Setswana, ChiShona, IsiNdebele, XiTsonga and ChiChewa – among others – owe their existence to the colonial project of linguistic encirclement, which they continue to sustain – albeit by stealth. These are languages of the state and not languages of the people. What this tells us is that the current discourse and praxis of African multilingualism that are built around these notions of language need to be rethought (if not completely revamped) and replaced with that premised on languages of the people. Such epistemic reconstitution of multilingualism is necessary because the current mainstream conceptions revolve around colonially imposed linguistic categories that are disconnected from the real language practices of real people – the languages of the people.

The second suggestion we proffer is that of *socially realistic multilingualism*. In a 2003 contribution to an edited volume on *Black Linguistics*, Donald Winford introduces the concept of 'socially realistic linguistics', which he uses as a summary term that describes languages that reflect people's everyday communicative practices. Winford (2003: 21) specifically uses the notion of 'socially realistic linguistics' in discussing languages of the new world black diaspora that 'are associated with the socially disadvantaged ... and are often perceived as corruptions or deviations, lacking expressive power and rules of grammar'. He goes on to say that these languages include what linguists refer to as 'Creoles' spoken in Africa, the Caribbean, in areas along the Indian Ocean and parts of the United States. The origins of these types of languages lie in the everyday social and communicative practices of people and are characterised by hybridity, fluidity and boundary crossing – as opposed to notions of fixity, purity, normativity and boundedness (Blommaert et al., 2012). Winford further argues that language varieties that are often accorded less prestigious statuses in national language policy regimes do, in fact, represent more socially realistic forms of human communication. Unlike the standardised languages of the state, these varieties are the 'languages of the people' in the sense that they emerge from the atoms of society and reflect users' creativity and innovation. We build on Winford's thesis and introduce the notion of 'socially realistic multilingualism' that can be used as an alternative paradigm to inform discourses on African multilingual education policy frameworks. We propose that we need to follow the route of socially realistic multilingualism if we are to push back the frontiers of linguistic encirclement, of which African multilingual education policies in their current iterations are a part.

This leads us to our third point on the way forward: the *disinvention and reconstitution proposal* (Makoni, 2003; Makoni & Pennycook, 2007). Although it is not necessarily a new concept, we believe disinvention and reconstitution deserve reiteration. For more than two decades, Sinfree Makoni has been calling for the disinvention and reconstitution of African languages and African multilingual policies. He is still pushing this argument, together with other like-minded scholars such as Christine Severo (Latin American context) and Alastair Pennycook (Indian subcontinent and elsewhere in Asia). These scholars' ideas have evidently been around for quite some time but have either been ignored and marginalised from mainstream social-scientific and policy debates; or alternatively most of us have not cared enough to listen to voices other than our own or familiar voices. We would argue that it is probably about time that we pay attention to the anti-conventional and anti-foundational ideas that are at the heart of the disinvention and reconstitution proposal.

The proposal to disinvent and reconstitute languages 'calls attention to the importance of reflecting on our tools of analysis and on the significant realization that linguists and non-linguists may be using terms differently' (Makoni, 2003: 141) when talking about or describing people's language experiences. Scholars pushing the disinvention and reconstitution proposal are building on LePage and Tabouret-Keller's (1985) as well as Fardon and Furniss' (1994) conceptualisation of African speech forms as constituting a continuum as described in the following terms:

> [...] a multilayered and partially connected chain, that offers a choice of varieties and registers in the speakers' immediate environment, and a steadily diminishing set of options to be employed in more distant interactions, albeit a set that is always liable to be reconnected more densely to a new environment by rapid secondary learning, or by the development of new languages. (Fardon & Furniss, 1994: 4)

Makoni and Pennycook (2007) have called for the disinvention and reconstitution of languages because, they argue, the idea of language as an object is part of Christian/colonial and nationalist projects in different parts of the world. The starting point of their argument is that the invention of language sits within the broader context of the colonial invention of tribal and ethnic identities. They see languages as inventions that were created during the processes of territorialisation and imperial conquests (Masuku, 2016). Standard African languages in particular were co-constructed with the crafting of African nation-state boundaries at the Berlin Conference of 1884/1885. These new territorialised versions of African languages were used to mark territorial spaces to enhance the imperial project of domination, control and exploitation. Such deployment of African languages towards enhancing the nation-state-centric political interests of governmentality (Foucault, 1972) and control are still ongoing under postcolonial regimes.

It is for this reason that Makoni and Pennycook (2007) argue for the disinvention and reconstitution of African languages, which they see as social and political constructs. For them, the creation of African nation-states brought with it African national languages that are currently viewed as prime markers of group and individual African identities (Masuku, 2016: 48). Makoni (2003) summarises the potential benefits of the disinvention agenda to educational linguistics in the following terms:

> Most learners of African languages, mother tongue and second languages alike, find themselves confronted with a sharp divide between the official language, as embodied in current written texts, and the speech used in the everyday drama of life, moment by moment, situation by situation. [...]

A shift away from African languages as discrete boxes to interconnected hybridized forms would make it possible to produce a set of materials based on the same orthographic system. (Makoni, 2003: 145)

This is about looking at languages through the prism or metaphor of 'frontiers', which challenges and unsettles the notion of languages as self-enclosed partitions. Through working on the basis of interconnectedness, the metaphor of frontiers enables us to talk about speakers' language repertoires as opposed to the 'number' of discrete language-things that a speaker supposedly moves in and out of (Fardon & Furniss, 1994; Makoni, 2003; Ridge, 2000). In other words, conceptions of language as interconnected patterns, frontiers and scrambled systems hold the promise for delinking the present sociolinguistic experiences of groups and individuals from the overwhelming hold of the past (read, colonial linguistics).

The disinvention and reconstitution project does not reject or deny the existence of standard language-things as a social reality. Neither is it a push for a return to arcane forms of African language speak. It is, instead 'a serious effort to capture current language practices, which are generally pan-ethnic in nature – hence, which cut across conceptualisations about language/society/ethnicity affiliation implicit' (Makoni, 2003: 145) in mainstream multilingual education policies. Disinvention and reconstitution, therefore, seeks to broaden the remit of our conception of what we should be looking at in reimagining languages, multilingualism and associated meta-discourses. We would add that we also need to understand that the process of imagining and inventing languages in particular ways was never a noble and innocent enterprise. Neither was it an ideologically neutral exercise. It was deliberately designed to meet those specific colonial interests of domination, control and governmentality as Foucault (1972) might have put it. It would, therefore, be naïve of us to assume that the very same objects (standard African languages) that were invented as technology for exploitation and domination would suddenly become bastions for empowerment and sociolinguistic justice in education and allied domains – simply because we are now in the so-called postcolonial or post-apartheid context.

We need to seriously consider the merits of the disinvention proposal, draw on its insights and reimagine languages and multilingualism in ways that accord with the contextual particularities of communities of the Global South. We scholars speaking from the South must exercise our inalienable right to imagine and theorise afresh – in a manner that is consistent with the real language practices and experiences of our communities. Imagining African languages as 'multilayered interconnected chains' (Makoni, 2003: 141) is one example of a perspective that can ideally form the basis for Southern conceptualisations of multilingualism. As demonstrated by the data we presented in Chapters 3, 4 and 7, this is a perspective that we can support empirically with narrative ethnographic and autobiographical data from local communities. For us to push forward a research agenda of this nature, we also need strong commitment to empirical evidence and methodological rigour. We must hasten to add this cautionary note though: in advocating locally grounded theorisation and methodological innovations, we are not in any way suggesting that we become a parochial, nativist and inward-looking community of scholars isolated from the rest of the world – doing our own thing and disconnected from the broader global network of knowledge societies. Rather, we need to remain part of the broader global network of knowledge societies – only that we have to do so from a position of strength whereby we bring Southern epistemologies, our own experiences and the experiences of our communities to the table of ideas on multilingualism and its applications in language education policy.

The fourth point is that of *ignored lingualism* (Ndhlovu, 2015a, 2015b). Through the notion of ignored lingualism, Ndhlovu has suggested the diversification of conceptual discourses on language and multilingualism by opening up to those philosophies and bodies of thought that proceed from perspectives other than normative Euro-modernist epistemologies. Ignored lingualism is a term that Ndhlovu adapted from Hélot's (2007, 2011) coinage of 'ignored bilingualism' in her description of the languages of immigrant children that are excluded from education systems in Europe and elsewhere. In an interview recorded for the Non-Native English-Speaking Teacher blog for August 2011, Christine Hélot says migrant background children 'are considered as having problems with the school language and their knowledge in their first language is not recognized'. Hélot gives examples of languages such as Arabic, Turkish and Polish spoken by immigrants in France but are not included in the school curriculum. She calls this practice 'ignored bilingualism'. Therefore, the related concept of ignored lingualism is an umbrella term that we use to capture those views about language that depart from traditional or mainstream understandings of what is meant by language and what language diversity entails (Ndhlovu, 2015b).

Hélot's (2007, 2011) and Ndhlovu's (2015a, 2015b) work hold the promise for fruitful insights we can draw upon to describe those conceptualisations of multilingualism that are currently not being recognised in the discourse and praxis of language and literacy education. The scholarly views that fall under this alternative framing of multilingualism include those that see languages as: 'plurality of consciousness', 'communicative ethos' (Khubchandani, 1997); 'transidiomatic practice' (Jacquemet, 2005); 'strategies of communication' (Canagarajah, 2007); 'attitudinal resources' (Higgins, 2009); as 'interpersonal strategies' (Gumperz, 1982); 'diversity of practices'; 'discursive practices' (Ndhlovu, 2013, 2014); 'creative linguistic practices' (Otsuji & Pennycook, 2010); 'plurilingual multimodal communication resources' (Piccardo, 2013); 'communicative resources' (Blommaert, 2010); and as 'local practice' (Pennycook, 2010). Rather than seeing languages – and by extension – multilingualism as compartmentalised systems of rules, the ignored lingualism perspective sees them as resources that can be employed strategically and socially in the form of language practices (Ndhlovu, 2015b). In this vein, we suggest integrating the ignored lingualism perspective into our conceptual toolkit for reimagining African multilingual education policies. Ignored lingualism complements options such as the disinvention and reconstitution project, the notion of languages of the people and that of socially realistic multilingualism discussed above.

Our fifth and final point is one about revisiting the *harmonisation project* pioneered by Jacob Nhlapo in the 1940s and 1950s and resuscitated by Alexander in the 1980s and 1990s. The back-story to the harmonisation idea is that in meddling with local language issues, colonial regimes had followed processes of language standardisation that sought to reduce language diversity. This untenable situation needed to be reversed in the postcolonial/post-apartheid dispensation. This is how harmonisation came in as a fruitful pathway for countering the putative language ideological regimes of the colonial past. Harmonisation seeks to address 'the residues of political systems based on segregation [that] contributed towards divergence or balkanisation of languages …' (Heugh, 2016: 239). Harmonisation thus came into the picture as a suggestion for how postcolonial African governments might want to address logistical and material challenges associated with offering literacy programmes for multiple languages. Harmonised writing systems for mutually related languages would help circumvent these challenges while ensuring that the diversity of language practices continues to flourish.

We, therefore, wish to revisit the harmonisation agenda in order to explore those spheres of possibility and promises it holds for mapping Africa-centred notions of multilingualism. Although the uptake of this idea among relevant academic communities has historically been rather tentative and lethargic, we believe it is worthwhile revisiting it once again. This is because our current social and political conditions are radically different from those of the 20th century, which may have fomented resistance from both the academic and non-academic communities. With specific focus on the South African context, Jacob Nhlapo 'proposed that the spoken varieties of Nguni and Sotho respectively be *standardised in written form* as a first step to a possible standardised indigenous African language' (Alexander, 1989; emphasis ours). Although he was not a linguist by training, Jacob Nhlapo had multiple professional and intellectual affiliations. He was a scholar, lawyer, journalist and political activist under the banner of the New African Movement and the African National Congress (Heugh, 2016). Owing to this rather diverse intellectual, professional and political background, Nhlapo's harmonisation project was not a purely linguistic enterprise. Rather, it was a project centred on the political economy of language – the potential for African languages to be deployed towards achieving the political goals of uniting and empowering African people (Hirson, 1981). The ethnolinguistic fragmentation of African people that prompted Nhlapo's ideas remains to this day, which means the political imperatives of harmonisation are still as relevant.

Nhlapo spelt out his vision for the harmonised Bantu languages of Southern Africa in a 1944 monograph titled *Bantu Babel: Will the Bantu Languages Live?*

> Joining languages together is a good thing [...] It is really happening and it will go on happening wherever two or more languages are spoken in the same place. All we need to do is to help the mixing of the languages, and try to show that mixing up the languages is nothing to be ashamed of … it is the way languages grow stronger and richer. (Nhlapo, 1944: 8–9)

This is precisely what harmonisation sought to achieve as envisaged by Nhlapo and others who came after him (see below). What is apparent here is that Jacob Nhlapo was well ahead of his time. We see him prefiguring what the current generation of sociolinguistic theorists is putting forward as a novelty. This is in relation to the idea of fluidity and boundary crossing that is at the heart of translanguaging and allied approaches to language as a translingual practice among speakers as discussed in Chapter 8. As a practical way of teaching literacy in mutually related language varieties, Nhlapo suggested that in addition to converging on a common Nguni or Sotho text, whichever the case may be, students would also be afforded the opportunity to read and engage material from related varieties. To illustrate this point, he gave the example of the Nguni cluster: 'if there are three books for the Nguni examination, one would be in

Xhosa, one in Zulu and one in Ndebele' (Nhlapo, 1944: 13). This, once again, resonates with the agendas of translanguaging scholarly communities who are currently trying to convince provincial, state, national and federal government departments of education to embrace strategies that utilise more than one language in the same assessment task (García & Kleyn, 2016).

The intention of harmonisation was and remains the development of uniform *orthographic or written forms* for mutually intelligible language varieties for literacy and other educational purposes. Harmonisation does not seek to tamper with the spoken forms of the language varieties in question. This means it does not seek to supplant, curtail or reduce the incidence of language diversity among the speaking populations. Speakers of related language varieties continue to speak or use their respective varieties in exactly the same way they have always done, only to converge in writing. What is common across all varieties is the written form to facilitate literacy and cross-linguistic/cross-cultural interchange both in and out of school contexts. This is the key point that sets harmonisation apart from the approaches of missionaries and other colonial linguists. The projects of colonial linguists effectively erased existing languages/speech forms and replaced them with dominant ones (at best) or erased and replaced them with newly invented languages of command (at worst).

The harmonisation project is solely concerned with uniform written forms of related languages for literacy and educational purposes. It proceeds from a frontier perspective (Makoni, 2003); one that looks at languages as constituting concentric circles of continua with varying degrees of relatedness, which then become a basis for determining which varieties can share common written forms. Here, we wish to underline the crucial distinction between harmonisation and colonial linguistics projects of standardisation and unification that were driven by exigencies of domination, control, manipulation and the exercise of power over colonial subjects and their languages. Harmonisation is, *ipso facto*, a counter-hegemonic strategy that aims to bring back into language and literacy education those elements of fluidity and boundary crossing that are intrinsic to the real communicative practices of real people in their real everyday lives.

South African sociolinguist and anti-apartheid political activist, Neville Alexander, picked up Nhlapo's (1945) ideas to support arguments for the role of African languages in forging national unity, development and cross-cultural understanding in a post-apartheid South Africa (see e.g. Alexander, 1989, 2000). Because South Africa's language policies have historically been linked to racial inequality from 1652, the promotion of 'non-racialism, anti-racism, and anti-ethnicism' (Alexander, 1989: 8) was foremost on his agenda for a post-apartheid South Africa. Among Alexander's main ideas was one on how to use African languages to enhance cross-linguistic exchanges among students and teachers through the harmonisation of mutually intelligible language varieties. He advocated this idea as an additive measure and not one to supplant the numerous African languages into some homogeneous standard form.

The premise of Alexander's argument was that most African languages of South Africa belong to two major language families: the Nguni and Sotho-Tswana groups. Although they are known by different names, languages that belong to either of these groups have high degrees of mutual intelligibility to the extent that speakers of related varieties can easily understand each other without resorting to interpretation. This is the singular most important element of the (South) African language ecology that holds the promise for rethinking multilingualism in a manner that has the potential to facilitate socially realistic multilingual and literacy education while simultaneously promoting the diversity of language practices both in and out of the classroom context.

As already indicated above, we are acutely aware that the idea of harmonisation was not well received among some sections of the academic and non-academic communities during both Jacob Nhlapo's and Neville Alexander's time. It remains a contentious issue even today. Nevertheless, most earlier critics of the harmonisation proposal (such as Raboroko, 1953; and Satyo, 1992) appear to have done so from a misunderstanding or misinterpretation of these ideas. For example, Sizwe Satyo, then a sociolinguist at the University of Cape Town, was one of the leading critics of both Nhlapo and Alexander. In his response to Neville Alexander's essay titled *Language Policy and National Unity in South Africa/Azania* where the harmonisation idea is canvassed, Satyo raised numerable objections. In his rejection of what he termed the 'Nhlapo/Alexander Option', Satyo (1992) argued in favour of the status quo – the current fragmentation of African languages into discrete entities. However, in his five-point plan that he termed 'The tongues option', Satyo (1992: 45) did not provide a concrete alternative apart from poking holes in the harmonisation project on the grounds of 'the pragmatic principle', which is effectively shorthand for maintaining the status quo. In the end, his default position was that of doing nothing but simply defer to the legacy of the racist and supremacist language policies of both the colonial and apartheid political regimes. Here is what Satyo had to say in his rebuttal to the harmonisation agenda:

What about a 'no more and no less' principle when it comes to the existing languages of South Africa? In other words, wouldn't it be expedient to try to accommodate the existing languages of South Africa (including English and Afrikaans) as they are? Shouldn't we refrain from tampering with them in any artificial way? (Satyo, 1992: 46)

But if agents of colonial imperialism, including colonial administrators, missionaries, colonial linguists and architects of the apartheid project of sociolinguistic engineering could tamper with languages (for all the bad reasons), why can't we do the same for a good cause? It would appear that in his defence of colonially inherited approaches to language policies, Satyo implied that scholars from the Global South (and their communities) had to give away their agency and be content with being suppliers of raw data and not producers of new and alternative theoretical frameworks. Admittedly, the quite contemporary ideas unsettling colonial imaginaries of language that we advance in this book may not have been in vogue at the time Satyo wrote his reply to Alexander's proposal. However, it is still worth pointing out that scholars speaking and writing from the Global South do have the right to theorise. After more than 500 years of coloniality and epistemic domination, it is about time that previously marginalised voices rise to the occasion – in defence of their inalienable right to theorise; the right to epistemic freedom (Ndhlovu, 2018b). As Ndhlovu (2018b) suggests further, decolonial and Southern theorists must be seized with the task of unmasking the role and purpose of research; they must shift the phenomenology of research in order to 're-position those who have been objects of research into questioners, critics, theorists, knowers, and communicators' (Ndlovu-Gatsheni, 2019: 4). This is because scholars of Southern and decolonial persuasions (and among them must be counted Jacob Nhlapo and Neville Alexander) have voices, which must not be silenced any longer.

As we indicated earlier (see Chapters 1 and 2), the versions of languages that Satyo fiercely defended are products of colonial and apartheid inventions that require disinvention and reconstitution if they are to serve the envisaged role of empowering marginalised sections of African society. The phenomenology of named African languages as we currently know them is traceable to the period of colonial encounters. However, as fate would have it, Satyo's arguments supporting colonial and apartheid versions of African languages and multilingualism prevailed. The current 12 official languages policy of South Africa follows precisely the very same colonial linguistics route of inventing, enumerating, picking and adding multiple language-things; and then calling it multilingualism.

Nevertheless, as we have come to know with the passage of time since the end of apartheid some 27 years ago, this approach to multilingualism and language policy is not working. It has failed to deliver sociolinguistic justice, cognitive justice and, above all, epistemic access for the majority of black Africans peripherised by the legacy of apartheid and the ongoing project of global coloniality.

The above setbacks notwithstanding, the harmonisation agenda did not die; rather it was only dormant for a short while. Subsequent to the pioneering work of Nhlapo and Alexander, later generations of critical social scientists have resuscitated the idea through projects such as those of the Centre for the Advanced Study of African Society (CASAS) at the University of Cape Town (see e.g. Chebanne, 2003; Prah, 2002). The projects of other prominent African sociolinguists such as Banda (2002, 2008), Banda, Chanda and Kamwendo (2002), Mtenje and Kamwendo (2002) and Prah (2008) – working individually and collaboratively – attest to the currency and viability of harmonising the orthographies of genetically related (southern) African languages for use as the medium of instruction at all levels of education. In Table 9.1, we provide a list of lexical items from mutually intelligible Nguni languages to illustrate the particular point about the prospects and feasibility of harmonisation to facilitate pan-African/pan-ethnic literacy and education. What we see from Table 9.1 is that vocabulary items currently written in slightly different ways in each group of languages can be easily reduced to one orthographic form without posing any major literacy acquisition problems.

Kwesi Prah in particular, has adopted a much more ambitious and far-reaching approach to harmonisation: one that is pan-African in outlook. Prompted by the need to develop policies and literacy materials that could be widely used across different polities of the African continent, Prah (2008) provides an outline of principles along which harmonisation may be developed in Africa (Makoni, 2016). Prah postulates that nearly 80–85% of Africans speak 15–17 'core' languages. If harmonisation were to be adopted, these 'core' languages could form the basis for Africa-wide language and literacy education. Leketi Makalela (2009) advanced similar arguments on a much smaller scale by focusing on the Sotho-Tswana group of languages. He investigated the degrees of mutual intelligibility among three structurally related Sotho-Tswana languages, namely Sepedi, Sesotho and Setswana. The outcome of his study has been the possibility of harmonising the orthographic representations and spelling systems of these languages towards a standard Sotho for educational purposes and for the purposes of cultivating cross-cultural understanding and social cohesion.

Table 9.1 Examples of words that can be harmonised[a]

Nguni languages→	IsiNdebele	SiSwati	IsiZulu	IsiXhosa
	Kumnandi	Kumnandzi	Kumnandi	Kumandi
	Ngisuthi	Ngesutsi	Ngisuthi	Ndihluthi
	Wenzani?	Wentani?	Wenzani?	Wenzantoni?
	Umuntu	Umuntfu	Umuntu	Umntu
	Ngiyaxolisa	Ngiyacolisa	Ngiyaxolisa	Ndyaxolisa

[a]Recent work by African languages experts shows that Xitsonga has similar morphosyntactic structures as the Nguni group and that the speakers comprehend each other without major difficulties. Tshivenda is reported to have a sizeable stock of words and pragmatic features similar to the South African Sotho/Tswana group of languages.

The 2016 special issue of *Language Policy* (Volume 15) is the latest attempt to revive scholarly conversations and debates on the viability of harmonisation. The special issue displays articles that draw attention to the history and future prospects for harmonising orthographic conventions of closely related language varieties for literacy and educational purposes. Guest editor, Sinfree Makoni (2016: 223) introduced the issue with a critique of how African language policy and planning regimes have traditionally been designed to serve as technology for 'romanticizing differences and managing diversity'. Makoni (2016: 231) commends the harmonisation project for holding the promise for generating fruitful ways of 'producing literacy material more attractive to publishers than producing materials that are used by a small number of people'. Nevertheless, he also raises alarm bells on the soundness and reliability of the underpinning methodology, particularly in relation to Prah's pan-African project.

> While Prah might be correct about the number of core languages and the percentages of Africans who speak them, how he arrived at the figures he treats as factual is not empirically self-evident. Efforts to establish common principles of mutual intelligibility are important insofar as they attempt to build consistency in measuring intelligibility; thus, it behoves him to explain theoretically why [and how] he arrived at an 80% cut-off point. [T]he sociolinguistic validity of the project becomes suspect because the methodology does not seem to be sensitive to context. As a result, he ends up in a situation that he may not have found productive: a one-size-fits-all approach. (Makoni, 2016: 231)

Makoni sums up the critique by questioning positivistic meta-discourses implicated in Prah's decision to use terms such as 'core' and 'cluster'.

These invoke logics of counting and enumerability that are at odds with quite contemporary sociolinguistic perspectives on languages as communicative practices that are inseparable from users.

We consider Makoni's critique to be a call to refine methodological instruments and not a casting of doubt or aspersion on the promise of the harmonisation option in acknowledging diversity in a way that simultaneously facilitates the development of literacy and access to education (van der Walt, 2016: 324). We, therefore, hold the view that now is not the time to give up on the proposal to harmonise African languages for literacy and educational purposes. Now is, in fact, the time to intensify our conversations on the prospects and possibilities for improving the literacy and educational outcomes of African children through harmonised versions of mutually intelligible African languages. In the penultimate article of the special issue, Crista van der Walt characterises harmonisation as a transformative force; a strategy to facilitate social equality and the development of an epistemology of African languages; and 'a key resource for empowering communities to combat marginalization, poverty and impoverishment' (Roy-Cambell, 2006, cited in van der Walt, 2016: 328). We find these arguments on the envisaged benefits of harmonising the written forms of mutually related African languages quite compelling and persuasive.

Conclusion

Our thesis for a socially realistic approach to multilingualism centres on shifting the focus from enumerable language-things to individuals and communities of practice. It is about how and where to search for the 'lingual' and 'lingualism', which for us, is located within individuals and communities. In the context of language and literacy education, the alternative approach we propose posits that individuals and members of communities of practice bring their varied linguistic repertoires to the object of engagement – the literary text coded through a shared orthographic convention. This is where the project of harmonisation and related strategies discussed above come in handy. A uniform orthographic representation of multiple, yet mutually related language varieties, means individuals deploy their diverse multilingual resources (however imagined or configured) to the task of decoding meaning from the shared text.

In other words, what this effectively means is we consider multilingualism to be a phenomenon that resides in individuals and communities of practice. It is not something to be theorised through looking at those bounded and boxed countable language-things. The analysis of multilingualism in terms of the number of countable objects recognised and included in national language policies is a futile and misleading enterprise. It both misses and obscures the crucial point about where diversity lies. However, having said this, the flipside of this permutation might raise perceptions of another conundrum: Doesn't the use of a uniform writing system in our approach equate with a monolingual way of seeing? Absolutely not. In our reframing of multilingualism, the experience of engaging material written in a uniform orthography is, in fact, a multilingual exercise. Students draw on their individual language experiences and the repertoires of their peers, thus resulting in a dialectical multivocal conversation and collaboration where every bit and piece of communicative resource and way of knowing matter in meaning making.

As a way to illuminate the above point further, we would like to take the reader back to the stories about the literacy practices of Finex's father and Leketi's mother narrated in Chapter 1. The two stories drew our attention to the partiality and incompleteness of a logic that only relies on quantitative and mono-epistemic approaches to diversity. As we saw in both stories, people from diverse ontological and epistemological traditions use differing ways to unlock their senses of cognition in order to figure out elusive notions of diversity and meaning making. In the case of our framing of Africa-centred multilingualism, the use of a uniform written text to represent a range of mutually related language varieties does not erase diversity. It simply means that we have invoked a different logic, ontology and epistemology of engaging with the social realities of literacy and language diversity.

Individuals from differing ontological backgrounds have capacities to tap into their wealth of diverse language practices and ways of reading and interpreting the world to decode meaning from a text written in an orthography common to all. This to us approximates socially realistic multilingualism. Unlike mainstream approaches that proceed through counting putative language-things, we believe an approach to multilingualism that puts emphasis on the language practices and experiences of individuals and communities of practice holds the promise for decolonising this field of study.

References

Alexander, N. (1989) *Language Policy and National Unity in South Africa/Azania*. Cape Town: Buchu Books.
Alexander, N. (2000) Why the Nguni and Sotho languages in South Africa should be harmonised. In K. Deprez and T. du Plessis (eds) *Multilingualism and Government: Studies in Language Policy in South Africa* (pp. 115–122). Pretoria: Van Schaik.

Banda, F. (2002) Towards a standard Bantu orthography. In K.K. Prah (ed.) *Writing African* (pp. 43–54). Cape Town: CASAS.
Banda, F. (2008) Orthography design and harmonisation in development in Southern Africa. *Open Society Initiative for Southern Africa* 12 (3), 39–48.
Banda, F., Chanda, V., Kamwendo, G. H. (2002) *A Unified Standard Orthography for South-Central African Languages: Malawi, Mozambique and Zambia*. Cape Town: Centre for the Advanced Studies of African Society Monograph Series.
Blommaert, J. (2010) *The Sociolinguistics of Globalization*. Cambridge: Cambridge University Press.
Blommaert, J., Leppänen, S., Räisänen, T. and Pahta, P. (eds) (2012) *Dangerous Multilingualism: Northern Perspectives on Order, Purity and Normality*. London: Palgrave Macmillan.
Brutt-Griffler, J. (2006) Language endangerment, the construction of indigenous languages and World English. In M. Pütz, J.A. Fishman and J.N. Aertselaer (eds) *Along the Routes to Power: Explorations of Empowerment through Language* (pp. 35–54). Berlin/New York: Mouton de Gruyter.
Canagarajah, S. (2007) Lingua Franca English, multilingual communities, and language acquisition. *The Modern Language Journal* 91 (1), 923–939. DOI 10.1111/j.1540-4781.2007.00678.x
Chebanne, A.M. (2003) *Unifying South African Languages: Harmonisation and Standardisation*. Cape Town: CASAS.
Clifford, J. (1997) *Routes: Travel and Translation in the late Twentieth Century*. Cambridge: Harvard University Press.
Connell, R. (2007) *Southern Theory: The Global Dynamics of Knowledge in Social Science*. Crows Nest: Allen & Unwin.
Cohn, B.S. (1996) *Colonialism and Its Forms of Knowledge*. Princeton, NJ: Princeton University Press.
Errington, J. (2001) Colonial linguistics. *Annual Review of Anthropology* 30, 19–30.
Errington, J. (2008) *Linguistics in a Colonial World: A Story of Language, Meaning, and Power*. Oxford: Blackwell.
Fardon, R. and Furniss, G. (1994) *African Languages, Development and the State*. London/New York: Routledge.
Foucault, M. (1972) *The Archaeology of Knowledge and the Discourse on Language*. New York: Pantheon.
García, O. and Kleyn, T. (2016) Translanguaging theory in education. In O. García and T. Kleyn (eds) *Translanguaging with Multilingual Students: Learning from Classroom Moments* (pp. 9–33). New York/London: Routledge.
Gumperz, J.J. (1982) *Language and Social Identity*. London: Cambridge University Press.
Hélot, C. (2007) Awareness raising and multilingualism in primary education. In J. Cenoz and N.H. Hornberger (eds) *Encyclopedia of Language and Education. Second Edition, Volume 6: Knowledge about Language* (pp. 371–384). Berlin: Springer.
Hélot, C. (2011) Interview for NNEST of the month, 31 August 2011. See https://nnestofthemonth.wordpress.com/2011/08/ (accessed 19 March 2021).
Heugh, K. (2016) Harmonisation and South African languages: Twentieth century debates of homogeneity and heterogeneity. *Language Policy and Planning* 15, 235–255.
Higgins, C. (2009) *English as a Local Language: Post-colonial Identities and Multilingual Practices*. Bristol: Multilingual Matters.
Hirson, B. (1981) Language control and resistance in South Africa. *African Affairs* 80 (319), 219–237.

Jacquemet, M. (2005) Transidiomatic practices: Language and power in the age of globalization. *Language and Communication* 25 (3), 257–277.
Khubchandani, L. (1997) *Revisualising Boundaries: A Plurilingual Ethos*. New Delhi/London: Sage.
LePage, R. and Tabouret-Keller, A. (1985) *Acts of Identity*. Cambridge: Cambridge University Press.
Makalela, L. (2009) Harmonizing South African Sotho language varieties: Lessons from reading proficiency assessment. *International Multilingual Research Journal* 3 (2), 120–133.
Makoni, S. (1998) African languages as European scripts: The shaping of communal memory. In S. Nuttall and C. Coetzee (eds) *Negating the Past: The Making of Memory in South Africa* (pp. 242–248). Oxford: Oxford University Press.
Makoni, S. (2003) From misinvention to disinvention of language: Multilingualism and the South African constitution. In S. Makoni, G. Smitherman, A.F. Ball and A.K. Spears (eds) *Black Linguistics: Language, Society, and Politics in Africa and the Americas* (pp. 132–151). London/New York: London.
Makoni, S. (2016) Romanticising differences and managing diversities: A perspective on harmonization, language policy and planning. *Language Policy* 15, 223–234.
Makoni, S. and Pennycook, A. (eds) (2007) *Disinventing and Reconstituting Languages*. Clevedon: Multilingual Matters.
Masuku, J.M. (2016) Language, discourse and survival strategies: The case of cross-border traders in Southern Africa. Unpublished PhD Thesis, University of New England, Armidale, Australia.
Mignolo, W.D. (2000) Geopolitics of knowledge and the colonial difference. *South Atlantic Quarterly* 1 (101), 57–96.
Mignolo, W.D. (2011) Epistemic disobedience and the decolonial option: A manifesto. *Transmodernity* 1 (2), 44–66.
Mtenje, A. and Kamwendo, G.H. (2002) On the harmonisation of orthographies: The case for Ciyao, Citumbuka and Cilomwe. In F. Banda (ed.) *Language Across Borders: Harmonisation and Standardisation of Orthographic Conventions of Central African Languages* (pp. 83–90). Cape Town: Centre for the Advanced Studies of African Society.
Ndhlovu, F. (2013) Language nesting, superdiversity and African diasporas in regional Australia. *Australian Journal of Linguistics* 33 (4), 426–448.
Ndhlovu, F. (2014) *Becoming an African Diaspora in Australia: Language, Culture, Identity*. Houndmills: Palgrave Macmillan.
Ndhlovu, F. (2015a) *Hegemony and Language Policies in Southern Africa: Identity, Integration, Development*. Newcastle upon Tyne: Cambridge Scholars Publishing.
Ndhlovu, F. (2015b) Ignored lingualism: Another resource for overcoming the monolingual mindset in language education policy. *Australian Journal of Linguistics* 35 (4), 398–414.
Ndhlovu, F. (2018b) Can the other be heard? Response to commentaries on 'Omphile and his Soccer Ball'. *Multilingual Margins* 5 (2), 43–50.
Ndhlovu, F. (2021) Decolonising sociolinguistics research: Methodological turn-around next? *International Journal of the Sociology of Language* 267–268, 193–201. DOI 10.1515/ijsl-2020-0063.
Ndlovu-Gatsheni, S.J. (2019) Provisional notes on decolonising research methodology and undoing its dirty history: A provocation. *Journal of Developing Societies* 1, 1-12. DOI 10.1177/0169796X19880417

Nhlapo, J. (1944) *Bantu Babel: Will the Bantu Languages Live? The Sixpenny Library (4)*. Cape Town: The African Bookman.
Nhlapo, J. (1945) *Nguni and Sotho*. Cape Town: The African Bookman.
Novoa, A. (2015) Mobile ethnography: Emergence, techniques and its importance to geography. *Human Geographies* 9 (1), 97–107.
Nyamnjoh, F.B. (2015) Incompleteness: Frontier Africa and the currency of conviviality. *Journal of Contemporary African Studies* 33 (1), 48–63.
Otsuji, E. and Pennycook, A. (2010) Metrolingualism: Fixity, fluidity and language in flux. *International Journal of Multilingualism* 7, 240–254.
Pennycook, A. (2010) *Language as a Local Practice*. London/New York: Routledge.
Piccardo, E. (2013) Plurilingualism and curriculum design: Toward a synergic vision. *TESOL Quarterly* 47, 600–614.
Prah, K.K. (2002) *Speaking in Unison: The Harmonisation and Standardisation of Southern African Languages*. Cape Town: CASAS.
Prah, K.K. (2008) *Africa in Transformation: Political Economic Transformation and Socio-Political Responses in Africa (2)*. Dakar: Codesria.
Raboroko, P.N. (1953) The linguistic revolution. *Liberation* 5, 14–19. See https://disa.ukzn.ac.za/sites/default/files/pdf_files/LiSep53.1729.455X.000.005.Sep1953.7.pdf (accessed 29 October 2019).
Ridge, S.G. (2000) Language policy and democratic practice. In S. Makoni and N. Kamwangamalu (eds) *Language and Institutions in Africa* (pp. 45–65). Cape Town: Centre for Advanced Studies of African Society.
Roy-Campbell, Z.M. (2006) The state of African languages and the global language politics: Empowering African languages in the era of globalization. In O.F. Arasanyin and M.A. Pemberton (eds) *Selected Proceedings of the 36th Annual Conference on African Linguistics* (pp. 1–13). Somerville, MA: Cascadilla Proceedings Project.
Salazar, N.B., Elliot, A. and Roger, N. (2017) Studying mobilities: Theoretical notes and methodological queries. In N.B. Salazar, A. Elliot and N. Roger (eds) *Methodologies of Mobility: Ethnography of Experiment* (pp. 1–24). New York/Oxford: Berghahn.
Satyo, S. (1992) A response to Neville Alexander's essay: Language policy and national unity in South Africa/Azania. *Southern African Journal of Applied Language Studies* 1 (1), 41–50.
Severo, C.G. (2016) The colonial invention of languages in America. *Alfa: Revista de Linguistica* 60 (1). DOI 10.1590/1981-5794-1604-1
Sheller, M. and Urry, J. (2006) The new mobilities paradigm. *Environment and Planning* 38 (2), 207–226.
Smith, L.T. (2012) *Decolonizing Methodologies: Research and Indigenous Peoples* (2nd edn). London/New York: Zed Books.
Strathern, M. (2004) *Partial Connections*. Lanham: Rowman & Littlefield.
van der Walt, C. (2016) Conclusion: Harmonization as a transformative force. *Language Policy* 15, 323–329.
Wa Thiong'o, N. (1981) *Decolonising the Mind: The Politics of Language in African Literature*. London: James Currey.
Wa Thiong'o, N. (2009) *Re-membering Africa*. Nairobi: East African Educational Publishers Ltd.
Winford, D. (2003) Ideologies of language and socially realistic linguistics. In S. Makoni, G. Smitherman, A.F. Ball and A.K. Spears (eds) *Black Linguistics: Language, Society, and Politics in Africa and the Americas* (pp. 21–39). London/New York: London.

Index

abyssal lines 99–100
academic justice 58
academic language 14, 55–74
ACALAN (African Academy of Languages) 94, 95, 96, 97, 103, 120
action research 45
Adamek, P.M. 12
additive bilingual education 17, 20, 76, 77, 78, 85
administrative convenience 31, 79
Adult Migrant English Language Programme 110–11, 118
Africa, idea of 101–4
African Englishes 116, 117, 118
Afrikaans 10, 57–8, 78, 82
Alexander, Neville 159, 165, 167–8, 170
Al-wer, Enam 80
Amadiume, I. 57
Amharic 115
Anderson, Benedict 33
Anderson, J. 112
Anderson, L. 146, 147
antecedent genres 65–6, 72
Antone, E. 40
apartheid 58, 67, 77, 78, 170
applied linguistics 99, 101, 143
Arabic 95, 115, 117, 120
Armstrong, J. 40
art 56
'asking for help' conversations 10–11
assessment tools 166–7
assimilation 63

Atkinson, J.M. 133
attitudinal resources 165
Australia 8, 86–7, 103, 109–28
Australian English 116–17, 118
autoethnographic research 131–2, 133, 144–8

Baker, C. 38, 60, 86, 117
Bakhtin, Mikhail 40, 46, 71
Banazak, G.A. 76–7
Banda, Kamuzu 98, 170
Bantu 6, 41, 56, 57, 59, 60, 70, 166
Baronov, D. 140
Barro, M. 120
Beberé 95
Benjamin, W. 13
Benson, Carol 15, 16, 88–9
Benton, M. 112
Berlin Conference of 1884/1885 162
Berthoud, Paul 29–30
Bhabha, Homi 34, 102
Bickerton, D. 124
bilingual education 17, 20, 37, 61, 76, 78, 79, 85
bilingualism through monolingualism 96
Blackledge, A. 61, 62, 86, 96, 102, 103, 139
Blommaert, Jan vii, 61, 85, 101, 132, 138, 161, 165
Bloomfield, Leonard 138–9
Bochner, Arthur 145
Bodwin, P. 112

Botswana 95
bottom-up practices 20, 37, 88
Bourdieu, Pierre 15, 80
Brock-Utne, B. 39, 68
Brown, M.E. 82, 117
Brutt-Griffler, Janina 7, 17, 26, 29, 75, 78, 139, 160
Burundi 115, 121

call-response cultural patterns 41
Cameroon 115
Canagarajah, S. 7, 14, 15, 132, 137, 139, 165
Carreira, J.M. 117
Castles, S. 110
Ceja, L.R. 76–7
census ideology 83
Centre for the Advanced Study of African Society (CASAS) 170
'certainties' 2–3, 5, 27, 159
Chanda, V. 170
Chang, H. 146
Chebanne, A.M. 170
Chewa dialect 98
ChiChewa 95, 98, 160
children and language acquisition 117–18
Chilisa, B. 88, 142
Chimhundu, H. 7, 28, 29, 75, 78
Chinyanja 82, 95, 98, 115
ChiShona 82, 160
Chivhenda 78
Chomsky, Noam 138–9
Christianisation 28, 30
Christianity 8, 27, 32, 33, 75, 97, 162
Church Manyika Language 28
circumlocution 41, 48
citizenship participation 82, 89, 103, 112
citizenship studies 110
Clifford, J. 158
Clyne, Michael 8, 9, 86, 87
co-construction of knowledge 43, 44–5, 88
co-construction of meaning 42–3
codemeshing 69, 132, 137
code-mixing 137

code-switching 65–6, 125, 137
codification 29, 30–1, 33 *see also* writing systems
cognitive domains 63, 67, 157
cognitive justice 157, 170
Cohn, Bernard 7, 160
co-learning 48
Coleman, S. 103
collaborative research 19, 88
collectivity 59, 60, 63 *see also* ubuntu values
Collin, P. 103
Colombo, M. 133
colonial ethnography 3
colonial linguistics vi, vii, 26–34, 156, 167
coloniality, strands of 16–17
coloniality of language 7, 17, 75–86, 88–90
coloniality of language by stealth 75
Comaroff, Jean vii, 142
Comaroff, John vii, 142
command over language 7, 29, 160
communicative currency 120
communicative ethos 165
communities of practice 148, 172
community collaboration 88
community-based knowledge 48–50
community-based learning 48
community-based participatory research (CBPR) 37, 43–5
concept literacies 62
conclusions, structuring 69
Connell, Raewyn vii, 3, 4, 122, 141, 142
constitutive hybridity 102
contact zones 59, 72
contextual cues 41, 70
continua, language/dialect 57, 59, 66, 84–5, 98, 162
conversational analysis (CA) 133, 136, 146
corpus planning 95, 96
'correct' usage 80
cosmopolitanism 85
co-teaching 48, 88
Coulmas, Florian 80
countable entities, languages as

colonial inventions 9, 31, 163, 169, 172–3
diversity not necessarily quantifiable 9, 10, 11
  national language policies 79, 83, 85, 87
  and research methodologies 133
  vehicular cross-border languages (VCBLs) 96, 97, 99
counter-hegemonic strategies 15, 167
counter-practices of research 142
Cox, R.W. 56
creativity 110–12, 126, 138, 165
Creese, A. 61, 62, 86, 96, 139
creoles 111, 123–5, 126, 161
Creux, Ernest 29–30
critical applied linguistics 14
critical ethnographic sociolinguistics 143
cross-border languages 94–107, 111, 120–4
Crystal, D. 119
cultural competence 46, 49, 56, 60, 64, 70, 72, 127
cultural oppression 98, 100
cultural uniformity 31
Cummins, Jim 137, 139
curricula 37, 42–3, 55
Czyzewski, M. 133

Daniel, S.M. 140
Davidson, A. 110
Davidson, B. 57
Davies, A. 119
Davis, B. 112
Day, R.R. 38
de Saussure, Ferdinand 138–9
de Sousa Santos, Baoventura vii, 5, 99–100
decolonial epistemology viii, 18–19, 88, 142
decolonial theory 76–7
decolonial turn 88
decolonising indigenous methodologies 142
deficit-based approaches 16, 39

Delamont, S. 147
democracy 82
denizens 108, 109, 110–12, 113, 115, 118, 126, 127
Derrida, Jacques 13
dialect/language continua 57, 59, 66, 84–5, 98, 162
diaspora communities 103, 108–30, 161
dictionaries 33
directness/indirectness 41–3
discontinuation continuation 47, 59, 60, 62, 63–4, 71, 72
discursivization 27
disinvention and reconstitution 159, 161–4, 169–70
displaced people 109
divide and rule 58
Doke, Clement Martyn vi, 28–9
DRC 115
Dussel, Enrique 76

ecological relationships 50
ecologies of knowledge 99–100
education
  Australia 117
  Bantu language education 6
  bilingual education 17, 20, 37, 61, 76, 78, 79, 85
  harmonisation project 172
  ignored lingualism 164–5
  language and literacy education 37–54
  language education policies 75, 77–8
  multilingual education 2, 78, 79
  multilingual habitus 15–16, 88–9
efficiency principle 69
Einzelsprache (language-with-a-name) 29–32, 63, 79, 137, 140, 169
elites 31, 32, 85
Ellis, Carolyn 145, 146, 147
Ellis, E. 8, 9
emancipation 85
empathy 148
Enfield, N.J. 136
English
  academic language 13, 14, 40–1

in African classrooms 40
African Englishes 116, 117, 118
assimilation by 63
in Australia 110–11, 116–18
Australian English 116–17, 118
circumvention by VCBLs 96
as colonial language 160
in encounter with Omphile 135, 136
and inclusion 14
Kriol and Pidgin English 123–4
as a lingua franca 14
literature 14
as medium of instruction 40, 64, 78
monolingual drone 14
multilingual Englishes 118–19
as 'neutral' 14
as official language 78, 82
replacing home languages 119
rhetorical organisation 41–3, 69–70
in South African education system 78
standard variety 120
as target language 62
in universities 55, 57–8
varieties of 116, 118, 119
Enlightenment, Western European 8, 27, 33, 38
'entities,' languages as 85 *see also* countable entities, languages as
enumeration *see* countable entities, languages as
epistemic justice 157, 158
epistemic violence 84–5
Errington, Joseph vi, vii, 26, 27, 29, 30, 139, 156
ethnography 18, 108, 133, 138, 141–2, 143, 144–8, 164 *see also* autoethnographic research
Eurocentrism 71, 83, 99, 104, 156
Euro-modernist epistemologies 2–4, 9–10, 19, 27, 32, 38, 77, 157
exclusion 3, 14, 17, 81–2, 100, 103, 112, 117, 141

fallacy of monolingual thinking 38
family systems 57, 115, 118

Fang, X. 125
Fardon, R. 26, 156, 162, 163
Fasold, Ralph 80
Fees Must Fall 55, 58
Ferguson, Charles 80
First International Free Linguistics Conference 101
'first' language, multiple 67–8, 72
first-person narratives 134–7, 145–6
Fishman, Joshua 80–1, 96
focus group methods 114, 138, 141
folklore 56
Foucault, Michel 33, 162
French 96, 160
frontiers 163, 167
funds of knowledge 11, 15, 39, 49, 70, 89
Furniss, G. 26, 156, 162, 163

Gambia 115
Ganguly, S. 82, 117
García, O. 15, 37, 55, 59, 60, 61, 62, 66, 71, 81, 132, 137, 138, 139
gaze 33
Gee, James Paul 39, 46
genre overlaps 68–9, 70, 72
Gentil, G. 55
Germanic rhetorical constructions 41
gesture 115, 136
'gestures of exclusion' 3, 141
Ghana 115, 123
Giles, Howard 132, 138
Glanz, C. 40
Glick-Schiller, N. 123
Global South, definitions of vii
globalisation 79, 85, 100
'goat of the road' stories 10
Goffman, E. 136
Gogolin, Ingrid 15, 86
'goodbyes' 11
governmentality 162
Graddol, D. 119
grammar 41
grammars 30–1, 33, 96
'grand erasure' 3–4, 142
Green, J. 133

Grosfoguel, Ramón 76
Guinea 123
Guldin, Rainer 18
Gumperz, John J. 132, 138, 165
Gurung, G. 112
Gwamba 29

Hajek, J. 110
Hall, S. 123
Hammar, Thomas 110
harmonisation project 159, 165–72
Harris, Roy 81, 125, 139
Haugen, Einar 80, 132, 138
hearer/reader-oriented structures 41, 42, 48, 63, 65, 70
hegemonic language ideologies 95, 100
hegemonic/subaltern relations 13
Heller, M. 55, 96, 143
Hélot, Christine 164–5
Heritage, J. 133
heritage languages, keeping up 126
heteroglossia 40, 70
Heugh, K. 165
Hibbert, L. 57, 62
hierarchies of ideas 41, 48
hierarchisation of languages 78, 81–2, 96, 98, 160
Higgins, C. 165
higher education 55–74
Hirson, B. 166
history of fluid multilingualism in Africa 27, 29, 32–3, 56, 57, 59
Hogan-Brun, G. 103
Holm, J.A. 124
Holmes, Janet 80
Holt, N.L. 144, 145
home, concepts of 67, 126
homogenisation 86, 139
honorifics 134
Hornberger, N. 1–3, 4, 6, 39, 59, 71, 139
Hountonji, P. vii
Hub for Multilingual Education and Literacies 44
Hudson, Richard 80
human rights 6

humility 148
hybrid language 65, 161

idea of Africa 101–4
idealised standard languages 80
identity
  Africa and African identity 7, 102
  African denizen 122
  colonialism 75, 78
  ethnocultural identities conflated with 'languages' 31
  group/collective 103, 125
  and language policies 81
  and language separatism 62
  multilingual citizenship 102–3
  multilingual identity construction 70
  national identity 103
  sociocultural approaches to 140
  transidiomatic identities 102
  transient postmodern 125
  transnational 124, 139–40
  'tribalism' 28
  in Zimbabwe today 29
ideology
  African denizen 123
  census ideology 83
  coloniality of language 79
  eradication of tribalism/ethnicity 29
  hegemonic language ideologies 13–15, 95, 100
  homogenisation 83
  ideologies about language 82
  language ideologies 82
  monoglossic ideologies 38
  national language policies 75
  nation-states 32, 33
  research methodology 141
  standard language ideology 81, 82–3, 84
ignored lingualism 15, 143, 159, 164–5
illiteracy 37
illusion of linguistic communism 80
imagined communities 33
indigenous knowledge systems (IKS) 37, 42–3, 45, 59

indigenous literacies 39
indirectness 11, 41, 48
individuality 59, 60, 63
inferences, drawing 41, 42
information flow 47
information organisation 41
input/output alternation 59, 60–1, 62
integration 1, 70, 94–8, 100, 102
integrationist theory 81, 125
intercultural communication 14, 57, 94, 97, 117
interdependence 46, 50, 59–60, 71, 137
    see also ubuntu values
interdisciplinarity 88
interethnic marriage 57
intergenerational transmission 115, 117, 118, 126
interlingual experiences 59
interlingual moves 66–7
internationalisation 14
interpersonal strategies 165
interview methods 114, 138, 141
Inyanga district 28
isiNdebele 9–10, 64, 78, 82, 160, 171
isiXhosa 62, 64, 78, 82, 171
isiZulu 64, 66, 78, 82, 134–5, 136, 160, 171
Islam 102

Jacquemet, Marco 102, 132, 165
Johnston, B. 32
Jones, S.H. 145
Jørgensen, J.N. 132

Kamusella, T. 28, 30, 34, 76, 102
Kamwendo, G.H. 170
kasitaal 65
Keane, M. 43
Kembo-Sure 56
Kenya 95, 115
Khoe people 56, 57
Khosa, R. 38
Khubchandani, Lachman 90, 132, 138, 148, 165
Kirundi 126

KiSwahili 95, 120–1, 122
Kleyn, T. 132, 137, 138, 139
Knight, N. 101
knowledge production
    co-construction of knowledge 43, 44–5, 88
    colonial understandings of legitimate knowledge 141
    colonialism 14
    community-based knowledge 48–50
    epistemological turn-around 156–9
    Euro-modernist epistemologies 2–4, 9–10, 19, 27, 32, 38, 77, 157
    funds of knowledge 11, 15, 39, 49, 70, 89
    indigenous knowledge systems (IKS) 37, 42–3
    and marginality 122
    pluralisation of 88
    Western knowledge systems 34, 49, 100
    world-centred approach to knowledge production 4
Koener, Conrad 6–7
Kollmair, M. 112
Kouwenberg, S. 124
Kriol 115, 123–4, 125
Kuku 117, 126
Kwindigwi, W. 43, 59
Kyratzis, A. 133

land, connection with 85
Lane, S. 39
language acquisition 117–18
language and literacy education 37–54, 170
language as a verb 85
language as capacity 81
language as process 132
language commissions 95
language education policies 75, 77–8
language maintenance 62
language nesting model 143
language objects 80, 81, 87, 97, 132
language of command 29, 98, 160

language of widest communication 120
language planning 81
language policies 75–93, 171
language separatism 61–2
languages as invented categories 7
languages of command 7, 29, 160
languages of the people 159–60
language-with-a-name (*Einzelsprache*) 29–32, 63, 79, 137, 140, 169
languaging 59, 61, 62, 131–54 *see also* translanguaging
Larsen, J.E. 112
Latin American scholarship on coloniality 76, 88
learner-centred approaches 47–8
Léglise, Isabelle vii, 124–5
LePage, R. 162
Lerner, G. 147
Letseka, M. 40
Li Wei 15, 37, 55, 59, 60, 61, 62, 71, 132, 137, 138, 139, 140, 143, 144
Liberia 115, 123
Limpopo Valley 59
lingua francas 14, 115, 116–17
lingualism 12, 15, 172
linguistic encirclement 160
linguistic habitus 15
linguistic homogenisation 31
linguistic imperialism 100
Link, H. 59, 71, 139
literacy
  academic literacy 55–74
  African languages and 40–1
  African literacy history erased by colonists 56–7
  African literacy in universities 57–8, 65–6
  African meaning making 11
  coloniality of language 33
  concept literacies 62
  harmonisation project 165, 167, 170
  indigenous literacies 39
  local language literacy 38
  monolingualism 57–8
  multilingual habitus 15–16

orthography 31, 33, 96, 163, 167, 170, 173
pan-African literacy 170–1
pre-historic African 56
sociocultural approaches to 39–40, 42, 46
uniform writing systems 170–3
Western systems of 9, 10
Liu, W. 1
locus of enunciation 82–3, 132
logical structures 41, 42, 48, 60
Love, Nigel 81
Luganda 119

Maadi 119, 126
MacSwan, J. 63
Madiba, M. 62
Madison, D.S. 147
Mahboob, A. 101
Makalela, Leketi 10, 38, 39, 40, 41, 42, 44, 45, 48, 51, 55, 56, 57, 58, 59, 60, 62, 63, 65, 70, 71, 72, 134, 170
Makoni, Sinfree vii, 6, 7, 9, 17, 26, 29, 34, 37, 39, 58, 59, 75, 78, 83, 84, 86, 98–9, 125, 138, 139, 156, 159, 161, 162, 163, 164, 167, 171
Makoni district 28
Malawi 95, 98
Malcolm, C. 43, 64, 66
Maldonado-Torres, N. 142
Mandenkan 95
Manyika Language 28
Mapungubwe 57
Maree, J. 87
marginality 112–14, 122, 125, 126
Marlowe, J. 110
Mashonaland vi
Massey, D. 127
Masuku, J.M. 162
Matolino, B. 43, 59
Mawere, M. 40
May, S. 38
Mazeland, H. 133, 146, 147
Mazrui, A.A. 102

Mbigi, L. 87
Mbiti, J.S. 43–4
McIntyre, E. 15, 89
McNamara, T. 103
meaning making
  blended use of languages 66–7
  co-construction of meaning 42–3
  negotiation 41
  through indirection 11
  translanguaging 63
  using any available resource 64–5
medium of instruction 55, 62, 64
Mende 126
Méndez, M. 133, 144, 146
Meneses, M.P. 5
meta-discourses 84, 101, 157, 163, 171
metalanguages 1, 144
meta-learning 50
metalinguistic awareness 16, 27, 50, 72, 89
metrolingualism 132, 143
metropole, reading from the 3–4, 122, 141
Midgely, Mary 1
Mignolo, Walter 34, 39, 76, 77, 82, 142, 156, 157, 158
migration 28, 103, 108–30
Milroy, J. 82
Milroy, Lesley 138
missionaries 28, 29–30, 32, 75, 97, 156, 169
mobility paradigm 108, 158–9
modernisation 79, 100
moment analysis 144
monoglossic ideologies 38
monolingualism
  bilingualism through monolingualism 96
  burden of the 'mono' in multilingualism 7–16
  and Christianity 32
  and colonialism 8
  and the concept of 'first' language 68
  curriculum designed for 49
  English 14
  fallacy of monolingual thinking 38
  hegemonic policy frameworks 2–3
  as idealisation 79–80
  and imperialism 8
  language and literacy education 39–40
  mindset 7–9, 15, 86–7, 126
  monoglossic ideologies 38
  monolingual drone 13–14, 15
  monolingual ways of seeing 12–13
  multiple monolingualisms 96–7
  as pathology 8–9
  presentist 12–13
  separate bilingualism 96
  two monolinguals in one body 61, 96
  universities 55, 56–8, 62, 63–4
  and VCBLs 96
Monomotapa, Emperor 56
'mother tongues' 61–2, 68, 110
Motlhaka, H. 41
Moyo, Themba 98
Mozambique 29
Mtenje, A. 170
multiculturalism 85
multidimensional pedagogy 47–8
multi-genre writing 68–9
multilanguaging 47
multilingual being 71
multilingual citizenship 102–3
multilingual data collection 45
multilingual education 2, 78, 79
multilingual habitus 15–16, 88–9
multilingual tutorials as research method 64–5
multilingualism
  colonial roots of vii–viii, 26–36
  human rights-inspired multilingualism discourse 6
  integrationist theory of 125
  the 'lingual' of 12
  mainstream understandings of 1–2, 6
  metaphors of 18
  misconceived as a disabler 38
  mono-epistemic paradigm 11–12
  myths 1
  as the norm 59
  prior theorisations 18

as resource 49
viewed as chaotic 38, 85
multimodality 61, 138
multiple first languages 67–8
multiple voices 40, 63, 71, 72
Musgrave, S. 110
mutual intelligibility 30, 31, 167, 168, 170
Mwaniki, M. 55

naming of languages 29, 97–8 *see also* *Einzelsprache* (language-with-a-name)
narrative research 133
national identity 103
national language policies 75–93, 161
national language status 17, 77, 80–1, 95–6, 98–100, 111, 158, 162
nationalist projects 162
nation-states 29, 31, 38, 58, 97–8, 120, 162
naturalisation 112
nature, relationship with 50, 85
Ndebele 30, 31, 64, 78, 82
Ndhlovu, Finex 7, 9, 15, 17, 26, 28, 29, 30, 31, 33, 34, 75, 76, 78, 79, 81, 85, 87, 96, 97, 99, 100, 101, 102, 103, 109, 110, 111, 119, 120, 123, 132, 138, 139, 141, 142, 143, 148, 156, 157, 159, 164–5, 169
Ndhlovu-Mhaso, James Mabuku 9
Ndlovu-Gatsheni, Sabelo 55, 58, 157
neo-colonialism 14
neoliberalism 14, 94, 102
Nguni languages 30, 31, 159, 166–7, 168, 171
Nhlapo, Jacob 159, 165, 166, 167, 168, 170
Nhlapo/Alexander harmonisation option 159, 168–9
Nigeria 115, 123
non-academic communities, researching with 18–19, 88, 159
non-linearity 41, 47, 61, 68
non-verbal communication 115
Norris-Holt, J. 117

Novoa, A. 158
Nustad, K.G. 141
Nyamnjoh, F.B. 46, 158
Nyanja 115

objectivity 142, 147
occupation of Zimbabwe 9
official languages
  Australian English 116–17
  coloniality of language 17
  diaspora communities 124
  national language policies 77, 78, 80–1, 82
  vehicular cross-border languages (VCBLs) 95
Omphile 131–54
one nation one language 33, 38, 49
one-ness ideologies 38, 49, 60, 63–4
ontologies 39, 99, 100, 173
oracy 33
orthodoxy 33, 39, 132, 139
orthography 31, 33, 96, 163, 167, 170, 173
Otheguy, R. 55, 63
Otsuji, Emi 132, 138, 143–4, 165
Ouane, A. 40

Pable, A. 125
Pace, Steven 145, 146
Pacheco, M.B. 140
Painter, Desmond 13–14
pan-African denizen communities 120
pan-African literacy 170–1
paragraphing 41–3, 48, 69, 70
parent-child communication 117–19
Paris Missionary Society 29
Park, J. 38
participant observation 141
participation, exclusion from 82, 89, 103
participatory research 43–5
Peet, R. 3, 141
Pennycook, Alastair vii, 7, 9, 11, 14, 29, 37, 59, 78, 83, 84, 97, 98–9, 101, 132, 138, 143–4, 159, 161, 162, 165

performative actions 136
Perry, K. 40
Phillipson, R. 14
Piccardo, E. 138, 165
pidgin English 123–4
pidgins 111, 123–5, 126
Piller, Ingrid 12, 13, 29, 30
plurality of consciousness 165
plurilingual multimodal communication resources 165
plurilingualism 8, 138, 139, 148
pluriversality 77
poetry 68–9
police brutality 60
political engineering 17
political participation 82
polylanguaging 132
Portuguese 82, 96, 160
positivism 2, 131, 140–1, 147, 148, 159
post-apartheid 77, 78, 163, 165, 167
postcolonial society
  coloniality of language 17, 75
  governmentality 162
  harmonisation project 165–70
  language standardisation 31
  monolingualism 38
  socially realistic multilingualism 163
  vehicular cross-border languages (VCBLs) 95, 100
postcolonial studies 77
postmodernism 58, 85, 125
post-nationalism 100
post-positivism 131
power
  assimilation of marginalised languages 63
  colonial matrices of 17, 18
  coloniality of language 75–9
  cultural oppression 79
  Euro-modernist colonial matrix 27
  hegemonic language ideologies 95, 100
  ideologies about language 82
  language as instrument of 28
  language of command 29, 98, 160
  and marginalised literacies 40
  renegotiation of 63
  to 'save/rescue' 33–4
  will to 33
pragmatic communication 115, 117, 125
Prah, K.K. 120, 170, 171
pre-service teacher training 50
prestige 161
print capitalism 33
proficiency 97, 110, 117, 119
proverbial lore 85
psycholinguistics 61
psychosocial distribution of multiple linguistic usages 109, 120–1
purism, linguisitic 63, 85, 136–7, 161

quantification of 'languages' 9 *see also* countable entities, languages as
Quijano, Anibal 16, 76, 77, 83

Raboroko, P.N. 168
Ranger, Terrence Osborne 7, 17, 27–8, 75, 78
rationality 99
Raum, O.F. 56
reader/hearer-oriented structures 41, 42, 48, 63, 65, 70
reflexivity 133, 136, 146
refugee journey languages 111, 113, 115, 120
refugees 109, 113
'regimes of truth' 1
research methodology 43–5, 64–5, 132–3, 140–4, 156–9, 164, 169
researcher-participant relationship 43, 133, 145–6
revivalism 59
rhetorical organisation 41–3, 69–70
Rhodes Must Fall 55, 58
Ricento, T. 38
Richards, R. 146
Ridge, S.G. 163
rock paintings 56
Ronga/XiRonga 29
Rowe, C. 103

Salazar, N.B. 108, 147, 158
San people 56, 57
Satyo, Sizwe 168–9
scaffolding 16, 89
Schegloff, E. 136, 147
Schieffelin, B.B. 82
Schiffman, H. 81
science, Western concepts of 99, 131, 138
    see also positivism
second generation immigrants 110
'second' languages 61–2
segregationist perspectives of linguistics 139
semiotics 62, 77, 99
Sepedi 10, 11, 30, 31, 46, 64, 66, 78, 134, 136, 170
sequences of acts 136
Seshadri-Crooks, K. 112, 113
Sesotho 30, 31, 64, 66, 78, 82, 170
Setswana 30, 31, 64, 65, 66, 68, 78, 82, 95, 134, 135, 136, 160, 170
Severo, Cristine 26, 27, 33, 156, 161
Sheller, M. 158
Shi-xu 87
Shohamy, E. 71, 82, 103
Shona vi, 29, 30, 31, 115
"showing" writing styles 145, 149
Siegel, J. 124
Sierra Leone 115, 123
Singler, J.V. 124
SiSwati 10, 31, 46, 64, 78, 171
Siwati 30
small data versus big data 147, 149
Smith, Linda Tuhiwai 4, 88, 142, 157, 158
social anthropology 3, 141–2
social capital 120
social cohesion 103
social engineering 79, 100
social isolation 121–2
social justice 58, 89, 103
social networks 111, 112, 116, 121–2
social transaction, language as 90, 99, 132, 138
socially realistic linguistics 160–1

socially realistic multilingualism 111, 159–72
sociocultural approaches
    to African languages 40, 78
    to diaspora 103
    to identity 140
    language policies 81
    languages as sociocultural activities 7, 17
    to literacy 39–40, 42, 46
    real language use 132
    to research 43
sociolinguistic justice 17, 78, 163, 170
sociolinguistics
    idealised standard languages 80
    integrationist theory of 81
    mainstream understandings of 6–7, 12
    research methodology 140–4
Somali 95
Sotho/Tswana languages 30, 31, 159, 166, 168, 170
South Africa
    language education policies 6
    language policies 78
    Leketi's mother 10
    Nhlapo/Alexander harmonisation option 166, 167–8
    official languages 95
    television 14
    Thonga language 29
    universities 55
South Sudan 115
Southern Theory 142
Soysal, Y. 100
speaker/writer-responsible structures 41, 42, 48, 63
speech communities, idealised 79–80
'spheres of possibility' 111–12
Spolsky, Bernard 80
standard language ideology 81, 82–3, 84
standard languages
    English 120
    ideology 81, 82, 84
    literacy 38

national language policies 75, 78, 79
socially realistic multilingualism 161, 162
vehicular cross-border languages (VCBLs) 97, 99, 100
standardisation 31, 38, 95, 165, 166, 167
storytelling 65, 88, 114, 145
straight to the point 11, 41, 69, 70
strategies of communication 165
Strathern, M. 108
Street, Brian 39, 46, 50
Stroud, C. 102
student protests 55, 58
Sudan 115, 120
Swahili 115, 121
Swaziland 29
symbolic communication 115, 117, 120

Tabouret-Keller, A. 162
Tanzania 95, 115, 121
teachers
  co-teaching 48, 88
  multidimensional pedagogy 47–8
  teacher education 37, 50–2
  translanguaging 50
technocracy 58
technologies of orthography and orthodoxy 33
"telling" writing styles 145, 149
territorialised languages 95, 162
TESOL (Teaching English as a second language) 139
texts (school) 49, 162–3
textual coherence 41–3, 69, 70
third spaces 63
Thompson, J.B. 79–80
Thonga language 29–30, 31
Toolan, Michael 81
topic promotion devices 67, 70
trade records 56, 57
transdisciplinary discourse 87
transfer theories 137
transidiomatic identities 102, 132
transidiomatic practice 165
translanguaging
  all-terrain vehicle metaphor 61
  assessment using 166–7
  versus code-switching 66
  communicative translanguaging 140
  critiques of 63
  as decolonising tool 71, 72
  harmonisation project 166
  and literacy development 51
  as pedagogic strategy 60–1, 134, 139
  psycholinguistics 61
  research methodology 133, 147
  in schools 62
  teachers' use of 50
  theories of 132, 137–40
  translanguaging spaces 61
  and transnational identities 139–40
  ubuntu values 46–7, 50, 58–64
  universities 56
  weak versus strong versions 137–8
translation 13
Transvaal 30
'tribalism' 7, 28, 58, 71, 162
Tshivenda 62, 64, 82, 171
Tswana/Sotho languages 30, 31, 159, 166, 168, 170
typologies of language policies 80–1

ubuntu research methodology 43–5
ubuntu translanguaging 46–7, 50, 58–64, 71, 72
ubuntu values 43, 46–7, 48–50, 56, 59–60, 71, 87–8
Uganda 115, 119
Umtali district 28
uncertainty 4–5
UNESCO 49
uniformity 31, 99, 159, 173
unilingual approaches 55 see also monolingualism
unintended consequences 75
universalism 12, 76, 83, 84, 85, 141
universality, assumptions of 3, 4, 5, 12, 77, 83–4, 131, 141, 148–9
universities 55–74

University of Cape Town 55, 62, 168, 170
Urry, J. 158
utopianism 60

van Binsbergen, W. 59
van der Walt, Crista 57, 62, 172
vehicular cross-border languages (VCBLs) 94–107
Viljoen, H. 112, 113
vulnerability indicators 112

Wa Thiong'o, Ngugi 160
Wallerstein, Immanuel 4–5, 15
Ward, J.R. 103
Wardaugh, Ronald 80
Watson, R. 133, 136, 146
Webb, V. 56
Western knowledge systems 34, 49, 100 *see also* Euro-modernist epistemologies
Western modernity 76, 83
westernisation 28

Williams, Cen 60, 139
Williams, E. 39
Winford, Donald 159, 160–1
Wolf, George 81
Woolard, K. 82
world views 85
world-centred approach to knowledge production 4
writer/speaker-responsible structures 41, 42, 48, 63
writing systems 33, 95, 167, 170, 173 *see also* orthography

Xhosa 30, 31, 64, 78, 82
Xichangana 29
Xitsonga 10, 29, 46, 64, 78, 160, 171

Zambia 95, 115
Zeleza, P.T. 27
Zhu, H. 15, 138, 139, 140, 143
Zimbabwe 28, 29, 115
Zulu 30, 31, 64, 78, 82

For Product Safety Concerns and Information please contact our EU Authorised Representative:

Easy Access System Europe

Mustamäe tee 50

10621 Tallinn

Estonia

gpsr.requests@easproject.com

www.ingramcontent.com/pod-product-compliance
Ingram Content Group UK Ltd.
Pitfield, Milton Keynes, MK11 3LW, UK
UKHW020238200525

458704UK00018B/99